Praise for **Sundowner of the Skies**
the story of Oscar [Garden]

'Beautifully written, *Sundowner of th[e Skies]* ... [this] [domes]tic family history is a profound exploration of [......] [tr]auma and its effects on individuals, families and their shared memories'
JUDGES, NSW PREMIER'S HISTORY AWARD

'A rattling, searing, soulful story that takes flight on the Gipsy Moth wings of the author's relentless research and willingness to pull back every curtain of this extraordinary man's life, sometimes at her own emotional peril. I didn't want this trip to end'
TRENT DALTON

'Author Mary Garden writes beautifully and honestly of her father, Oscar Garden, a hero from the golden age of aviation when intrepid men in tiny biplanes crossed the globe in flights that startled the world' GRANTLEE KIEZA

'An important piece of aviation history and a courageous personal story, vividly told. I found it enjoyable in every way. Beautifully told and bravely too, the width of research is astonishing. *Sundowner of the Skies* should find enthusiastic readers, grateful readers in the aviation world, and thoroughly engaged ones in the wider one' MAURICE GEE

'I have just read your book *Sundowner of the Skies* again. What a fascinating story. Your father was an incredible person. That was an extraordinary flight he did from Wyndham, over Halls Creek and then to Alice Springs using dead reckoning alone. I think it took amazing skill to find Alice' DICK SMITH

'This bare bones outline of an aviator's career is simply the skeleton which Mary Garden, with an objectivity rare in a daughter's account of a father's troubled life, fleshes out with solid research into family history, recollections from friends and colleagues and extracts from the files. *Sundowner of the Skies* is a fine biography and aviation fans will love every mile of it, while the social historian will revel in the stories of how things were so different' JIM SULLIVAN, *OTAGO DAILY TIMES*

'Mary Garden has done us all a great service by bringing to public gaze this fascinating tale about her highly talented but hugely troubled father and the impact he had on her. The Sundowner came and went but his story now remains'
ROSS FITZGERALD, *WEEKEND AUSTRALIAN*

'... maps out a cascade of acrimonious family dysfunction, religious zealotry, bitterness over unequal inheritance, alcoholism, and grudges nurtured for generations. Oscar Garden's achievements were noteworthy and he deserves to be remembered'
GARRY SHILSON-JOSLING, *AUSTRALIAN AVIATION*

'It's no hagiography – warts and all she promises and doesn't hold back about a man who was much better with planes than people'
JIM EAGLES & MARK FRYER, *NEW ZEALAND HERALD*

'Mary Garden's portrait of her father could be read as an attempt to retrieve his lost fame, but it's probably best read as a daughter's homage to a father who is at once familiar and a mystery ... Garden's deep affection for her flawed father shines through'
STEVEN CARROLL, *SYDNEY MORNING HERALD*

'A searingly honest and well-written narrative, packed with fascinating and surprising detail' CHRIS CLIFFORD, *FLYPAST*

'Oscar Garden's daughter makes no secret of the fact that her father was a difficult person and the exposé of fractured family relationships permeate the whole book from the first page to the last. Oscar was a pilot and he achieved a great deal, but he was also a human being and Mary Garden has held nothing back in telling this story of a man who might for some odd quirk in history, until now, have been labelled "The Forgotten Aviator"' STUART MCKAY, *THE MOTH*

'The author has candidly described her father's life – warts and all. One of her greatest strengths is her ability to write disarmingly of the main characters in her story, including of herself. This style has made this book a great biography of one of the world's unknown aviators. Mary has done her father Oscar proud. She has assured him of his place in aviation history' MARTIN PLAYNE, *ANCESTOR*

'Oscar has arrived. What a triumph. A searingly honest, raw and expressive narrative. He is no longer forgotten and his unique Scottish spirit intact'
MARK CHITTICK

'It's a beaut story of a forgotten figure, sensitively but honestly told' ROBYN ANNEAR

'A fabulous book ... which shows painstaking research, including a family tree, and it is all very well written. The story needed to be told'
ROB CHARLTON (FRAES)

SUNDOWNER OF THE SKIES

The story of Oscar Garden
THE FORGOTTEN AVIATOR

Mary Garden

NEW
HOLLAND

First published in 2019 by New Holland Publishers
This edition published in 2021 by New Holland Publishers
Sydney • Auckland

Level 1, 178 Fox Valley Road, Wahroonga, NSW 2076, Australia
5/39 Woodside Ave, Northcote, Auckland 0627, New Zealand

newhollandpublishers.com

A catalogue record for this book is available from the National Library of New Zealand.

ISBN 9781760793838

Group Managing Director: Fiona Schultz
Publisher: Alan Whiticker
Project Editor: Elise James
Designer: Luke Harris
Production Director: Arlene Gippert
Printed in China

10 9 8 7 6 5 4 3 2 1

Keep up with New Holland Publishers:
 NewHollandPublishers
 @newhollandpublishers

Front cover: Oscar Garden flying to Essendon aerodrome, Melbourne, on 10 November 1930. AUTHOR'S COLLECTION.

Back cover: Passengers and crew disembarking from the TEAL Short S25 flying boat ZK-AME at Mechanics Bay, Auckland. Photograph by Whites Aviation, March 1947. Ref: WA-05916-G, ALEXANDER TURNBULL LIBRARY, WELLINGTON, NEW ZEALAND.

Here you go, Mum. Warts and all.

GARDEN FAMILY TREE

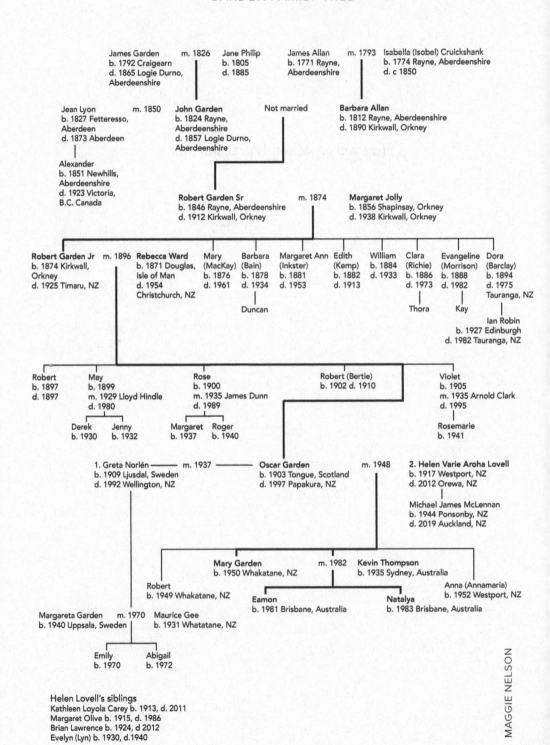

James Garden
b. 1792 Craigearn
d. 1865 Logie Durno,
Aberdeenshire

m. 1826

Jane Philip
b. 1805
d. 1885

James Allan
b. 1771 Rayne,
Aberdeenshire

m. 1793

Isabella (!Isobel) Cruickshank
b. 1774 Rayne, Aberdeenshire
d. c 1850

Jean Lyon
b. 1827 Fetteresso,
Aberdeen
d. 1873 Aberdeen

m. 1850

John Garden
b. 1824 Rayne,
Aberdeenshire
d. 1857 Logie Durno,
Aberdeenshire

Not married

Barbara Allan
b. 1812 Rayne, Aberdeenshire
d. 1890 Kirkwall, Orkney

Alexander
b. 1851 Newhills,
Aberdeenshire
d. 1923 Victoria,
B.C. Canada

Robert Garden Sr
b. 1846 Rayne, Aberdeenshire
d. 1912 Kirkwall, Orkney

m. 1874

Margaret Jolly
b. 1856 Shapinsay, Orkney
d. 1938 Kirkwall, Orkney

Robert Garden Jr
b. 1874 Kirkwall,
Orkney
d. 1925 Timaru, NZ

m. 1896

Rebecca Ward
b. 1871 Douglas,
Isle of Man
d. 1954
Christchurch, NZ

Mary
(MacKay)
b. 1876
d. 1961

Barbara
(Bain)
b. 1878
d. 1934

Duncan

Margaret Ann
(Inkster)
b. 1881
d. 1953

Edith
(Kemp)
b. 1882
d. 1913

William
b. 1884
d. 1933

Clara
(Richie)
b. 1886
d. 1973

Thora

Evangeline
(Morrison)
b. 1888
d. 1982

Kay

Dora
(Barclay)
b. 1894
d. 1975
Tauranga, NZ

Ian Robin
b. 1927 Edinburgh
d. 1982 Tauranga, NZ

Robert
b. 1897
d. 1897

May
b. 1899
m. 1929 Lloyd Hindle
d. 1980

Rose
b. 1900
m. 1935 James Dunn
d. 1989

Robert (Bertie)
b. 1902 d. 1910

Violet
b. 1905
m. 1935 Arnold Clark
d. 1995

Derek
b. 1930

Jenny
b. 1932

Margaret
b. 1937

Roger
b. 1940

Rosemarie
b. 1941

1. Greta Norlén
b. 1909 Ljusdal, Sweden
d. 1992 Wellington, NZ

m. 1937

Oscar Garden
b. 1903 Tongue, Scotland
d. 1997 Papakura, NZ

m. 1948

2. Helen Varie Aroha Lovell
b. 1917 Westport, NZ
d. 2012 Orewa, NZ

Michael James McLennan
b. 1944 Ponsonby, NZ
d. 2019 Auckland, NZ

Mary Garden
b. 1950 Whakatane, NZ

m. 1982

Kevin Thompson
b. 1935 Sydney, Australia

Robert
b. 1949 Whakatane, NZ

Eamon
b. 1981 Brisbane, Australia

Natalya
b. 1983 Brisbane, Australia

Anna (Annamaria)
b. 1952 Westport, NZ

Margareta Garden
b. 1940 Uppsala, Sweden

m. 1970

Maurice Gee
b. 1931 Whatatane, NZ

Emily
b. 1970

Abigail
b. 1972

Helen Lovell's siblings
Kathleen Loyola Carey b. 1913, d. 2011
Margaret Olive b. 1915, d. 1986
Brian Lawrence b. 1924, d 2012
Evelyn (Lyn) b. 1930, d.1940

MAGGIE NELSON

Sundowner: An Australian swagman who arrives unexpectedly out of nowhere on sundown, and disappears the next morning. The *Sun* newspaper called Oscar Garden *Sundowner of the Skies* after he flew into Wyndham on 4 November 1930 after his last hop on the flight from England.

Kia Ora: A Māori term which is used as a greeting but it also means to wish someone or something good luck. Oscar Garden named his Gipsy Moth plane *Kia Ora*.

MR OSCAR GARDEN.

Postcard portrait of Oscar wearing flying costume.
Taken in England, July 1931.

Contents

Contents

Author's note

My father, Oscar Garden, was once a famous aviator. He achieved notoriety in 1930 when he became the youngest and most inexperienced pilot to fly solo from England to Australia. His flying career went on to span 17 years, and in 1943 he became Chief Pilot and Operations Manager of Tasman Empire Airways Limited (TEAL), the forerunner of Air New Zealand. Some of the pilots he trained said he was the 'Father of Air New Zealand'.

When he was alive the idea that someone might write a book about him came up in conversations. He seemed quite keen on the idea, although he was adamant that his son-in-law, Maurice Gee, should not write it. Maurice, an acclaimed New Zealand author, is married to Margareta, my father's daughter from his first marriage. My father reckoned there was too much sex in his books. Not that Maurice could write much about the sex in my father's life. According to Mum, they only had sex a few times and after she became pregnant with my younger sister, Anna, that was it.

In the 1990s, I had toyed with the idea of writing a book about my father, which would mean going over from Brisbane to Auckland to interview him at length. But I didn't. I couldn't afford it, for a start. By then I was a single mum struggling to bring up two children. As well as airfares, I would have to pay for a motel room, as my father could not cope with visitors. And I was ambivalent. Until I embarked on this journey,

1

I knew little about his flying days. Was he really *that* famous, and worth writing about? He seldom talked to me about anything, except to bark orders. He commanded our family as if he was still the captain of a flying boat. And I remember overhearing someone (perhaps it was Aunt Ola, my mother's sister) talking about his epic solo flight from England to Australia in 1930 and calling it, 'a lot of fuss about nothing'. Mum used to downplay it too, by saying, 'He was only the fourth, you know.'[1]

But in 1992 I did write something, not that the results were encouraging. I wrote an article – essentially an overview of his flying years – drawing on some newspaper and magazine articles, extracts from aviation books and a few interviews. I sent a draft to my father to check. He was chuffed and scribbled a few corrections in pencil in various places. I posted the final version to the *Sydney Morning Herald* and mentioned I had photos that could be used if they were interested. We were all taken aback by the type-written reply: 'The Editor of the *Sydney Morning Herald* thanks you for submitting the attached contribution but regrets he is unable to make use of it. Unfortunately, the SMH doesn't publish fiction.' I didn't try to find another home for it.

In 2005, I decided to have another go. The notion of writing a book was even more out of the question, for by then my father was gone. He died in 1997. I'd left it too late to talk to him about his life. Mind you, had I talked to him, it is unlikely I would have extracted the truth out of him; that is, the full story. He wasn't much of a talker and, as I was to discover, he often exaggerated and sometimes lied to the press. Besides, talking about feelings was strictly off-limits in our household. I doubt whether he would have told me how he felt about the things that had happened to him as a child and during World War I.

But I was curious about his 1930 flight from England to Australia, and, after researching it, I realised my mother was wrong. Even though my father had not broken any records, what he did was remarkable. He was the first aviator to risk landfall at Wyndham and the first to fly over the harsh deserts of central Australia. He also broke a record for novice aviators. So, I wrote a long-form feature article on this flight and submitted it to *The Australian Financial Review* (*AFR*). The editor, Chris Short, replied: 'Mary, it's not our usual fare but I've read it a couple of times and it has a growing appeal. I think I can find a home for it.' The article, 'Sundowner of the Skies – Mary Garden takes flight with her father' was published in the centre mid-spread pages of the *AFR's* Easter edition, 24–28 March 2005.

There was a huge response. I received emails from people all over the world. Deepak Somar, a retired pilot for Air India, said, 'I consider your father's solo flight from England to Australia in 1930 the single most sustained feat of courage in aviation, since he had little flying experience, he did the maintenance himself, and navigated with just an old-fashioned compass. It would make a good movie.' Rakesh Sharma, the first Indian astronaut into space, said it was an awesome story, describing Oscar as the 'magnificent man in his flying machine'. He pointed out that 'only a very few could appreciate the extent of my father's commitment and the enormity of his achievement.' Ian Mackersey, a New Zealand writer acclaimed for his deeply researched and revelational biographies, including those of aviators Jean Batten and Charles Kingsford Smith, wrote: 'He was a remarkable man. Because he was so low-key about it, his aviation career is little known here.'

I was hooked. I decided to write other articles. However, a book still seemed out of the question. Even though the internet had arrived, a Google search revealed only one entry on Oscar Garden, a piece in the *Dictionary of New Zealand Biography*[2] compiled in 2000 by my half-sister, Margareta Gee, and Stephen Berry, a former flight attendant for Air New Zealand. Ray Richards, a New Zealand literary agent who had been a distinguished navy flyer in the Pacific War, wrote to me in 2006, saying, '*The Australian Encyclopaedia* appears to have only one line for Oscar

Garden. That's in a four-page chart of landmarks in Australian aviation! He's a forgotten hero, perhaps waiting to be reconstructed in a biography.'

I began researching his life – combing microfilms of old newspapers and magazines, sending queries to librarians and archivists, and placing requests for information on various aviation online forums. I subsequently had articles published in newspapers such as the *Southland Times, Timaru Herald, Otago Daily Times, Christchurch Press* and *Bay of Plenty Times* as well as Scotland's *Northern Times*. I wrote articles that were snatched up by aviation magazines in Florida, California, South Africa and Australia, as well as *New Zealand Geographic* and *New Zealand Memories*. At the end of each I included requests for information about my father. At one stage I wondered whether I was overdoing it. Wouldn't people become sick to death of hearing about my father? Bruce Cavanagh, curator of Gore Museum (New Zealand), reassured me: 'Don't worry. We can't get enough of stories of Oscar Garden. Can't wait for your book.'

As well as emails from aviation buffs and aero philatelists[3], I heard from people whose relatives – an aunt, grandmother or uncle – had gone for a joyride with my father during his 1931 tour of New Zealand. They'd send handwritten letters and enclosed photographs. Air New Zealand paid for me to fly to Auckland to interview some of the surviving TEAL pilots. Bill Salt, a retired pilot and engineer, contacted me. He had owned Bay Aircraft Services at Mt Maunganui, New Zealand, and 25 years ago, in amongst paperwork, came across the logbooks[4] for *Kia Ora*, the Gipsy Moth plane my father flew to Australia. Bill had kept them all this time but was about to sell them (along with other aviation paraphernalia) when he read one of my articles in an aviation magazine and decided they would be better back with our family. Remarkably, he was living at Caboolture, a 20-minute drive from my home on the Sunshine Coast. I felt as if I had entered Aladdin's Cave. As well as discovering gems from my father's flying days, there was a treasure trove of his own family history, especially that of his grandfather.

However, there are gaps in my story. It was difficult to piece together much of his personal life up to the time he married my mother, Helen Varie Lovell, in 1948. He had not kept in touch with the friends he made in Christchurch and Sydney in the 1920s, and he was not close to any of his early aviation peers. During the TEAL years (1940–1947) he kept to himself and was regarded as a loner. He never kept diaries and seldom wrote letters, although I managed to track down some he wrote to his mother, Rebecca, in the 1930s and a few he wrote to his parents when he was a young child at boarding school in Scotland. Rummaging around the National Archives of Scotland, I also stumbled upon Rebecca's petitions to Scotland's Supreme Civil Court after she'd run away from Robert, her husband. I obtained my father's file from the New Zealand Defence Force, and found to my surprise that it contained letters Rebecca had written between 1934 and 1937 to Prime Minister Michael Savage and the Minister of Defence, John Cobbe. She kept requesting that they see if they could find a job for 'my boy'. For a while my father had been 'stuck' in England, at first unemployed and then, when he did procure a flying position, hankering for work in New Zealand or Australia. He found the English winters unbearable.

I was, however, able to procure transcripts of several interviews: one by Eric Tucker, a retired Operations Manager of British Airways; another by Ken Ellis (New Zealand Radio and Television), and interviews done by Margareta Gee and her daughter Abigail. My father wrote two feature articles: 'My flight to Australia: with Oscar Garden over the Hinkler route', *New Zealand Free Lance*, 3 December 1930, and 'Garden's story: How 'plane capsized; nearly killed at Munich; peril of ocean hop; thrills in the desert', *The Sun* (Sydney), 9 November 1930. Unless cited, all personal quotes are from these letters, interviews and articles.

My recollections of my father and my childhood may differ from those of other family members, but nobody has a monopoly on the shared past. Thankfully, in the decade before she died, I spoke to Mum for countless hours and wrote down her recollections and shared with her my finds. She hoped my book would be a 'warts and all' account, which was strange coming from someone who never wanted neighbours knowing what was going on and who once – when I was an adult – shut the windows because she thought I was laughing too loudly My father would not have been happy about the skeletons I uncovered, nor my mentioning his failures as a father and a husband. He would have only wanted people to know about 'the good bits', his self as a pioneer aviator. And yet history, going back, can be a healing process. Digging up his past and going on this journey helped me, and my mother, understand in part why he became who he was.

My Sister's Book

Soon after the first edition of *Sundowner of the Skies* was published in June 2019, my sister Anna (Annamaria) began writing her own book. I first heard about *Oscar Garden: A Tale of One Man's Love of Flying* on 18 October 2020, the day before its release. No-one in the family, apart from my brother Robert, knew about it.

It was a huge shock, and I felt betrayed.

Anna wrote on the NZ Booklovers site, 'I disagreed so strongly with my sister's rendition of my father that I put pen to paper and wrote furiously, putting together my tale on Dad.' Yet the draft manuscript of *Sundowner of the Skies* had been given to family members, including cousins, for feedback. No-one had come back to me and challenged anything I'd written about Dad or said he was 'not like that'.

A Tale of One Man's Love of Flying is a hagiography – excessively flattering and ignoring many of Dad's faults, especially his cruel streak.

In January 2019 I gifted my extensive collection, including Dad's logbooks, photos, letters and newspaper clippings, to Auckland's Museum of Transport and Technology. It was a treasure-trove, and Anna accessed it. I was surprised to see many of the same photos, letters and anecdotes that I used in *Sundowner of the Skies* pop up in *A Tale of One Man's Love of Flying*.

My sister says in the author's note, 'It took only eight months to write the basics.' Unfortunately, I discovered that her book is riddled with factual errors, especially errors regarding dates and ages, and even includes some of Dad's tall tales. I made plenty of mistakes when I first set out on my journey in 2005. I realised Dad often exaggerated, came up with stories that were not true or was mistaken on some points. If articles or books on aviation history are to be of any value, they require meticulous research and fact-checking, especially with regard to sources.

A number of my articles on this family saga have been published. One is reprinted in the Afterword on page 252. In this I write, '*Oscar Garden: A tale of one man's love of flying* is the book he [Dad] would have wanted,' as it glosses over his character flaws. On reflection, I'm not so sure. Dad was a perfectionist. He liked to get things right; he liked dates and figures to be correct.

N.B. In the 1980s my sister changed her name from Anna to Annamaria, the name under which her book is published. In my articles I call her Annamaria. In this book, I have left her name as Anna, which is what Dad and Mum always called her, as have Robert and I.

Whenever I hear a small plane droning overhead, I think of my father. Sometimes I imagine him sitting up there, perched in the cockpit. It has been like this for as long as I can remember.

TAKEN ON LANDING AT
MASCOT AERODROME
SYDNEY, AUSTRALIA

Oscar in the cockpit of *Kia Ora*, his De Havilland Gipsy Moth aircraft, on arrival at Mascot Aerodrome, Sydney, on 7 November 1930, after his solo flight from England to Australia.

Introduction

In the early morning of 16 October 1930, Oscar Garden set out from Croydon Aerodrome in South London in a second-hand, open-cockpit Gipsy Moth. On his feet he wore carpet slippers, and he had half a dozen sandwiches on his lap. His plan was to fly to Australia. He was 27 years old and had just learnt to fly, with a mere 39 flying hours under his belt. There was only one person there to see him off – a representative of the Vacuum Oil Company, who had agreed to provide fuel supplies of Plume and Mobiloil at his planned stops along the 12,000-mile route.

At that time, the flight from England to Australia was considered to be 'the most formidable feat in aerial navigation and the sternest test of pilot and machine'.[5] Many aviators failed; some lost their lives. If Oscar's father's flying instructor, First Officer Reginald James Bunning, an ex-wartime pilot, had known of his plan he would have tried to talk him out of it. Bunning only found out after he had left. He told reporters Oscar was foolhardy and didn't have a hope in Hades.

It is difficult today to imagine the courage, endurance and foolhardiness of pioneer aviators. Apart from the compass, they had no instruments, relying on dead reckoning and their wits. They had to fly at low level through turbulence, dust storms and the darkness of tropical storms. They would sit hunched up in their tiny cramped open cockpits for hours at a time with no protection from the weather. They had no radios or toilets.

Miraculously, Oscar made it. Eighteen days after leaving Croydon, he landed at Wyndham Aerodrome in Western Australia. He was lucky to survive the trip, as he had several forced landings, including a spectacular crash in darkness near Jhansi in central India. He found himself hanging upside down in the seat's safety straps listening to petrol dripping out from the rear tank and watched with horror as a local Indian ran towards him with a hurricane lamp. Like most of the people he encountered, the Indian spoke no English.

Oscar became the fifth aviator to complete a solo flight from England to Australia. Even though he was the youngest and the most inexperienced, at 18 days his flight was the third-fastest after veteran pioneer aviators Charles Kingsford Smith and Bert Hinkler. Hinkler took 15 days in 1928, and Kingsford Smith, who left England a week before Oscar, took 10 days. They both had flown during World War I and each had over a decade of flying experience before their flights. Oscar just beat Amy Johnson, who had taken 19 days earlier that year. She had had several crash landings over Burma (now Myanmar) and Thailand. And he easily beat Francis Chichester, who departed in December 1929 but took 41 days due to a crash landing in Libya.

The day after Oscar reached Australia, *The Sun* reported:

Oscar Garden, the casual flier, blew in to Wyndham yesterday evening, after his last hop on the flight from England. Kingsford-Smith [sic] has dubbed himself a Vagabond of the Air. Garden, then, is the Sundowner of the Skies. The airman took Wyndham by surprise. There was no definite news there that he would arrive, and the landing ground at 'Three Mile' held no welcoming crowds. His arrival was not actually known until a motorist brought the news to town from the landing ground.[6]

'Sundowner of the Skies' became a nickname that stuck to Oscar throughout his life. Not that it was used on a day-to-day basis. It would crop up in the press when someone managed to track him down, even years after he had turned his back on the world of aviation.

Sundowner describes an Australian swagman who arrives unexpectedly out of nowhere on sundown and disappears the next morning. The name suited Oscar perfectly. He was forever on the move. Even though he was born in Scotland, at the time of his initial flight to Australia, he had also spent time in the Isle of Man, Manchester (England), Australia and New Zealand. When he finally settled in New Zealand, he moved house countless times.

Oscar was one of the few survivors of those early years of long-distance flying. Many died in crashes, including Hinkler, Kingsford Smith and Johnson. Of those who survived, he was one of a handful who went on to a career in commercial aviation. He worked first in England and then in New Zealand where, in 1943, he became Chief Pilot and Operations Manager of the fledging airline TEAL, the forerunner of Air New Zealand. By then he was considered 'one of the most capable airline pilots in the world' and 'one of the British Empire's most noted and experienced commercial pilots'.[7] He left TEAL in 1947, three years before I was born, and became a tomato grower in Tauranga, in New Zealand's Bay of Plenty. He never flew a plane again.

After that, he was soon forgotten. In 1979, Ian Driscoll, a noted aviation writer, pointed out that 'Oscar Garden must be the most unnoticed of New Zealand's airline pioneers.'[8] What puzzled me was: if he was that famous and successful, why was he forgotten? And if he was so successful at navigating the skies, why was he such a failure on earth and at family life? Mum had always described him as 'a bastard of a father. And a bastard of a husband.'

He was certainly not my hero when I was growing up. My aim was to leave home as soon as possible, to get right away from him and my odd, dysfunctional family. 'The mad Gardens,' Mum called us. They were Scots, after all, she'd add.

MAP OF ENGLAND AND SCOTLAND

SHETLAND

ORKNEY
Shapinsay
Kirkwall

Tongue

WESTERN ISLES

Rayne

Aberdeen

SCOTLAND

Atlantic
Ocean

Stirling

North
Sea

Glasgow

Edinburgh

Ramsey
Douglas

ISLE OF
MAN

Irish
Sea

Manchester

WALES

ENGLAND

Southend-
on-Sea

London

English Channel

MAGGIE NELSON

0   100   200 km

0   100   200 miles

CHAPTER 1

Merchant Prince of Orkney

Oscar was a Scotsman. Even though he lived in New Zealand for most of his life, he still considered himself a Scot and, more importantly, a Highlander. Our Gardens have been Highland Scots for centuries. One researcher claims we can be traced back to a John Garden born in 1480, whose son George was sent by James I to Denmark in 1589 to deliver the marriage treaty to Princess Anne, and that another ancestor, Beatrix Garden, was maid of honour to Mary Queen of Scots.

Oscar was born in Tongue, a small village of about 500 people in the far north of mainland Scotland, once an historic crossroad for Gaels, Picts and Vikings. His date of birth was 21 August 1903 – just months before the Wright brothers inaugurated the aerial age with their first powered flight. While few would have heard of it, I've known about Tongue since I was a child. It was one thing about my father that made me smile. The name tickled my fancy. One Christmas, a Scottish relative (it may have been his aunt Dora) sent us a board game, that had a large map of Scotland on it. We would throw dice and move little metal cars around to various towns. Tongue was there, right up the top. This board game is the only thing of my childhood I still have. I picked it up from my mother's place one day after I had children of my own. It was remarkable that she still had it, given that she was good at getting rid of things. As was Oscar. The only things he kept from his past were bits and pieces from his flying days that he stored in a camphor laurel chest.

In 2005, after Scotland's *Northern Times* published one of my articles on Oscar, I received an email from an Allan Burr, who subscribed to that newspaper online. Allan, a doctor, was living in Buderim, on Queensland's Sunshine Coast, a short distance from where I was living at the time. I met up with Allan for coffee. Incredibly, he had also been born in Tongue and spent summers working in one of the stores that my great-grandfather Robert Garden Sr, a merchant trader in Orkney, had established years before. In 1974 he had cared for one of Oscar's sisters at Aberdeen Royal Infirmary. Later, at Deception Bay in Queensland, he had a patient who had been an employee of Robert Garden Sr.

Allan said the thing that struck him more than anything else was that a pioneer aviator could have sprung from Tongue. Tongue of all places. Tongue is in the Shire of Sutherland, a bleak and isolated part of Scotland. To this day there are no airports in Sutherland. The land is rugged and sparsely populated. At the time of Oscar's birth, there were about 19 dwellings surrounded by crofting country – crofts were units of agricultural land on large estates, and rented from the landowner.

The area was ravaged during the Sutherland Clearances – the forced and brutal evictions of small crofters by the Duke and Duchess of Sutherland between 1806 and 1820. Sutherland suffered more from the clearances than in other parts of the Highlands. Houses were destroyed or burnt, and people starved or froze to death. Some people were given small allotments in coastal villages where they tried to scrape a living by fishing; others were given assistance to emigrate to North America and Australasia. It has been said that the Highland Clearances left scars on the psyche of Highlanders for generations to come. Even for those who went away, there was an incredible sense of nostalgia and empathy with their former homeland, and also a high degree of romanticism. This was evident in my father. We were given constant reminders of Scotland throughout our childhood. One of our few family outings was the Christmas Carnival at Tauranga's Soundshell at Memorial Park. There would be marching by the local Scottish Pipe Band as well as Highland dancing. I have always found the sound of bagpipes haunting and rousing; no doubt it was for my father.

But it wasn't just his nostalgia. As Margareta, my half-sister, pointed out, 'I always felt he was trapped in north Scotland. Strange things happen to kids when their parents split up.' When I was growing up, I knew little about my father's Scottish childhood; I only knew his parents had separated. And that his grandfather had been disinherited from the Garden fortune. That Garden fortune was amassed by my great-grandfather, Robert Garden Sr. His story is a remarkable one: born into poverty, he became one of the wealthiest traders of Orkney and north Scotland, earning himself the moniker 'Merchant Prince of Orkney'.

Robert was born in 1846 in Rayne, a small village about 26 miles from Aberdeen, nestled in the foothills of Bennachie. Family rumour suggests we are related to one of the Bennachie colonists who were subjected to the Highland Clearances in 1859 but this is yet to be substantiated. His parents were also born in Rayne: John Garden in 1824 and Barbara Allan in 1812. I had assumed they were married, as this was indicated in various documents. Barbara's death certificate had her as 'widow of John Garden – General Labourer' and in the 1881 Census she was listed as 'widowed'. However, after extensive searches I was unable to locate a marriage certificate. In fact, there was none, as they never married. Eventually I located the local parish record of his birth:

1846 August 17 John Garden and Barbara Allan had a son in uncleanness named Robert, baptised on 21st December before witnesses Robert Allan [Barbara's brother] and John Philip [John's uncle]

'In uncleanness' means illegitimate. This is not big deal these days, but to have a child out of wedlock in Scotland back then was a source of great shame and was condemned by the community. Robert would have been called a bastard child. Such was the shame that families went to great lengths to keep their secret under wraps, and they would lie about it, as Barbara did, simply pretending she had been married and had become a widow. It is not known why John and Barbara did not marry, as there would have been pressure for them to do so. However, there was quite an age difference – Barbara was 13 years older than John. She was 35 years old, and to be unmarried and have her first child at that age is unusual.

It is not known how they met; perhaps Barbara was working as a servant on the farm where John was working, and the pregnancy was the result of a casual encounter. It is also unusual that he allowed his son to take his surname. It is likely that he left her to fend for herself as a single mother, soon after the birth. I have no idea if Oscar knew that his grandfather was illegitimate; if he did, I doubt whether he would have told me.

However, John Garden had another child who had a luckier start in life. A few years after Robert's birth, he married Jean Lyon, and their son Alexander was born in 1851. By then John was working as a brewery carter, a wine merchant. I managed to track down the great-granddaughter of Alexander, Barbara Yablonksi, now living in Canada. Barbara has a keen interest in family history, and she, too, had been searching in vain for John Garden and Barbara Allan's marriage certificate. John died in 1857, and the cause of death is stated as 'supposed to be drowning by falling into the Denburn River – not certified'. Perhaps he was drunk, as I was finding that alcoholism coursed through the Garden tree. As Eoin MacGillivray, one of my distant cousins, pointed out to me, 'Denburn is not too wide a

Opposite: My great grandfather Robert Garden Sr in his kilt. He was born into poverty in Rayne, Aberdeenshire, and became one of the wealthiest men in north Scotland. c 1880.

burn and I would have thought he must have been very drunk to manage that or was helped!'

Barbara and Robert lived with her mother, Isabella, for some years in Rayne. Barbara and Isabella worked as stocking knitters; knitting was a thriving cottage industry in rural Scotland at the time. Next door to them lived Barbara's older brother, Robert Allan, his wife and their four children. Robert Allan was renting a small croft of 6 acres. It would have been a hard life in very harsh conditions; they would have worked long hours for meagre rewards and had a poor diet. There was a local parish school, so presumably Robert Garden would have gone there for a few years and learnt to read, write and do basic arithmetic.

The family then experienced upheaval. Isabella died, and Robert Allan and his family emigrated to Canada. In 1856, at the age of 10, Robert Garden went to work on a farm at Culsalmond, about three miles from Rayne, where he became what was known as a herdy boy, tending cattle and sheep. He eventually left the farm and returned to Rayne to live with his mother, now a washerwoman. There he worked as a roof slater.

Evidently Robert was thinking of following his uncle and emigrating to Canada with his mother, but a chance conversation was to change their lives. The story goes that in 1873 Robert met an Orcadian who complained to him about the scarcity of shops in the rural districts of Orkney, and the high price and lack of variety of goods. Orkney is an archipelago a few miles off the north coast of Scotland. Robert had a brainwave. He thought of the pedlars that serviced his little farming community, and he had an idea: he could do the same in Orkney. So he sailed to Kirkwall, the largest town and capital of Orkney. According to anecdotal evidence, he arrived in Kirkwall with a barrow-load of onions.[9]

He was soon travelling the country roads with a horse and wagon, selling goods such as groceries and hardware items at a small profit. He also traded in kind and would accept items including eggs, butter, woollen socks and vegetables, which he would then sell on. His travelling shop

– fitted with shelves on the inside and racks on the outside – was an instant success, and by the end of the year he had acquired more horse-drawn wagons, as well as a six-horsepower steam traction engine, which 'puffed around the mainland roads much to the astonishment and delight of the natives, and to his own profit'.[10] He then opened a grocery store in Kirkwall, and it was here he met Margaret Jolly, whose parents owned a shop around the corner. The Jollys obtained their supplies from Robert.

Margaret Jolly was born in 1856 in Westhill, Shapinsay, one of the islands of Orkney and a few miles north-east of Kirkwall. The Jollys had also come up to Orkney from Aberdeenshire and managed to work themselves up to owning a farm of 106 acres. They eventually sold this farm and moved to Kirkwall. Shortly after meeting Robert, Margaret became pregnant. Sex outside of marriage was fiercely frowned upon during this time, and yet, for some unknown reason, they waited seven months before getting married. They married in September 1874 and their son, who they also named Robert, was born two months later. Unlike his father, he was not born out of wedlock, although he came pretty close.

Robert Sr bought a large house in 18 Bridge Street, Kirkwall, and his mother came up from Aberdeen to live with them (she stayed until her death in 1890). From a life of poverty, they were now living in luxury – a 14-roomed house. They not only had two servants, but also a boot man and a horseman. Robert and Margaret had eight more children, including another son, William; their youngest, Dora, was born in 1894.

In 1890, Robert also bought the Kirkwall Hotel on Bridge Street, turning it into a retail and wholesale business complex, with separate departments for groceries, furniture and other goods. The complex also had an aerated waters factory making lemonade from local spring water, a seeds and manure store, a weaving business and a bakery. The building had historic significance having been built in 1433 and at various times been home to several earls. As well as establishing other stores – mainly grocery and bakeries – in other towns on Orkney, he also built a row

Robert Garden Sr and his family in Kirkwall, Orkney, in 1894. His eldest son (my grandfather), also called Robert, is standing at the back. William is at the front. Dora, the youngest, is sitting on her mother's lap. Dora's son Robin moved to Tauranga, New Zealand, in the early 1950s. Dora settled there in the late 1960s.

of terraced houses, called Garden Street, to accommodate his workers, which he let at very low rents. (These houses still exist today.)

Apart from his growing family and business success, it seems all was not rosy in the Garden life. According to Eoin, a distant cousin, the Jollys owed Robert Garden a substantial amount of money. As the story goes, they obtained a loan and then bought their supplies direct from Aberdeen instead of Robert. Evidently, Robert was furious about this and was seen ripping their sacks of supplies down at Kirkwall harbour. Eoin says, 'There was bad blood between them after this ... apparently he was not the nicest of men.'

Robert realised there was an untapped market in the north and west of Sutherland, one of the most desolate and sparsely populated parts of

Scotland, and he established a string of shops around the coast – most were simple buildings of corrugated iron and wood – with the most prestigious store at Tongue. He clearly made an important contribution to sustaining communities in the north-west of Scotland. One local described him as 'a wheeler-dealer and shrewd businessman who conducted often complicated business dealings informally, usually with nothing in writing; such deals might typically be sealed with a handshake.'[11]

His most brilliant idea was floating shops. In 1884 he bought a schooner, *Zuna*, and converted it to a floating shop, with departments for drapery, groceries and agricultural requirements. A succession of boats followed. These were used to service Orkney, Shetland and the north of Scotland, and down the west coast as far as Ullapool. To access islands that had no piers, the ships would anchor in the harbour, and in response to a signal, a dinghy would go to shore to ferry customers out to the shop. Alexander MacLeod[12] recalls the two floating shops that made monthly visits to Tanera Island, off Scotland's north-west coast. He said he would gather winkles and be given a few shillings, or he would barter them for sweets, biscuits or chocolate.

Although Robert Garden became Orkney's and north Scotland's biggest merchant of the day, he was not just focused on business success. Not surprisingly, considering his impoverished beginnings, he was very generous and helped many Orkney and north Scotland crofters to buy their holdings. He also played an active part in public life and served as a councillor on Orkney County Council, where he advocated for increased allowances to the poor, especially for widows and orphans. He was also involved in the restoration work of the famous Magnus Cathedral, known as the 'Light in the North', founded in 1137 by the Viking Earl Rognvald.

Robert had a fascination for the travels of some of the Norse Earls of Orkney. Between 1906 and 1909 he and Margaret travelled extensively, visiting Norway, Denmark, Sweden, Morocco, Canary Islands and the Near East (now referred to as the Middle East), including a trip to

My great grandparents, Robert and Margaret, in Egypt, 1909.

Jerusalem. He sent back regular reports published in *The Orcadian*, which were later published in a book *Old Cities and Old Countries*. Copies were leather-bound, and I am lucky to have one in my possession. Considering his limited and basic education it is remarkable that he could write so well.

Robert thought Old Cairo was 'the most undesirable place on the earth to live in. The sanitary conditions are shocking, signs of poverty, filthiness, degradation are on all hands.' He describes it as 'overcrowded and such tumble-down buildings and hovels as one could not expect to see anywhere. People and animals are huddled together so that in some cases you could hardly tell which is which.'

Robert's writings show the influence of his puritanical Presbyterian faith. In one report, he writes that he was shocked to see young American ladies with 'faces artificially polished and coloured and their eyebrows blackened'. And he railed against the evils of drink, condemning the scenes of drunkenness he encountered in Aberdeen before they left. Yet he must have known his older son (my grandfather) was an alcoholic. Robert Garden Jr died in 1925 when he was only 50, and his death certificate states cause of death 'chronic alcoholism for 36 years', which suggests he had had a drinking problem since the age of 14! Robert's younger son William was also an alcoholic and died in 1933 at the age of 49 – surprisingly, his death certificate also states cause of death to be chronic alcoholism. Perhaps he had managed to conceal his alcoholism from his father.

On 4 September 1912, Robert died at the age of 66 after a short illness. The cause of death was 'dilation of heart; gangrene of feet for 28 days'. Some said he had worked himself into the ground. There was an outpouring of grief in the community. On the day of his funeral, flags flew at half-mast on public buildings and on all vessels in the harbour. Members of his staff carried the coffin to his grave in the churchyard of St Magnus Cathedral. The headstone of Robert Garden states that Barbara Garden, his mother, was a widow, even though we now know she was never married and he was illegitimate.

The Scotsman wrote that Robert Garden was identified with the trade and life of the county as no other man had been, and his success was phenomenal. The full-page obituary in *The Orcadian* noted:

> *Mr Garden's name has been a household word in every parish and island in Orkney for wellnigh 40 years, and the news of his death will evoke a widespread feeling of regret, for he has been universally held in high esteem not only for his incomparable ability as a business man, and but also for his deep and practical interest in the welfare of Kirkwall and the county generally … His love of work, combined with the gifts as an organiser, the originality of his ideas, and the courage which he brought into his undertakings, pre-eminently fitted him for a successful business career.*

He left a fortune of £821,795, worth today about £77,340,000.[13] A few days before his death, Robert Jr got his clerk John Mooney, who had begun working for Robert in 1884, to draw up a will. In this, he left his business empire to his wife and their youngest son, William. My grandfather, his eldest son, received about £8000, worth today about £752,900. Embla Mooney, John Mooney's daughter, recalled: 'To his son, Robert, with whom he had always quarrelled, and to his daughters, he left legacies. Robert as elder son was advised by lawyers to contest the will, but no flaw was found in it.'[14] At the time of Robert Sr's death, Robert Jr had been married to Rebecca Ward for 16 years, but they had separated in 1910, which no doubt played a role in embarrassing the family. The story I heard from a cousin was that Robert was disinherited from the family fortune because of this separation. Mum said, 'They hated Rebecca [my grandmother] you know. It was such a scandal at the time, separating like that.' However, Embla's letter does not mention this being a reason for the disinheritance.

I have no idea of the nature of the conflict between Robert and his eldest son, but the disinheriting is harsh and cruel. Such acts are a kind of final payback, a blow from the grave. His son would have felt rejected and unloved. And Robert's younger son William repeated his father's pattern. In 1903, William married his first wife, Barbara, who was eight years older than he was (an age difference unusual for the time) and had a seven-year-old illegitimate child. They were an unlikely match. Barbara was to have eight children with William but died in 1915 during childbirth. William went on to marry Robina, with whom he had six children. A few years before he died in 1933, Maggie Garden, one of his daughters of his first marriage, wrote, 'He doesn't seem to care the least little bit for his first family at all, but takes a very keen interest in the welfare of the second.' William left his estate to the children of his second wife, which not surprisingly intensified the bad feeling between the two families. Such unfair bias popped up in later generations. Rebecca would disinherit her two eldest children. And my father took no interest in my two children, the grandchildren from his second marriage, but always had a keen interest in the two granddaughters from his first marriage.

Although Robert Garden Sr remains a legend in Orkney, the troubles that beset his family are not mentioned in any of the articles written about him. They were never discussed in our family. We were only given a sanitised and distorted version. Before I began my research, I knew only the rags-to-riches story, the tale of the poor herdy boy who became a wealthy merchant trader. I did not know of the marital conflict between my grandparents, let alone my grandmother's petitions to Scotland's Supreme Civil Court, except snippets from Mum who said there were 'so many tensions in that family, so much bitterness'.

My mother always said my father had not a chip on his shoulder but a huge plank. This disinheritance from Robert Garden's fortune was certainly the bottom layer. The bitterness, laced with envy toward the wealthier Gardens, also infected his siblings, seeping through the generations.

CHAPTER 2

Family ruptures

Mum always said it was his mother's fault that Dad turned out the way he did. She said Rebecca Garden was stark raving mad and a lying toad. On the other hand, even though she never met him, she'd say that Robert Garden Jr was 'highly thought of' and say of him: 'The poor man, what he had to put up with.' This was the version of Oscar's family history I grew up with. It is only one version.

My grandmother, Rebecca Jane Ward, was not Scottish but a Manx woman, born on 22 March 1871 in Douglas, Isle of Man. Her father, William Henry Ward, was a grocer. Rebecca was brought up a strict Wesleyan Methodist, but in 1887 a branch of the Salvation Army opened in the Isle of Man and she was accepted as a cadet. She was first sent to East End London; in 1891 was promoted to the rank of captain and posted to Harlem, New York. After about a year, she returned and was promoted to officer-in-charge of Belfast, Ireland. Mum said she had heard a story that Rebecca was once put in a barrel and rolled down a hill after she had gone to a pub and ranted and railed about the evils of the demon drink.

In May 1895, Rebecca was appointed to the command of the recently opened branch at Kirkwall, Orkney. This was where she met Robert

My grandparents, Robert Garden Jr and Rebecca Ward, with members of the Salvation Army in Kirkwall in 1895, a year before their marriage.

My grandfather standing in front of *Dunvarrich* c. 1902.

Oscar and his siblings in front of *Dunvarrich* c. 1907. From left to right: Oscar, Robert (Bertie), Violet, Rose and May.

Garden Jr, the oldest child of Robert Garden Sr. It was said that he joined the Salvation Army to get her attention, even though his parents were strict Presbyterians. He only remained a member for a year, and Rebecca left soon afterwards.

Their marriage took place on 22 July 1896 at Douglas, Isle of Man. For their first year they lived in a small tenement house in Glasgow, where Robert worked as a grocer. His father had arranged for him to be the manager of his Tongue store and to live nearby in *Dunvarrich,* a magnificent house made of local granite that he had had built in 1894. They moved there in August 1897, and their first child, Robert, was born soon after. However, the child was a haemophiliac and died 19 days later. Robert and Rebecca were to have five more children in quick succession: May on 2 May 1899; Rose on 2 December 1900; Robert (Bertie) on 23 March 1902; Oscar on 21 August 1903 and Violet on 4 February 1905. Oscar was named after one of Rebecca's twin brothers. A few months after Violet was born, Rebecca's father died, and Rebecca went to the funeral. She had experienced six births and two deaths in the course of seven and a half years. This would have been a harrowing time for her.

It may seem odd to name daughters after flowers (Rose, May and Violet) with a surname like Garden, but not only was Garden a common Scottish name, but Rose Garden, May Garden and Violet Garden were not uncommon at the time. However, Mum and her two sisters – Ola and Margaret – often laughed about it. To them it was more evidence that the Gardens were mad. They thought it was kinky but typical of Rebecca. Mum loved to tell the story of when she visited me in Brisbane in 1983 soon after the birth of my daughter, Natalya. She was sitting at a bus stop at Indooroopilly and began chatting with a woman next to her. They must have shared names with each other as the woman said, 'There's a woman in New Zealand and she had three children: May, Violet and Rose Garden. Have you ever heard anything like it?' 'Really?' Mum replied, pretending to be as shocked as the lady sitting next to her. I'd hear her tell this story to people and laugh out loud. My Aunt Ola would say, 'What a reflection on her intelligence to call her daughters Rose, May and Violet.'

The only letter written by Robert Garden Jr that I have been able to locate is dated 6 December 1900. It was to his parents in Kirkwall after the birth of Rose:

I have always been going to write to you ever since the event happened or rather took place on Sunday night, but have always had something do; your letters came tonight and glad to see that Miss Dunn is on the way [the servant]. We have a nurse and a woman in at present but would rather have some other one... Re [Rebecca] and baby are coming on extra well so far. Re [Rebecca] will likely be writing to you as soon as she is able which won't be long if she gets on as she has done only it is better for her to be careful for a bit. Very sorry to hear of you both keeping so poorly, as it makes one miserable when they are like that. I reckon I have had a good share of it, only I am glad to tell you that I was never better and always plenty to do. I think the bakehouse will do all right ...

The joiner is still here making alterations and improvements, he has been since 1st of July, but another month will about finish him here. Have also got an extra man for one of the shops which up to now was only opened twice a week, will now be opened every day. Another new man at the Rispond shop about a month ago, he isn't going to do, so another one went yesterday and I will have to go away on Monday again to take stock, which takes about two days, that is the place my uncle left fully a year ago. I have a lot of letters to write so you will have to excuse me writing more in the meantime. May is very much taken up with her sister, she is coming on splendid. I shall now close with best love from Re and all.

Yours Bob

Oscar used to brag that on Sundays they would spend most of the day at church, the historic St Andrews built in 1724. He even scratched his name into the back of the one of the pews. It was still there when he and Mum went to Tongue for a visit in 1979. The church was a Free Presbyterian Church of Scotland (commonly referred to as The Wee Respond Frees), an ultra-conservative Calvinist church, where the Bible is taken literally – regarded as the inspired and infallible word of God. Until the day he died, my father believed this. And believed he was going to heaven.

The Wee Respond Frees was featured in the movie *Breaking the Waves*. For many years on a Friday, to escape Oscar, Mum would take the train from Papakura in South Auckland into the city to see a movie. Once, in 1996, she rang me from a pay phone. I have never heard her so angry. My mother, whose anger was usually held inside and only seeped out in tight grimaces or a high-pitched voice, was shaking with fury. She had just seen *Breaking the Waves*, set in north Scotland, where the chief gathering place was an austere little church, a Free Scottish Presbyterian church, much like the one in which Oscar spent his Sundays. One reviewer called the movie a masterpiece, 'a blistering critique of the repression and denial that faith-based moralizers confuse with principles and decency'.[15] I just had to see the movie, Mum said. That bloody church. She said she had no idea how narrow-minded they were, how cruel and cold. No wonder your father turned out the way he was, she seethed. (It wasn't *only* Rebecca's fault!)

When I was a child, we had to go a Presbyterian Church and Sunday school. Dad seldom went to church, except at Easter and Christmas. He said he had learnt all he needed to know from his mother and so didn't need to go. Thankfully, religion was never discussed at home and the Bible was never mentioned, although for some years I was convinced there was a God up there and there was a heaven, a hell and a devil. By the age of 11 or 12, I had discarded it all. Other things were more important, like boys, Elvis and the Beatles. Perhaps Mum had an influence, as she was an atheist and had not grown up in a religious household. The Scottish Gardens, however, were staunch Presbyterians, and religion played a central role in their lives.

Not long after Oscar was born, his father bought the first car (a little Peugeot) in the district and by 1904 was running a lorry service and a car-hire service. In recognition of this, on 4 February 1909, he was presented with an illuminated address[16] and a gold appendage.

I never took much notice of it when I was a child, but this address hung in the various lounge rooms of my parents' homes. It has a walnut frame and at the top there is an inlay of mother of pearl, with a carving of a motorcar. The address itself is in old English script in five colours and is interspersed with miniature watercolour paintings of various scenes, including Sir John Square, the Melvich Hotel and *Dunvarrich*. The *Northern Times* reported:

> *An event unparalled in the history of the district, took place in Tongue hotel … when Mr Robert Garden was presented with an illuminated address and gold appendage, in recognition of his invaluable services in opening up the country and facilitating the means of transit of passengers and goods by substituting motor power for the slow and cumbrous means formerly in use.*[17]

The *Northern Times* also reported a Mr Lennox as saying, 'One obstacle had yet to be overcome, and that was the snow which sometimes prevented mails from reaching their destination for a week. Perhaps Mr Garden would in the future carry them over that obstacle on the wings of an aeroplane.' (Some 26 years later Oscar was employed as a pilot flying Fox Moths for Scottish Motor Traction, the first airline to service the north of Scotland.) The address reads:

> *Sir, we the undersigned representing Traders & Residenters in the*

My grandparents Robert and Rebecca in a red Baby Peugeot, the first car in the district, in front of their home *Dunvarrich*. The car was registered in Robert's name in 1904.

My grandfather introduced motor transport to the north of Scotland. These are his cars and he is driving the one on the right hand side – NS-10.

Counties of Sutherland and Caithness desire to convey to you their high appreciation of the benefits which have resulted to them since you introduced locally in the year 1904 a System of Service by Motor Carriage. The only means of public road conveyance throughout the Counties prior to your introducing a Motor Service was by coaches and horse traction generally and in consequence the transit of persons, mails and good was limited, slow and expensive. Happily, these restrictions no longer exist and the change can be traced to you.

Your business foresight, your mechanical skills and your enterprise as pioneer in these parts of the modern system of carriage in which you have now indeed many followers has brought the different places of populations and trade in a wide and scattered area within closer relations and facilitated business dispatch and postal communication in every way. For these considerations, we would express our sense of gratitude and the sincere hope that you may long enjoy the business success, which you have well earned by contributing so signally to the prosperity and commercial development of the North.[18]

Robert's good reputation and business success were short-lived. Less than a year after the presentation, the marriage fell apart. In January 1910, while Robert was away on a business trip, Rebecca ran away with the five children. In a small town with only 500 people, where the family was well known and influential, this would have been scandalous. As Robert was to later state in a response to a court petition, 'They were the talk of the neighbourhood.' In Scotland at that time, women were expected and pressured to stay in unhappy marriages, especially as fathers had common-law rights to their children as property and women were financially dependent on their husbands. Not only that, but Rebecca was a staunch Christian and a member of the Free Church of Scotland congregation. Adultery and desertion were the only biblical (and legal) grounds for a divorce.

As there were no trains or buses to that part of Scotland at that time, presumably Rebecca took the four-horse mail coach to Thurso, about 50 miles away, and caught a train from there.

Rebecca and her children travelled a huge distance – at least 700 miles – from the far north of Scotland to Southend-on-Sea, Essex, on England's south coast. Here they stayed at a holiday home called *Elinsville*. During this time Rebecca applied to the Court of Session (Scotland's Supreme Civil Court) for separation and aliment (in Scottish law, aliment means maintenance and alimony) and gave the grounds as [Robert's] adultery with their servants and other women, and of indecent conduct towards one of their children.

Then disaster struck. The oldest child, Bertie, who was eight years old, became sick with acute nephritis and died on 11 May 1910. (Dad always said that Bertie died of consumption, but this is not the case.) Even though Robert did not know of the child's illness until after his death, it seems this led to some reconciliation, at least for the short term. According to Rebecca, in June 1910 Robert promised 'amends' and she abandoned the court action and returned to Tongue. However, he claimed she returned against his wishes.

In October 1910, Robert sent the two oldest girls to a private boarding school at Bridge of Allan at Stirling, in central Scotland, about 300 miles from Tongue. May was 11 years of age and Rose was only nine. Robert states in his responses to Rebecca's subsequent petition to the court that this was necessary in order to remove them from her influence and so they were not affected by local gossip. He claimed that Rebecca frequently made unfounded accusations of his 'drunkenness, indecent conduct and adultery', and even told the neighbours that he was committing adultery with the female servants. He also complained about the way she treated the children, as she 'encouraged them to resist his authority and took their part against him when it was his duty to reprove or punish them'. Corporal punishment was common in those days; parents and teachers had the right to spank or cane children when they thought it was appropriate. For Rebecca to try to intervene was highly unusual.

Robert admits that Rebecca was 'highly incensed' that the two girls were sent away, but said he allowed her to visit them at the school. In July 1911 Rebecca lodged with criminal authorities a charge of 'indecent behaviour' towards one of his daughters (which one is not mentioned), although, surprisingly, she continued to stay at *Dunvarrich*. In May 1912, Robert decided to send Violet and Oscar to boarding schools. Violet, who was only seven, joined her older sisters at Bridge of Allen; Oscar, who was eight years old, went to the Dollar Academy, in Clackmannanshire, about 12 miles from his sisters' school and 35 miles from Edinburgh.

Robert claimed that while he was away making these arrangements, Rebecca left and informed Robert that she would not be returning. However, her version was that she had been 'kicked out' of her home. Regardless, she went to live in Edinburgh. Earlier that year, on 6 January 1912, Rebecca's mother died, and in November she received £420 (worth about £39,530 today).

In a letter to his parents dated 23 August 1912 (two days after his 9th birthday), Oscar seems unaware of their separation. He thanks them for a flash lamp, and tells them of the game of trains he received from May and Rosie, which he and his classmates play with every day. He says he was also given a box of chocolates and a [toy] yacht. He mentions he is going home on 31 August and draws pictures of *Dunvarrich* and a box of chocolates. While Oscar was on holiday at *Dunvarrich*, his grandfather Robert Garden Sr died. As mentioned, Robert Garden Jr received £8000 from the estate; however, there was no property settlement in those days, so Rebecca would not have been entitled to receive any share of Robert's wealth, including the inheritance from his father.

On 21 February 1913, the business that had been carried on by Robert Garden Sr was transferred by the executors to Margaret, his widow, and William, his youngest son. Robert Jr had to cease working in the family business, although he still retained his motor business. This surely would have made him furious: not only had he lost his main source of income but his marriage had fallen apart. Peter Burr, who had been managing a few of the Garden stores on Orkney, moved to Tongue to manage the store and rented most of *Dunvarrich*. His grandson, also named Peter, told me that the Burr clan at that stage comprised of Peter and his wife, their nine children and one on the way! Robert kept just a few rooms for himself. (The Tongue store was purchased by Peter Burr in 1932. He retired in 1939 and his two sons, Gordon and Leslie Burr, bought him out.)

In June 1913 Rebecca applied to the court for permission to be able to return to the marital home, and if this was not granted then she requested aliment and custody of the children. Clearly, it was unbearable for her to be separated from the children. However, when Robert agreed to place the children near Edinburgh during the school holidays so she could see them periodically, she withdrew the application.

Robert did not stick to his agreement. Oscar returned to Tongue, Violet went to stay with one of Robert's sisters at Aberdeen, and the two eldest girls stayed in Edinburgh. Evidently, Rebecca was only given 5 minutes' access to May and Rose on the first day and 10 minutes on the second visit and then denied access altogether on the third. Robert then demanded an undertaking that Rebecca not enter the county of Sutherland, which was quite absurd but a reflection of the hostility growing between them. In Robert's case it was compounded by being disinherited. He must have felt cast out of his Orkney family and now his own family, was breaking up. His drinking would not have helped his state of mind.

On 9 September 1913, Rebecca lodged a petition[19] to the Court of Session for access to her children and requested that they be placed in neutral custody near Edinburgh; in the following month she petitioned for adherence and aliment.[20] In these applications, she alleged that for several years his conduct had been 'very cruel, due chiefly to his being much addicted to drink' and she had been 'forced by his mistreatment to leave the house'. She claimed he was almost daily under the influence of liquor and frequently beat her in front of the children. He denied these allegations and said the marriage had never been a happy one due to Rebecca's 'excitable and emotional temperament, hasty temper, extreme and intolerant views on temperance, and her jealousy and suspicion'. He claimed she was 'mentally abnormal in sexual matters', possessed of a hysterical temperament and morbid imagination, and constantly concocting false stories about him being immoral and a drunkard and discussing these with neighbours, relatives and their children. She tried to alienate the children by calling their father a 'drunkard and adulterer'.

What can we make of these allegations? Mum was adamant that Rebecca lied. She used to call her a 'lying toad'. And she had evidence! She told me that when she and my father visited Tongue in 1979, she went for a long walk one morning and met up with the eldest person living in the town who evidently said to her, 'Terrible what Oscar's father had to put up with, with that woman. The judge didn't believe a word she said.' In a letter to Margareta Gee (Oscar's daughter from his first marriage) in 1993 she wrote, 'When it comes to family history, there are so many versions. Rose may have been the most reliable one to ask questions, she did tell me a lot, much of which rocked me, but neither Oscar nor Violet would go along with that.' But why did Mum assume that Rose told her the truth? Some of what Rose told her son, Roger, was not true at all.

Roger believes that Rebecca's feisty nature would have taken a toll on the marriage and that 'Robert ultimately found her forthright and fervent nature somewhat of a strain'. Both Mum and her sister Ola found Rebecca forthright. Ola told me:

I'll always connect his mother with marmite. Brown bread, chives and marmite. That's all she knew about. She came out to visit me twice, and that was all she would have. I passed her cake once and she thrust

39

it back, saying 'muck'. She was full of him, your father. Religious crank.
Over brainy but odd, definitely odd.

Roger had the view that it was Robert's decision to leave her and split the family in half. This was not the case. It was Rebecca who decided to leave, who ran away. Roger also had been told that Robert had left Rebecca reasonably well off when the marriage collapsed. Again, this is not true, as there was no property settlement. Robert only paid her maintenance. This version of the marriage breakup is one that Robert seems to have fed to his two eldest daughters (May and Rose), who would have passed it on to their children (my cousins).

In 2006, after I had sent Margareta extracts from the court documents, she replied, 'It is hard to tell who's telling the truth but one didn't get a real sense of severe scarring from May and Rose so I imagine some of it was hatched for a divorce/separation case. Oscar and Violet seemed to be in a far worse state! Who knows? What a pity we never thought to really question them on everything, but then, on the other hand, many people feel happier that things are "forgotten", not dredged up and so on.'

Why would Rebecca lie? In the early 20th century in Scotland divorce and separation was a rare occurrence, especially when initiated by the wife. The only two grounds for divorce were adultery or desertion. At that time there were only about 200 divorces a year in Scotland. Domestic violence was not considered justification for a divorce, only separation. Alcohol was viewed as the cause of most common violence. Men were not blamed; rather, the violence was attributed to the effects of alcohol. In addition, provocation was a valid defence for cruelty. Scottish judges could conclude that the husband's violence was justified, and therefore should only be regarded as chastisement. The wife deserved discipline![21]

Women were financially dependent on their husbands, and the social stigma of marital breakdown was strong. While marriage represented a unity between a man and a woman, this unity did not mean equality. The wife was not considered equal under Scottish law: marriage placed her under the control of her husband. She was duty bound to have sex with her husband – rape did not legally exist within marriage – and the children of the marriage were, for purposes of guardianship, custody and access, the husband's. To end a marriage was difficult due to costly and lengthy legal processes, and requirements of evidence.

My cousin Rosemarie, Violet's daughter, recalled her mother telling her that Robert was a wonderful business-man, but had a nasty side: he loved whisky and the maids in *Dunvarrich*, and had a very bad temper. Rosemarie said she was told that Robert used to bang Rebecca's head down on the taps at *Dunvarrich*. The letter written by Embla Mooney, mentioned in the previous chapter, points towards a fractious relationship with his father, with whom he 'always quarrelled'. Robert admits that he 'punished' the children, which in those days meant beating or caning. It seems plausible that he was also abusive to Rebecca, his temper fuelled by alcohol, because the one thing we know for certain is that Robert was an alcoholic. Mum excused his drinking problem. She'd say, 'What man wouldn't be driven to drink with a wife like that?' However, Robert had been an alcoholic for some years before he met Rebecca.

Luckily, my father was not an alcoholic; nor is anyone in my immediate family. Interestingly, in January 1985, Gordon Burr discovered a hidden whisky cache of 11 bottles of Dewar's in the office desk of the Tongue store. They took a bottle for analysis to Dewar's of Perth in Scotland, who determined that Robert Garden Jr was the original owner. Surprisingly, when Cathie MacLeod, a neighbour of my brother Robert who lived in Auckland, was on holiday in Scotland, and read about the find in the *Northern Times*, she realised that it was Robert's grandfather who had concealed the whisky. One of the bottles was given to her to take back to our family in New Zealand.

Perhaps Robert *was* an adulterer. He had said Rebecca was 'mentally abnormal in sexual matters', and one of my cousins told me that on their wedding night she had run out into the streets screaming. Maybe she had never been told about sex or the facts of life. On 12 December 1913, a child, Williamina, was born to Robert's servant Kate Macpherson.[22] This is the child that Rebecca claimed in court documents was Robert's. The birth took place at *Dunvarrich*, and for some reason Oscar was home at the time. Peter Burr and his family were now living there, so presumably they were also aware of the birth. Amidst all this drama, the day after the birth Robert went down to Southampton to see his sister Edith, who was very ill. He arrived there just in time; she died on 15 December at the age of 31. Robert's problems were snowballing. He would have felt blindsided by what life was throwing at him.

Even though Robert denied the child was his, Kate continued to stay in the house until March 1914, at which time Robert made arrangements for her to stay elsewhere in Tongue. If the child was not his, why did Robert allow the birth to take place at his house and for her to stay for months afterwards? Why didn't she go back to her parent's home or to a relative? Unfortunately, the child died of pneumonia when she was nine months old, and my attempts to track down any of Kate's descendants have proved fruitless.

All these events and the fighting between his parents must have been hugely traumatic and confusing for Oscar who was only 10 years old at the time of Williamina's birth and who had been told by his mother that the baby was his father's! School was no respite either. Dollar Academy at that time, like most boarding schools, would have been a harsh environment, with corporal punishment universally used in Scottish schools. A child would be traditionally hit with a tawse, a stiff leather strap with two tails, across the hands or on the bottom.

On 19 March 1914, Oscar wrote to his mother, 'I have done the best in my exams. They are all finished now.' He tells her that he will meet her at the Alloa train station (about 7 miles away from his school) on that Saturday. In another letter dated 3 May 1914, he writes:

I have lots of things to tell you. May and Rosie are ill in Kirkwall. Violet is going to stay in Currie [about 8 miles from Edinburgh] I think. Dad is going to stay at Edinburgh. Him and Aunt Dora were here yesterday and I got a camera from them. Come here on Saturday if you like. The long weekend, I think. Dad is going to put me to Currie with Violet. The holidays are on 28 June. Am I coming back after summer holidays? I will know better what to do now.

Clearly, Robert had kept Rebecca in the dark regarding the children's whereabouts during the upcoming school holidays. Consequently, she decided to abduct Oscar and Violet from their schools. Violet's daughter, Rosemarie, said her mother told her that Rebecca grabbed her while she was marching with the class. A court order instructed Rebecca to return the children, and said she was prohibited from removing them from Scotland. She obeyed, but after a week removed them again and fled to the Isle of Man. They travelled more than 200 miles by train down to Heysham and caught a ferry across to Douglas. Rebecca ignored a court order to return the children within three days. Police were instructed to search England for the children and deliver them into the custody of Robert Garden.

It was too late. Not only was the Isle of Man independent of England, but on 4 August 1914 Great Britain declared war on Germany, the beginning of World War I. Soon after, Robert left Scotland with Rose and May and sailed to New Zealand on RMS *Tainui*. No doubt he wanted to escape the war, but he also wanted to get as far away as possible from Rebecca. He claimed his reputation had been ruined in both Tongue and Orkney because of her 'false allegations'. Other members of our Garden family had migrated to Canada. Robert was the first to settle in New Zealand. Perhaps it was further away from Scotland than Canada and he hoped he could leave his past behind him, reinvent himself in a place where no one knew him.

Oscar and his sisters after their return to *Dunvarrich* after Bertie's death in 1910.

Oscar and his youngest sister Violet in 1912.

Neither Robert nor Rebecca wanted to split up the family. In the early stages both had sought custody of all the children. Rebecca had argued that 'all the children should be brought up together, as they are all very much attached to each other.' This splintering of the family was traumatic for all concerned, especially the children, and has had ramifications to this day. Growing up I had little to do with Oscar's sisters or my cousins, who were between 10 and 20 years older than I was. Unlike in Mum's family, there were no Garden reunions or social get-togethers to celebrate Christmas or other events. Not only was there a split in Oscar's family, but it was as if we were all cut off from the Garden side. Not surprisingly, I was not aware of the rift between the two oldest children, Rose and May, on the one hand, and Violet and Oscar on the other.

Many years later, Violet and May lived near each other in Christchurch, but nothing was resolved. One of my cousins said this 'probably inflamed the animosity between them.' It is likely that neither of the pairs of siblings ever discussed the past with one another, or tried to heal things. The tensions were fuelled by misinformation and half-truths as to who was to blame for the breakup of the family. Who could they believe? Rose and May defended their father, while Violet and Oscar defended their mother. Not surprisingly, there are tensions even today between some of my cousins. One of them was shocked and saddened to hear another cousin's opinion of Rebecca and the family history, adding, 'They [the Gardens] were a very strange lot.'

CHAPTER 3

War and peace

Rebecca and the two children stayed on the Isle of Man for almost two years, during which time Oscar attended Douglas Secondary School. I have no knowledge of where they lived, or what life was like for them there. In no interview did Oscar mention what it was like to be estranged from his two older sisters and his father, and the impact that had on him. In one interview, he mentions that they went to the Wesleyan-Methodist church, which Rebecca had attended as a child. While in Douglas, Rebecca joined the International Bible Students Association (IBSA), later known as Jehovah Witnesses. The IBSA was opposed to military service in the war. In Britain, all the Germans had been rounded up and sent to two prison camps that were established on the Isle of Man, known as The Manx Alien Camps. The smaller of the two was at Douglas. There were several Germans who were IBSA members and Rebecca would visit them once a week.

Apart from this, all I have are reports from Oscar's school. One, dated autumn 1916, says, 'Excellent progress – a very reliable boy'. He received the highest grades possible for science, mathematics and French. A report from spring 1917 states, 'Excellent progress; pupil possesses excellent ability'. He left the school at the age of 13 on 5 April 1917, and this was the end of his schooling. A letter by the headmaster, AJ Ridge, dated 14 November 1919, states, 'Oscar was a very capable and painstaking boy who could always be relied on to do his best and consequently he invariably took a high position in his form. His conduct was always excellent.'

In April 1917, Rebecca moved to Higher Broughton, Manchester, to look after the home[23] of a doctor (Doctor Hudson) who had been imprisoned at Dartmoor Prison for being a conscientious objector. (Perhaps he was also a member of IBSA.) Evidently, he had refused to be a stretcher bearer. As well as having free housing, Rebecca was paid 10 shillings a week (worth approximately £26.63 today), and she let out one of the rooms for the same amount. Even though she also received £1.50 maintenance per week from Robert, Rebecca evidently still struggled to keep the children fed and clothed.

At 13 Oscar was now expected to be the breadwinner, and he applied for a job as an office boy with a Norwegian importer. About 27 boys turned up to be interviewed, and Oscar was given the job because he had the neatest handwriting. His work was addressing envelopes for 11 hours a day for 5 shillings a week. On Saturdays, he received a small allowance for lighting fires on the Jewish Sabbath with a Jewish friend. This work did not last long because Oscar became very ill with an abscess on his left leg and spent months bedridden. Oscar recalled that he eventually had three large holes 'spewing out pus and muck and what-have-you' and an Austrian doctor would come twice a week and burn off the proud flesh that kept growing with prussic acid. 'It was absolutely dreadful, my left leg, one side of the shin bone, was practically all eaten away inside.' It reached the point where the doctor could not do any more. He was taken to a specialist and told the leg would have to be amputated below the knee, and might have to be amputated further if that didn't resolve the problem.

Rebecca received a letter from the Manchester Royal Infirmary

Hospital stating that the operation would take place on 5 November 1917. As Oscar recalls, 'You couldn't imagine anything worse than that.' At the bottom of the letter (I have the original in my possession) it says: 'You must provide a proper change of linen weekly, and bring with you two towels and soap or you cannot be received into the Institution.'

Luckily, another letter arrived a few days later to say the operation was to be postponed due to the huge influx of wounded soldiers from the battle at Passchendaele. About that time Rebecca acquired a new boarder, an Egyptian man named Pizarro who had just qualified as a doctor. For a few weeks, Pizarro removed 'the muck from the wound' using a syringe and some salts, and then operated on the leg with Rebecca holding a pad with chloroform on it over Oscar's face. Miraculously, within a few weeks the holes had begun closing up and he was able to walk. Oscar said Pizarro took him back to the specialist who couldn't believe his eyes.

Dad loved telling us snippets of this story. Apart from his tale about scribbling his name into the back of the church pew at Tongue, it is the only thing I can remember him telling me about his childhood. Even though it was a horrific experience, he would make light of it. It was one of those rare occasions when you'd see him grin. He'd enjoy pulling up his trouser leg and showing us this large dent in his calf. For three years he had to wear a special shoe jacked up at an angle (and modified every few months) while new flesh grew against the shin bone. During these years he went to night school to learn electrical engineering, and for his last 18 months in Manchester he worked as an apprentice at a garage maintaining cars, 'grinding valves … and cleaning the damn things'.

Meanwhile, Robert Garden Jr was reinventing himself as a business-man in New Zealand. Scottish migration to New Zealand was mostly to the Otago and Southland regions; beginning in 1840, Scots made up about a third of the total population in these provinces by 1871. So it is not surprising that this is where Robert and his two eldest daughters headed. They first settled in Cave, about 14 miles from Timaru. Cave was a tiny town with a population of about 90 people, even smaller than Tongue. Robert went on a spending spree. He may have been disinherited from his father's business empire, but the legacy of £8000 he had received was not insignificant. He may also have gained some money from the lorry service and car hire business that he had in Tongue.

In January 1915, he bought the Cave general store and post-office as well as a property on 17 Anne Street that had an old house on it. He replaced the house with a contemporary six-roomed house for the girls and himself. He also built four other houses in town, including three more on Anne Street.[24] In those days of mostly horse-drawn transport, he owned a car as well as a Buick truck that he used for deliveries in the country area. As previously in Tongue, in Cave he was the wealthy merchant. And once again May and Rose went away to boarding school (Strathmore School in Timaru) but would return home for weekends and holidays. However, although Robert had escaped Rebecca, he could not escape his alcoholism. His drinking habit is mentioned in a 1990 publication on Cave that I discovered in the Timaru Museum: 'Mr Garden had a problem – periodically he would go on a drinking spree, and then refuse to hand out the mail.'[25]

In 1918, Robert moved to Timaru and bought a house in 16 Sarah Street. The next year, he sailed from Wellington to London on the *Athenic*, apparently with the intent of bringing back Oscar, as indicated in this letter:

Sunday July 25 1919

Dear Dad

Mother has told me you came to the door a fortnight ago asking to see me and she has also shown me the various notes you left stating you wished to see me, but we recieved [sic] information before you arrived that you were coming to take me from mother back to New Zealand. As I have no desire to be taken away from her, I think it would be best for you and I if you left me alone. I am quite content and happy where I am, and I have not forgotten how I was treated at Dollar Academy, when sent there by you before the War ... and yet you would see her working day and night with lodgers, even when I was ill in bed, to keep us in food or clothes. I shall not forget that either. I suppose you know that I am old enough now to choose by law who I go with so you will not be able to take me by fair means – I do not want to hurt your feelings in any way Dad, but I just want you to see that I do not want to be parted from my mother who has loved and cared for me all these years. You do not need to persuade me further to go to NZ with you.

From your son Oscar.

Oscar did in fact go back to New Zealand, but with Rebecca. In 1921, she decided to migrate. Oscar claimed that this was so she could 'extract 50 shillings more a week' maintenance. Roger told me that Rebecca only came to New Zealand because 'she couldn't stand the idea that Robert might be prospering and she wasn't there to reap some benefits.' The poor man, Mum used to say. He escaped to New Zealand to get as far away from her as possible. When he heard that she was moving there too, he fell to his knees and sobbed. I never asked who told her this story. Was it Aunt Rose? Of course, there was the possibility that Rebecca might have also been missing her two eldest daughters. And because they had separated, there would have been no chance for Rebecca to reap any benefits.

Rebecca, Violet and Oscar sailed on the SS *Ormonde* and arrived in Melbourne in May 1921. They went from there by steamer to Port Chalmers, Dunedin. Oscar stayed with his mother for six months living with his mother at Pine Hill, Dunedin, working as an apprentice electrician, before going north to Timaru – about 120 miles away – to work in his father's factory. In 1920, Robert had bought an aerated water factory (soft drink and cordial business) in 34 Wollcombe Street, renaming it R. Garden and Company. He would have been familiar with such production because in the late 1800s his father, the Merchant Prince of Orkney, had established an aerated waters factory in Kirkwall as part of his complex on Bridge Street; it used fresh water from a nearby spring and was called Garden's Lemonade Factory.

In several interviews, including one in 1990 for the *Otago Daily Times*,[26] Oscar said he had been persuaded to join his estranged father 'for the good of the family' but did not explain who talked him into this. Was it his father or mother? His older sisters? However, the situation came about, no good came of it. It wasn't long before 'a row drove him

The aerated waters factory my grandfather, Robert Garden Jr, bought in 1920 in Timaru, New Zealand. Oscar is wearing an apron and standing to the right of his father. c. 1922.

back to his mother', who had moved to Riccarton, a suburb a few miles from the centre of Christchurch. What the row was about Oscar never explained, and unfortunately those who interviewed him did not ask. Perhaps it was about his father's drinking or the way he had treated his mother in Scotland; or the way he had treated the children. I don't know what Oscar's relationship was like with his two older sisters after he arrived in New Zealand in 1921, but it was likely to have been strained because May and Rose had clearly sided with their father and believed his version of events. It would have also been difficult for Rebecca, knowing that she was cast as the villain in the drama. The Scottish way was to never discuss things but instead keep them close to one's chest. Rather than abating, the resentments and unresolved issues would have kept seeping through.

In Christchurch, Oscar found a job working for a restaurant where he would deliver food in a light van. 'One day,' he recalled, 'I was walking in and I had a can [this was before septic tanks or modern sewerage systems: the toilet would be outside the house and would often consist of a seat over a collection pan] and I slipped. That was the end of that job.' His next job as a chauffeur to a Jewish family didn't last long, either. He had to drive the man into Christchurch every morning to work and then go back to the house in case the wife wanted to be driven anywhere. One day she said, 'I've got an extra job for you to do, Oscar. I'd like you to clean the windows.' He replied, 'I don't clean windows.' She told him they would not need him anymore. I doubt whether Oscar cleaned a window in his life. After he married my mother, he did not lift a hand to help her in the house, even when she or we children were sick.

Then Oscar met a man who told him there was a lot of money to be made rabbiting, so he went up to a farm at Culverden in North Canterbury, found the person in charge and convinced him to give him a chance. Oscar told him he was a good shot (even though he had little experience) but fortunately they rarely had to use guns because poison was used instead.

At the time, rabbiting was then subsidised by the government, so the pay was good. May, interviewed in 1930, said her brother 'knew no more about country life than the man in the moon, but he went rabbiting and was successful at it'.[27] He earned £300 from this venture.

Soon afterwards Oscar spent some time in Christchurch hospital with appendicitis. Marion Shepherd, who was doing nursing training, met him when he was a patient. She recalls that after he was discharged, he would gather up a group of nurses for car outings:

> One memorable patient was Oscar Garden who was admitted with acute appendicitis. His irrepressible personality made a lot of friends among the nurses. After he regained his health, he took us out in his car for picnics, deliciously prepared by his mother. My first impression was that he was a reckless and foolhardy driver. When we approached what I thought was a river he did not slow down. I closed my eyes expecting the end. A minute or two later I found myself on solid ground. It was only a flooded water race but it looked terrifying, especially as all country roads were shingle and could be very rough. We marvelled at his sense of direction. A vague idea was enough for him to find his way.
>
> I was thankful that there was one outing with Oscar that I missed. He was showing off and, driving too fast, struck a large bump and the back-seat passenger hit her head on the roof. Her top denture broke; she cut her forehead and started nose bleeding. As a country hospital was nearby, they called in for help. Unfortunately, the sister of the back seat passenger was on the staff and was most displeased. To add to it, the girl was admitted to the ward where her sister had been on duty that morning. Oscar told us about the frosty reception from their mother when he visited her the next day with £5 for denture repairs. These outings ended when Oscar left the city and started a bicycle business in the country.[28]

Irrepressible personality! Lots of friends! This personality had long vanished by the time he became my father. He had no friends. He was a loner and had shut down emotionally.

The bicycle business Oscar bought was the Spreydon Cycle Depot about three miles from Christchurch. In the mid-1920s bicycles were very popular, as cars were still the preserve of the rich. Christchurch with its flat terrain had always been ideal for cycling, and in 1892 the first cycling club in Australasia for women was established there.[29] In 1924, the city council's motor inspector estimated that there were about 40,000 cyclists in the city, more than half Christchurch's population.[30] It was the opportune time and place for Oscar to buy such a business. How strange that, decades later, I was to marry someone in Australia who had his own bicycle business and had also been a racing cyclist. This business is now owned by our children but managed by our son. I work in the business and do the accounts and secretarial work. We sell bicycle parts and accessories Australia-wide. The Garden entrepreneurial spirit lives on.

While Oscar was busy selling bicycles and accessories, Rebecca was busy finishing things with Robert. I do not know what contact they had had since she arrived in New Zealand, but it could not have been amicable. On 17 April 1924, she made an application in the Supreme Court of New Zealand for a divorce, the grounds being 'mutual separation of three years and upwards'. She stated they had separated by mutual consent and since she had come to New Zealand Robert had been paying her maintenance of £1. This application came to light when I was ordering the wills of both Rebecca and Robert; an archivist at Christchurch asked if I was also interested in their divorce file. No one in the family knew of this.

Rebecca's divorce application was heard on 24 September 1924, and on 26 January 1925 she was granted permission to apply to have *Decree Nisi* made absolute. For some reason she never applied for this. At the time Robert was back in Scotland (who was he visiting and what was he doing there?). Shipping records show he sailed back to New Zealand on the *Aorangi*, arriving in Wellington on 28 February 1925. He was not well and a few months later, on 20 May 1925, at the age of only 50, he died at his home in Sarah Street. Even though Dad always said his father died of a heart attack, the cause of death, as already mentioned, was alcoholism. The death certificate actually states the cause of death as 'chronic alcoholism – 36 years; fatty degeneration of the heart – 5 years 5 months; syncope'. The doctor had seen him two days before. Unless the doctor had miscalculated, Robert had been drinking since he was 14.

His will, dated 24 March 1919, directed his trustee to invest £1000 Sterling, and to pay the income from such investment to his wife Rebecca Jane Garden so long as she remained his widow. However, due to her application for a divorce, he added a codicil dated 28 June 1924:

Whereas steps are now being taken by my said wife to obtain through the Supreme Court a legal divorce from me now I hereby revoke this bequest and direct my Trustee to pay the said sum of £1000 equally between all my children and further I direct my said Trustee to pay to my daughter Rose Garden a legacy of 500 pounds to be in addition to her one fourth share of my Estate.

I have no idea why Rose was given extra money. Had she been caring for him in those last months? The rest of his estate, valued at £6939, worth about NZ $558,503 today, was to be divided between his four children. However, at the time of his death Rebecca was still legally his wife, as the divorce had not been finalised. She continued to receive money from his estate for her living expenses until her death in 1954.

In June 1926, Oscar sold his bike shop and bought a garage with living quarters attached in Southbridge, a small town 17 miles southwest of Christchurch with only a few hundred residents. He called the garage Garden's Southbridge Garage. As well as selling petrol, oil, tyres and accessories, the garage provided servicing and repairs to cars and bicycles. It was also an agent for Hudson and Essex cars, and hired-out cars. Oscar

Southbridge Garage near Christchurch that Oscar bought in 1926. He is standing in front with hands on hips.

On the ship to England in early 1930. Oscar is on the left.

had been around cars from his childhood with his father introducing the first motor vehicles to Sutherland and Caithness in north Scotland. In Manchester during the war, he had worked as an apprentice at a garage maintaining cars. However, until the mid-1920s, few people could afford them. In New Zealand, between 1925 and 1930, the number of cars on the road more than doubled. With about one car for every nine people, it had one of the levels of car ownership in the world.[31]

Oscar soon introduced some of the earliest hand-pumped petrol bowsers; he also sold Plume Motor Spirit. It was through the sale of this petrol that he became a client of the Vacuum Oil Company, which later provided fuel supplies on his flight to Australia. He placed regular advertisements in the papers and claimed he could beat Christchurch prices for new bicycles and accessories of all kinds. Moreover, because Garden's Southbridge Garage were the sole manufacturers of the 'famous Peerless Racing Cycle', cyclists were urged: 'See us before you buy your next mount. Come in and have a chat with us about it.'

I also discovered that Oscar's reckless driving landed him in court. On 1 December 1926, he was caught speeding and driving dangerously on the Leeston-Christchurch Road. On 25 February 1927, he was convicted and fined 5 shillings and costs. When he was first charged on 28 January 1927, Constable Moriarty said to him, 'You have a reputation for fast driving. Hasn't the local constable warned you about fast travelling?' 'No,' Oscar replied.'[32] Oscar the speedster had long vanished by the time he settled down to family life. He was overcautious and so slow that if I was in the car and saw any children from primary school, I'd hide down behind the back seat and hope they wouldn't see me. He also had a habit of turning off the ignition whenever he went down a hill, believing this would save petrol.

Oscar's sisters were all living in Christchurch by this time. Rose had trained to be a nurse and was working at the St Saviour's Baby Home, an orphanage at Sumner, Christchurch. Violet was working as a receptionist at the St Helens Maternity Hospital in Christchurch. May had gained a teaching certificate and taught pianoforte (an early piano which had a revival in the 20th century) from home, later teaching at a studio in Victoria Chambers in town. In 1928 she went to Sydney to the Bjelke-Petersen School where she was taught 'medical gymnastics, corrective and health exercises, folk and country dancing, rhythmic exercises, fencing etc.', before returning to Christchurch.

Oscar then decided to move to Australia. I have not been able to find out the reasons for this sudden decision. In Christchurch he had friends and a successful business, and was near his family. Why Australia? Was it a woman? A failed relationship he was escaping? Family dramas? Rebecca and her four children were now all living near each other. It is tempting to put it down to his restlessness, but I believe his need to keep moving, to keep looking for something better, was in part an attempt to escape his tension-filled upbringing. Knowing him as I did, I also believe that it may have been the first early signs of the depression, the Black Dog, that was to plague him for the rest of his life. I, too, have been chased by the Black Dog, especially in my late teens and early twenties. I'd feel the fog of depression begin to creep up on me, and I'd move house. I'd be on the run.

In August 1927, Oscar sold the Southbridge Garage to a Mr AD Harrison and sailed across the Tasman to Australia. He bought Colebrook Garage, situated at 202a New South Head Road, Double Bay. New South Head Road was by then a major route linking the wealthy suburbs on the harbour foreshore to Sydney's centre. The business also offered exclusive hire service for wedding and theatre parties, and according to the advertisements he began placing in the *Sydney Morning Herald*, the service was 'under Royal and Vice-Regal Patronage'. Rebecca followed him over and lived with him for a few years, no doubt being his housekeeper.

The period between the two world wars – the 1920s and 1930s – became well known for two culturally and historically important reasons. The first was for the good times and economic prosperity experienced after the devastation of World War I – the emergence of the Roaring Twenties. The second was brought on by the extensive progress in aviation, earning this era the reputation as the Golden Age of Flight.

Many aviation firsts occurred during this period. Oceans and continents were conquered, and lives were lost. Men and women set out to fly long distances and disappeared without a trace in the oceans. One particular flight 'brought the world to a halt'.[33] In May 1927 an American pilot, Charles Lindbergh, in a Ryan single-engine monoplane, *The Spirit of St. Louis*, made a death-defying nonstop flight across the Atlantic. He flew 3600 miles in 33.5 hours, and a crowd of more than 100,000 were waiting for him to touch down in Paris.

The following year two Australians would earn world-wide acclaim for their long-distance flights. In February 1928, Bundaberg-born Bert Hinkler, who used to fly in crumpled double-breasted suits, made the first solo flight from England to Australia. It took him 15 days in a single-engine Avro avian biplane made from wood and fabric. His arrival in Darwin created a media sensation and Hinkler became a celebrity. Months later, on 31 May 1928, exactly one year and one week after Lindbergh's success, Brisbane-born Charles Kingsford Smith and Melbourne-born Charles Ulm made the first trans-Pacific flight from the United States to Australia.

Kingsford Smith, Ulm, and their American crew, Harry Lyon and radio operator Jim Warner, left Oakland, California, in a blue Fokker aircraft called the *Southern Cross*. They were to fly more than twice the distance of Lindbergh, refuelling in Honolulu and Fiji. On 9 June, shortly before 10.15 am they landed in Brisbane. The flight of 7200 miles had taken eight and a half days. In Brisbane, about 15,000 people had been waiting patiently in the frost since 3 am. The flight had brought Australia to a standstill, with millions of people staying up all night following their progress by radio.

The next day they flew on to Sydney, and their arrival there 'still ranks as one of the most memorable events in the city's history'.[34] It is difficult today to imagine a crowd of about 200,000 – about a fifth of the population of Sydney – pouring onto a small, muddy cow paddock at Mascot, with people dressed in their Sunday best. Some men even wore top hats. Surely Oscar was in that crowd, although he made no mention of it in subsequent interviews. In those he only talked about himself.

If anything would have put Oscar off flying it was some bad publicity that followed this flight. Kingsford Smith and Ulm wanted their trip to be an Australian triumph, and it is estimated that they made about £30,000 from it, a huge amount at the time. However, the American crew received nothing, based on an agreement made between Ulm and Lyon and Warner. However, what was not known until after the flight was that Lyon and Warner had replaced Australian aviator Keith Anderson and air mechanic Bob Hitchcock at the eleventh hour. This led to rancour and litigation as the two Australians claimed they were victims of broken promises. Hitchcock lost his case, but Kingsford Smith made an out-of-court settlement of £1000 to Anderson. He used the money to buy a small aircraft, a Westland Widgeon III, which he christened the *Kookaburra*. Remarkably, Anderson and Hitchcock joined the search party to look for Kingsford Smith when he later went missing.

On 30 March 1929, Kingsford Smith and Ulm, along with a wireless operator and navigator, set off in an attempt to fly from Sydney to London. They were forced to land on the mud flats in the north-west of Western Australia when they became lost and ran out of fuel. They had very little to eat or drink, but they did have a bottle of brandy, which they mixed with coffee. They drank to celebrate the fact that they were still alive, and Kingsford Smith named the mudflats Coffee Royal. After they were rescued came devastating news. The *Kookaburra* had been found in the Tanami Desert; both pilots had died of thirst. Events then took a bizarre turn, with some newspapers falsely accusing Kingsford Smith and Ulm of having staged the whole thing as a hoax or a publicity stunt. It became known as the Coffee Royal affair.

The Roaring Twenties came to an abrupt end in 1929 with the Great Depression, a world-wide economic recession marked by widespread unemployment, triggered when the New York stock market crashed. It lasted for almost a decade and brought years of gloom and hardship. People lost their jobs and homes. At its worst, unemployment in New Zealand and Australia hit 30 per cent. My father never talked about these years, except that on occasion he would yell at us, 'You should have lived through the Depression!' Like many children of my era, we were never allowed to leave the table until we had eaten everything on our plates. When the Great Depression hit, Oscar was lucky to be self-employed and to have his own business, but he would have witnessed the devastating impact it had on society.

During the Roaring Twenties, the decade of great optimism and progress, enormous technological advances and improvements in communications and transport were made. The years that Oscar spent in New Zealand and Australia in the 1920s seem to have been the happiest times for him. I have a photograph album of that period of his life: there he is picnicking and partying with friends, his arm around various ladies and invariably a bottle or cigarette in his other hand. Other photos show him with some of the nurses from Christchurch Hospital whom he had taken on outings in his car. There are photos of him on visits to the Jenolan Caves in the Blue Mountains. In these I recognised a woman I later discovered was Elizabeth (Betty) Whye, who was there to greet him when he arrived in Sydney after his epic flight from Australia. She is clearly his girlfriend. They are touching and embracing each other. I never once saw him be affectionate like this with Mum. Not once. I never saw him hug her or put his arms around her.

In these photos, Oscar looks happy. He has a wide grin on his face. I wonder: Who is this man? This Oscar Garden in his twenties is a foreigner to me. His carefree and affectionate nature had long vanished by the time I was born. However, his restlessness hadn't. He was forever on the move, looking for something better. In January 1930, his restlessness caught up with him again and he decided to go back to England for a holiday. He sold his business and sailed back to Christchurch to visit family members. There are photos of him on the wharf before leaving, his arm around Betty Whye, who presumably was there to see him off. They look happy together. He looks happy. But you can never tell from photographs.

CHAPTER 4

The Flight

In various interviews over the years Oscar would say that on the way across the Tasman he struck up a conversation with a young architect from Auckland called Lands. I have not been able to find any record of an Auckland architect with the surname Lands, although I did find an architect with the name Lance V Moses, so maybe Oscar got the name wrong. This 'Lands' asked him what he was going to do with his life. Oscar told him he had no idea, although when he mentioned that he had owned a small motor business in Sydney, 'Lands' suggested he learn to fly. Oscar had been around cars since he was a child. He knew how engines worked, and how to service and repair them. Perhaps 'Lands' had this in mind, because the early aviators often had to do their own maintenance and repairs.

Oscar said he had never given flying a thought before then. But this is not true. I tracked down several newspaper articles that quote a Captain Les Holden who said that Oscar decided to learn to fly in late 1929 after he, Holden, had taken him on two flights around Sydney Harbour. Holden recalled Oscar's 'extraordinary enthusiasm for aviation'.[35,36] And when Oscar was later interviewed at Broken Hill on 6 November 1930, he said that his first flight had been in Australia with a Captain Leslie

ENGLAND. **RECORD OF FLIGHTS.**

Date.	Aircraft.		Pilot.	Journey.	Time in Air.		Remarks.
	Type.	Markings.			Hrs.	Mins.	
				Brought forward...			
2/7/30	DH 60.	GEBQX	J. Bunning			55	Straight flying
3/7/30	"	"	"		1	30	Climbing & gliding
4/7/30	"	"	"		1	35	" "
5/7/30	"	"	"			25	Approaches
6/7/30	"	GEBZW	"		1	10	Landings
8/7/30	"	" QX	"		2	5	"
9/7/30	"	" "	"			15	"
9/7/30	"	" ZW	"			35	"
				Carried forward...	8	30	

ENGLAND. **RECORD OF FLIGHTS.**

Date.	Aircraft.		Pilot.	Journey.	Time in Air.		Remarks.
	Type.	Markings.			Hrs.	Mins.	
				Brought forward...	8	30	
10/7/30	DH 60.	GEBQX	J. Bunning		1	30	Landings
18/7/30	"	" QX	"		1	0	" & taking off
20/7/30	"	" QX	"		1	20	"
" "	"	" QX	O.G. Self.			25	1st Fresh...
25/7/30	"	" "	J. Bunning			10	Landings
" "	"	" "	Self.		2	35	Fig. of eights.
27/7/30	"	"	Self.			45	Landings
28/7/30	"	"	Self.			50	Height test & Landings
			Solo 4.10.	Carried forward...	17	5	
			Dual 12.55				

Pages of logbook of Oscar Garden, showing his first solo flight on 20 July 1930.

Holden and 'that gave him the idea of learning to fly.'[37] Hence it is not clear why years later he came up with the Lands story.

When Oscar arrived in Christchurch, his family were astonished when he told them he was going to be the first man to fly from England to New Zealand. This was something that no aviator had even attempted.

Shortly after arriving in Southport, England, on 16 April 1930, Oscar bought a second-hand Chrysler car so he could visit relatives in the Isle of Man, Scotland and Orkney. This would have been the first time he had gone back to Tongue or Kirkwall since 1913 or 1914, those traumatic tumultuous years of his parents' separation. I wonder what memories would have come back when he saw *Dunvarrich*, his childhood home? The church he used to spend *all* day Sunday in? His grandmother was still alive, and presumably he visited her in Kirkwall.

Oscar's father's cousin Thora recalled his visit to Aberdeen and told me how she and another cousin, Kay, had looked at this about-to-be-heroic figure in awe. When he eventually made the flight, she sat with her parents every evening and listened to reports of his progress on the radio. 'It was so exciting,' she said. 'We could hardly wait for the next episode.' Kay wrote to me, saying, 'Oscar was an absolutely astounding person. He was certainly a wonderful man – quite fearless and full of adventure – one in a million! Thora and I idolised him when we were young!! He was so good-looking. He was the greatest of all my cousins (I had 27 cousins).'

After his visits to Scotland, he went back to England and began searching for a place to learn to fly. He was put off the first two places he visited because he claimed that the pilots, including instructors, were 'all pretty high on the bottle'. But when he visited the Norfolk and Norwich Aero Club at Norwich, there wasn't 'a sign of booze on the horizon anywhere'. The sole instructor, First Officer Reginald James Bunning, an ex-wartime pilot, was a stone-cold sober man. Oscar decided to start there straight away.

On 20 July 1930, after 12 hours and 20 minutes' dual instruction with Bunning on a DH.60/80hp Moth Cirrus II, Oscar obtained his 'A' licence and was able to fly solo. His sights were now set on obtaining a commercial licence, which required 100 hours of flying time at a cost of £5 an hour, plus a few comparatively simple exams. Oscar came up with the idea of buying a second-hand plane and flying to Australia, and on to New Zealand, as a cheaper alternative. He also hoped he would be the *first* person to fly from England to New Zealand. Two birds with one stone: a record and a commercial pilot's licence.

As previously mentioned, the flight from England to Australia was considered the most formidable. A few months before, a young Australian aviator, Eric Hook, and Jack Matthews, who had worked as Bert Hinkler's mechanic, had made a forced landing in the deep jungle 150 miles from Rangoon. Both survived the crash, but Hook became sick and died while they were struggling through the jungle in monsoonal rains. Regardless, Oscar went looking for a plane. In early September, he came across a metal-fuselage DH.60M Gipsy Moth in the aviation department of Selfridges. Selfridges was London's first fully-fledged department store and had opened in 1909. Owner Harry Gordon Selfridge was an aviation enthusiast, and on 4 April 1930 he launched an aviation department staffed by ex-RAF personnel. As well as stocking several types of aircraft, they sold accessories, flying clothing and a selection of aeronautical literature.[38] Imagine going to Myers or David Jones to buy a plane!

The de Havilland Moths were a series of light aircraft designed by Geoffrey de Havilland, an avid lepidopterist. The DH.60M Gipsy Moth was launched in 1925. This was a straight-winged biplane two-seater with wings that could fold backwards against the fuselage, just like a moth! The early models had a plywood-covered fuselage protected on the inside by varnish and on the outside by a layer of doped fabric.[39] However, by 1927, it was discovered that the wooden structure holding the engine had a tendency to shrink, a problem that was solved by making the fuselage of welded steel tubing. This new model was the DH.60M, the 'Metal Moth'.

The blue-coloured version Oscar spotted in Selfridges had already seen many hours of flying. Originally registered G-AASA on 9 November 1929, it belonged to Harry Selfridge's son, Gordon, who had crashed it into a tree. His father had insisted he get rid of it and put it up for sale in the store aviation department. With a bit of wrangling Oscar bought it for £450 plus his car, which he traded in for £50. In his later years, he would boast that he was the first person in the world who traded in a second-hand car for a second-hand plane.

Oscar moved his plane to Brooklands and began preparing for his flight. He named the plane *Kia Ora*, Māori for 'good luck', and painted these words in silver on the front. Now short of funds, he saved £18 by making his own maps. He went around scouring London for bits of strip maps and spent hours putting them together and marking out distances. All other aviators had flown to Darwin, but Oscar noticed that the over-water distance between Koepang (now Kupang in Indonesia) and Darwin was further than if he flew direct to Wyndham.

Oscar was to later regret his decision to land at Wyndham. 'I was all for cutting down the distance over the water, being a novice. It was silly thing to do because I had an awful trip after that to get to Alice Springs.'

Oscar's first flight in *Kia Ora* was on 12 September, and over the next few weeks he flew cross-country flights to Manchester, Edinburgh and Blackpool to improve his navigation and flying skills. He also learnt how to read a compass. On one flight he nearly hit Edinburgh Castle. On board was his Uncle Marshall, one of Rebecca's twin brothers. Near Edinburgh they ran into thick haze, and visibility was so bad that Oscar was about to turn back when he saw a stone wall of Edinburgh Castle practically touching the wing tip. Luckily, he then flew into clearer air. He said he found himself very unpopular at Donibristle Aerodrome (8.7 miles north-west of Edinburgh) as it was Sunday, and the aerodrome was meant to be closed. It was covered with sheep, because on Sundays they were let loose there to keep the grass down. With the help of a few men

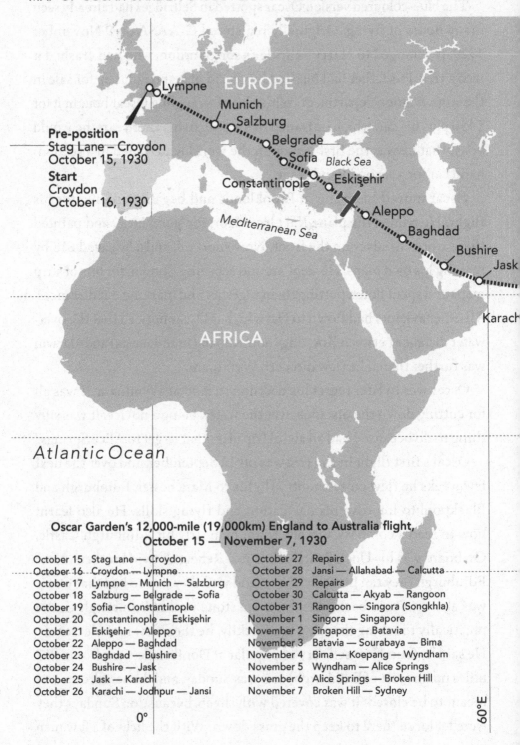

MAP OF OSCAR GARDEN'S 1930 FLIGHT FROM ENGLAND TO AUSTRALIA

EUROPE

Lympne

Munich

Salzburg

Belgrade

Sofia

Black Sea

Constantinople

Eskişehir

Pre-position
Stag Lane – Croydon
October 15, 1930

Start
Croydon
October 16, 1930

Aleppo

Baghdad

Bushire

Jask

Mediterranean Sea

Karach

AFRICA

Atlantic Ocean

**Oscar Garden's 12,000-mile (19,000km) England to Australia flight,
October 15 — November 7, 1930**

October 15	Stag Lane — Croydon		October 27	Repairs
October 16	Croydon — Lympne		October 28	Jansi — Allahabad — Calcutta
October 17	Lympne — Munich — Salzburg		October 29	Repairs
October 18	Salzburg — Belgrade — Sofia		October 30	Calcutta — Akyab — Rangoon
October 19	Sofia — Constantinople		October 31	Rangoon — Singora (Songkhla)
October 20	Constantinople — Eskişehir		November 1	Singora — Singapore
October 21	Eskişehir — Aleppo		November 2	Singapore — Batavia
October 22	Aleppo — Baghdad		November 3	Batavia — Sourabaya — Bima
October 23	Baghdad — Bushire		November 4	Bima — Koepang — Wyndham
October 24	Bushire — Jask		November 5	Wyndham — Alice Springs
October 25	Jask — Karachi		November 6	Alice Springs — Broken Hill
October 26	Karachi — Jodhpur — Jansi		November 7	Broken Hill — Sydney

0°

60°E

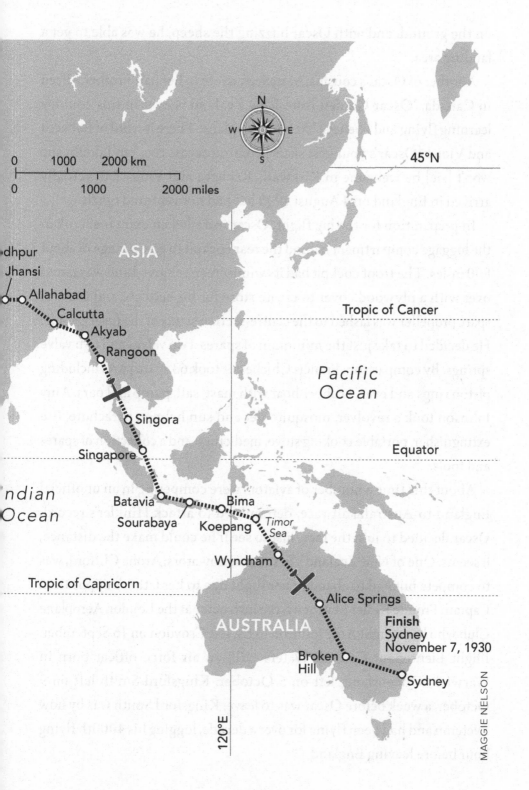

N
W   E
S

45°N

0   1000   2000 km

0   1000   2000 miles

ASIA

Tropic of Cancer

dhpur
Jhansi
Allahabad
Calcutta
Akyab
Rangoon

Pacific
Ocean

Singora

Singapore

Equator

ndian
Ocean

Batavia
Sourabaya
Koepang

Bima

Timor
Sea

Wyndham

Tropic of Capricorn

AUSTRALIA

Alice Springs

Finish
Sydney
November 7, 1930

Broken
Hill

Sydney

120°E

MAGGIE NELSON

69

on the ground, and with Oscar buzzing the sheep, he was able to get a landing area.

Another of Oscar's cousins, Margaret, wrote to her half-brother Alfred in Canada, 'Oscar Garden from New Zealand is over in this country learning flying and I believe has bought a plane. There is word of Rebecca and Violet [Oscar's youngest sister] coming across too, but I doubt she won't [sic] be welcome in Kirkwall.' Rebecca and Violet had actually arrived in England on 4 August 1930 but had not ventured north.

In preparation for the big flight, Oscar installed an extra fuel tank in the luggage compartment behind the rear cockpit to give a range of about 800 miles. The front cockpit had its windscreen removed and was faired over with a plywood cover to create store for his suitcase and tools. A spare propeller was lashed to the centre-section struts of the fuselage side. He decided to take just the minimum of spares: two valves and two valve springs. By comparison, Francis Chichester took 63 spare parts including piston rings and even a rubber boat with mast, sail, pump and oars. Amy Johnson took a revolver, mosquito net and sun helmet, parachute, fire extinguisher, portable cooking stove, medicines, and a collection of spares and tools.

About this time a number of aviators were competing in an unofficial England-to-Australia air race, determined to attack Hinkler's record. Oscar decided to join the race, just to see if he could make the distance, it seems. One of New Zealand's first women aviators, Aroha Clifford, was to compete but had to abandon her flight due to her father's opposition. Captain Froude Ridler Matthews, the instructor at the London Aeroplane Club who had taught Amy Johnson to fly, left Croydon on 16 September. Flight Lieutenant Cedrick Waters Hill, an air force officer born in Warwick, Queensland, left on 5 October. Kingsford Smith left on 9 October, a week before Oscar was to leave. Kingsford Smith was by now a veteran and had been flying for over a decade, logging his 4000th flying hour before leaving England.

The early aviators were a particularly competitive group, vying to see who could fly the fastest, the highest, the farthest. Many of them battled to see who could achieve an aviation first. Even though Oscar said his aim was to fly 'in leisurely stages to Canberra',[40] rather than break the England to Australia record, or be the first to fly from England to New Zealand, he wanted to keep his options open. He told a reporter the day before he left, he could not say definitely that he was trying to break the record until he was on his way. To stand a chance he would have to do 15 or 16 hours a day, and his longest flight had only been between five and six hours. He was unsure whether he could stand the longer period necessary. However, he said he hoped to be the *first* to fly from England to New Zealand.

In the early morning of 16 October 1930, Oscar taxied his tiny machine across the aerodrome in the grey light and, with a wave of his hand to the only person there to farewell him, took off. That person was a representative of the Vacuum Oil Company, who were providing fuel supplies of Plume and Mobiloil at his planned stops along the 12,000-mile route.

Unlike other early aviators, Oscar sought no publicity. On the day he left, *The Sun* wrote:

A young man landed on Croydon airport in a light plane yesterday afternoon and from it stepped a young man who announced his intention of starting at 4 am today, on a flight to Australia. After stating that his name was Oscar Garden and that his home was in Christchurch, New Zealand, he climbed back into his machine and flew away. Aerodrome officials have no idea where he came from.

This was the first anyone knew of his intentions, apart from Vacuum Oil Company, who had agreed to keep his plan secret. A reporter managed to contact Oscar's sister May, in Christchurch, who told him she had

Oscar standing in front of *Kia Ora* at Croydon airport, the day he left.

Oscar in the cockpit of *Kia Ora* before taking off on his solo flight to Australia on 16 October 1930.

received a letter from him a week ago, but he had made no mention of the flight. She said her brother had unusual determination and initiative. 'He's always done everything he said he would, and unless he has bad luck, I'm sure he'll get through.' She added that his destination was probably New Zealand.

Oscar said he tried to keep his date of departure secret from his family and friends, as he did not want to be talked out of going. He had visited Rebecca a fortnight before but had not told her. He had been going to take her for a flight in his plane, but she was not feeling well. She told the *News Chronicle*, 'He kissed me, and flew into the sky like a bird. I was nearly ill when I read in the paper that he had left Croydon. He is well named "the mystery man" for he tells nothing of his movements, and is full of daredevilry... [but] I am proud of my boy. He neither drinks nor smokes.' She was also concerned he was not wearing a hat – like all good mothers at that time!

When Bunning, his flying instructor, found out about his plan, he said Oscar was foolhardy and didn't have a hope in Hades. Bunning had a point. Oscar was a novice. He had been flying for only three months and had a mere 40 hours' solo flying experience.

Oscar had a bad start. After leaving Croydon on that first day, poor weather and fog forced him down at Lympne, near Folkestone. This meant that his official departure from England was not until the next day, 17 October, when he set off at 6.18 am. The weather conditions were not ideal; a southerly breeze was blowing banks of fog in from the sea. By the time he reached Munich, 9.5 hours later, he began to question whether the whole thing was such a good idea: 'Whatever am I doing, I must be mad.' When it was time to leave Munich, the journey almost ended there. The usual procedure to start his plane was to stand in front and turn the propeller. But when he tried this time, the plane suddenly 'became alive, plunging and buckling like a runaway horse'. He said:

I am usually very careful, so perhaps the accident may have been due to someone else's mistake; but, whatever the reason, when I swung the engine over, after re-fuelling, the throttle was wide open. That usually ends in disaster, sometimes for both the pilot and the plane. As the 'prop' [propeller] roared around, I dashed to one side and laid hold of a wing, with the idea of climbing along it to the cockpit and stopping the engine. But the machine was plunging so wildly that it was all I could do to hang on. I called to a German mechanic and he grabbed the wing, while I tried to climb aboard. But ... I saw the 'prop' coming straight for me, and I fell face down on the ground. It passed directly over me, as did one of the wheels.

When he staggered to his feet, he was hit by the other wing tip and knocked to the ground. The German mechanic let go in a panic and another dashed in to steady the plane while Oscar, dazed, climbed along the wing into the cockpit and turned off the throttle.

Fearing that he might not be believed, he wrote, 'By the way, this is quite OK – everything happened just as I am telling it.' He said that 'he was done to a turn' after this mishap. Even after he had been checked by a doctor, the German police tried to persuade him to remain there a day to rest. but he decided to push on. He flew to Salzburg (Austria), although he almost turned around because of the thick fog, which eventually melted to a haze.

The following day, 18 October, he ran into more fog on the way to Belgrade and had to climb 9000 feet to clear the Alps. From Belgrade he continued to Sofia in Bulgaria, where he landed in darkness. He claimed that 'two hundred men' had 'rushed' him there, 'and not a single one of them could speak a word of English.'[41] A man who could speak English was fetched from the city, and he told him his passport was in order for him to land, but it was not good enough for him to leave. After arguing for several hours, the Director of Air Services arrived and sorted things out. Other aviators had faced similar difficulties, although Kingsford Smith avoided such trouble by flying via Rome. Oscar later said that the British Air Ministry's arrangements – for which he had paid £18 – were 'by no means perfect'. Apart from passport problems, he was also given the wrong locations for five aerodromes.

The next day, after flying for four hours and 20 minutes, Oscar realised the plane had a leaking oil pipe. There was a prohibited landing area near Constantinople and aviators were supposed to fly over the water, but Oscar decided that was too risky: 'Better going down on any kind of land than in the water.' At Constantinople, he was again held up with passport troubles – he claimed that every airman who landed in Turkey had experienced similar difficulties. While his passport was being sorted Oscar was able to fix the leaking pipe.

By this stage two of the aviators were out of the running for the race. Flight Lieutenant Hill crashed on 17 October when taking off from Atamboea (Indonesia) on the final leg to Darwin. He resumed his flight on 9 December and reached Darwin the following day, which meant his total time was 7 weeks and 5 days. Matthews was on track to breaking Hinkler's record, but on 18 October he crashed in bad weather near Bangkok. After repairs to his plane, he eventually arrived in Darwin on 21 October, after a 32-day flight. Kingsford Smith arrived the following day. He had survived without mishap, and his 10-day flight had broken Hinkler's record. His Avian biplane had been modified for the flight. The fuselage was strengthened to take the extra weight of a 91-gallon fuel tank in the front cockpit, giving it a total fuel capacity of 115 gallons and a range of 1700 miles, twice the range of *Kia Ora*. Breaking the England-to-Australia flying record was now no longer an option for Oscar.

On the fourth day, Oscar had a further delay. After flying for only two hours and 50 minutes, he was forced by engine trouble to land on a Turkish military airfield near Eskisehir. Because his passport did not allow for him to land on a military aerodrome, he was stuck there until he obtained permission to leave, which was not until the next day. He said the officers were very hospitable and insisted on paying his hotel expenses, even giving him 20 tins of cigarettes when he left.

The next leg of the journey was to Aleppo in northern Syria, a flight of seven hours. Having been given the wrong directions, he ran out of fuel and had to make another forced landing 10 miles south of the town, near a railway line. After walking a couple of miles along the railway line he reached a telephone manned by an Arab policeman. Oscar said it took another several hours before he could talk with somebody who could speak English. In some interviews, he said he was on the phone for two hours; in one article, he wrote he said it took four hours, which seems a long time to be standing in the desert heat talking to people at the other end of the phone who could not speak English. Eventually a man appeared with a little oil and petrol. When he returned, the plane was surrounded by about 200 Arabs who were scared stiff and afraid to go near it. By this time, he was as 'thirsty as a wooden god and to make matters worse, it started to blow a parching wind'.[42] He tried to indicate through sign language that he needed water, but they kept bringing him hard-boiled eggs. He claimed that he ate about 20 of them. That night he slept on the floor of the village headman's hut, with locals outside keeping watch over the plane.

The next morning, 22 October, he flew the 10 miles to Aleppo, where he refuelled and went on to Baghdad. It was an incident-free flight that took six hours and 35 minutes. However, the following day, he ran into a severe sandstorm on the way to Bushire (now Bushehr) in Iran. That night he stayed at the same palatial house in which Kingsford Smith had recently stayed, a house that belonged to a 'rich old Persian'. Oscar said, 'The food was very greasy, but he had to swallow it,' and he slept on a hard board for a bed.

On 24 October, he flew for seven hours and 35 minutes to Jask in the Gulf of Oman. One of the first people to meet him was Mrs Victor Bruce, another aviator who was trying to set her own record of being the first woman to fly solo around the world. She wrote in her memoir[43] that Oscar looked tired and very dusty. She had set out from Heston Airport on 25 September 1930, wearing a skirt and pearls. (She was to finish her flight on 19 February 1931 – although she crossed the Pacific Ocean and Atlantic Ocean by ship, with her plane on board). Even though Oscar had intended to reach Charbar, 200 miles further on along the coast of the Gulf of Oman, Bruce persuaded him to stay the night at Jask and said she would be 'delighted to have his company in the air for the rest of the journey to Rangoon'.

The following day, 25 October, they flew in tandem as far as Charbar, at which point Oscar suddenly flew inland over the hills while Bruce flew low along the water's edge. When they arrived at their destination of Karachi in northern India (now Pakistan), Oscar told her that he had 'a horror of the water and preferred the hills and mountains' whereas she said she had 'a positive terror of the mountains'. She added that, 'in this part of the country', they were 'particularly forbidding'.[44]

The next day, Oscar headed off alone, as Bruce had been persuaded by the agent for the De Havilland Company to stay another day so they could check over her machine. Oscar had told Bruce he was trying to set a record for flying to Australia, so presumably he had not heard the news that Kingsford Smith had arrived in Darwin a few days before. Oscar flew east to Jodhpur and on to Jhansi in northern central India in the face of strong headwinds. He had by now been flying for 11 hours and 40 minutes but was unable to find the Jhansi aerodrome using the directions he been given by the Ministry, who had said it was 10 miles north of the town. It was actually a mile north-east. After circling around in near darkness for about half an hour in the hope of signals, he decided to 'take pot luck' and ended up crashing between two trees in a ploughed field. *Kia Ora* overturned, smashing the propeller and damaging the rudder.

Oscar was hanging upside down in the seat's safety straps listening to petrol dripping out from the rear tank. He was horrified to see a local approaching with a kerosene lantern; the plane was in danger of catching fire. As soon as he freed himself, he plugged up the petrol tank outlets. Other Indians were soon on the scene, and by using sign language he got them to help him right the plane by removing its wings from one side. The wings were then mounted again and the spare propeller he had brought with him installed. Oscar sat under one wing and waited for daylight. Some of the locals sheltered next to him. None of them could speak English. He was hungry and thirsty, but every time he motioned for food or water, they would give him 'vile beedie cigarettes'. He was also cut, bruised, tired and stiff. A couple of his companions must have realised this, because suddenly they rolled him over and gave him a vigorous massage, which, he said, 'despite its roughness, really did me a lot of good'.

At about 4 am it started to rain heavily, the 'heavens began to teem', Oscar recalled. Within a few minutes the ploughed field became a muddy bog and water began rising up the plane. Oscar set out through the mud, at times plunging up to his knees, until he found a relatively dry strip of land about two miles away. It took several hours for about 50 Indian helpers to tow the plane using a stout rope. About 100 trees that were in the way had to be cut down.

I spent six years in India during the 1970s and travelled through Jhansi on several occasions, as it is a major intercity hub situated on the main Delhi–Bombay (now Mumbai) and Delhi–Madras (now Chennai) railway lines. If only I had been interested in my father's story, then! I could have tracked down some of the Indians who had helped him and interviewed them using an interpreter. Some of them would have never seen a plane before. Were they frightened? Was my father's story correct? Were one hundred trees really cut down? How muddy was it? What did they think of my father? What were their impressions? These are things I would love to know.

Oscar was just getting ready for take-off when one of the locals, who had a long stick in his hand, perhaps fascinated by the sight of the propeller turning over, decided to put the stick into it. He got as much a shock as Oscar.

On take-off, an unexplainable and peculiar thing happened: 'It felt like the whole plane was being twisted by some giant invisible hand holding the front while another tried twisting the rear.' It lasted about two minutes before the plane settled down and he was able to fly to the Jhansi airfield. It was now about midday, and after he had a wash and something to eat, he checked the plane over. When he could find nothing wrong, he decided to stay the night at Jhansi and have the plane checked out at Calcutta.

The following day he flew to Calcutta via Allahabad. He had the same unnerving experience during take-off as the previous day, with the plane weaving and twisting for a couple of minutes. He arrived at Dum Dum Aerodrome, Calcutta, at 5.30 pm, after a flight of 10 hours and 50 minutes. When he jumped out of the plane he cheerfully said, 'I must have been born lucky,'[45] referring to his narrow escape at Jhansi.

One day later he discovered the problem he had been having on take-off. When the plane was stuck in the mud in Jhansi the wheels had sunk up to the hubs. The wheels were wire wheels with canvas covers, and the mud had oozed inside and dried out. This meant that during take-off, they acted as huge but unevenly balanced weights. Mrs Victor Bruce had arrived at Calcutta earlier that day, and she was surprised to be greeted by Oscar, as she thought he would have been well on his way to Australia. However, she was 'jolly glad' that he had to stop for repairs to his plane as this meant she would have his company on the leg to Burma. Part of this route crosses the Arakan Yoma range of mountains, where the Australian flyers, Eric Hook and Jack Matthews, had crashed a few months before. (Both survived the crash, but Hook became sick and died. Bruce wrote in her memoir that Hook had 'been eaten alive by leeches'!) Bruce said she and Oscar 'made an arrangement that if either had to come down, the other would fly on in search of help, for it would be useless to land, as both of us would probably be helpless.'[46]

Oscar shaking hands with Mrs Victor Bruce at Calcutta on 30 October 1930. Mrs Bruce's Blackburn Bluebird aircraft is in the background.

The next day they flew for eight hours to Akyab (now Sittwe) where they stopped for half an hour to refuel. The small group of people waiting had warm coffee for them, even though it was a sweltering hot day. Bruce wrote, 'I had never felt so hot in my life.'[47] They then flew across the Arakan Yoma range and along the Irrawaddy River to Rangoon. There was a glorious sunset as they came down to land, and they could see the glittering golden spire of the famous Shwedagon Pagoda dominating the skyline.

They parted ways the next morning. It was 31 October.[48] Bruce headed eastwards towards Japan. Oscar flew south to Singora (now Songkhla) in Southern Thailand, a trip of 12 hours, with a stop at Mergui. The Mergui airfield was not in a proper state to allow a take-off, so Oscar had to organise for the holes in the field to be filled. He said the natives had never seen a plane before.

Over the next two days Oscar flew to Singapore (a flight of 7.25 hours) and on to Batavia (now Jakarta), a flight of 7.45 hours. He arrived at Batavia about midday but was not allowed to carry on because it was a Sunday. He said in a later interview that the town was a 'small paradise', reminding him of the trees and flowers of Australia: 'The town is well laid out, and the Dutch residents there show the most wonderful hospitality. Most of them seemed to know a bit of English, and could not do enough to make my short stay as enjoyable as possible.' On 3 November, Oscar headed for Sourabaya, the capital of East Java, where he met Flight Lieutenant Hill, who was waiting for a ship to take his damaged plane to a repair shop. He continued on to Bima on the island of Soembawa (now part of Indonesia). He again had help from locals, this time from a tribe reported to be headhunters.

As usual, after arriving, he carried out his maintenance work on *Kia Ora*.

I was up there, getting one of the natives to stand beside me with a torch while I checked all the gear. I was dead tired and I was being bitten alive with millions of mosquitoes. I got on top of the engine and had a look. And I found two broken valve springs and I was just dead lucky that I had these two spare ones. So, I finished up by replacing them and getting it sorted out.

Valve springs close the engine valves which act as gatekeepers for fuel and air to enter and exit the combustion chambers of the engine. Had Oscar not replaced the springs, the engine would have failed.

At midnight he was taken to the chief's hut, where he was fed. He had been given a pocket watch as a souvenir by the Vacuum Oil representative at Surabaya, which he lent to the chief. Using sign language, he showed him where the hands would be at 4 am, the time he wanted to be woken up. Oscar said that on the dot of 4 am he was shaken awake. When he emerged from the hut, he was startled to find about 50 locals sitting on rope beds placed all around the plane.

I couldn't take it in, that they would guard the plane like that. And I thought, my God, what a marvellous thing to do! When it was time to say goodbye, they gave me something quick to eat for breakfast, goodness knows what it was. I had about 10 pounds in different currencies left. I knew if I came down in the Timor Sea that would be the end of that, I'd be gone, so I thought better for the chief to have it. So, I gave him this money and I sort of pointed to all the villagers and he nodded his head; he knew what I was talking about.

On 4 November, after flying to Koepang to refuel, he braced himself for the perilous flight over the Timor Sea. It was this last hop aviators dreaded: 500 miles of shark-infested waters. Oscar had no lifejacket or inflatable dingy. Fortunately, there were no incidents, and it was with great relief that he reached Wyndham at nightfall. Nobody was expecting him. He had completed the England-to-Australia flight in 18 days,[49] beating Amy Johnson's record. It was a new record for a novice pilot and the third-fastest time.

Oscar took the town of Wyndham by surprise. *The Western Australian* reported that, 'Most residents of the town, who could not see him, thought when they heard the sudden roar that a plane had been blown up with its passengers.' When Stanley Brown, a pilot for Western Australian Airways (which had a twice-weekly run to Perth), heard the sound overhead, he quickly drove out to the airstrip. He was stunned to find Oscar standing on a drum doing engine maintenance. His first request was for a cigarette, but Brown had none. He would have needed one. That last leg had been in his mind from the outset. As he said, 'There was no doubt that every

Pages of logbook of Oscar Garden, showing sections of his flight from England to Australia. He arrived in Sydney 7 November 1930: his logs books are out as he missed 31st October!

aviator coming to Australia must have a certain amount of dread of the last long, lonely hop over the sea in a one-engined machine.'[50]

Rebecca was relieved to hear he had landed safely in Australia. 'Thank God it's over. I am delighted with the performance. My boy has done what he set out to do. I did not sleep on Monday night, wondering how my only son was faring.'[51] The *Isle of Man Daily* wrote, 'Bravo! Oscar Garden, the Manx pilot, arrived safely. Yesterday he was unknown; today he ranks with Hinkler, [Kingsford] Smith and Miss Johnson.'[52] They added, 'He neither drinks nor smokes, but lives mostly on natural foods – fruit, nuts and raw vegetables. Although not exactly a vegetarian, he is what is known in New Zealand as a 'green-leafer' of whom there are a large number in that country.' This is rubbish and something Rebecca must have told them. Oscar smoked, drank and was far from a vegetarian.

Regardless, the flight captured the world's imagination. With few preparations for the long journey, he had given the impression he was just setting out on a short pleasure trip.[53] 'A casualness typically Australian characterised Oscar Garden's flight from England to Australia. It was commenced without blare of trumpets, and the wires were not burned up to report its progress to the world. Garden just slipped off quietly in his Gipsy Moth … There was no apparent effort or fuss, just a "leisurely flight" as the easy-going Aussie naively described it.'[54] Note that *all* the countries he had lived in wanted to claim him as their own. He was called at various times the Manx, Aussie, New Zealand or Scottish aviator.

It is difficult today to imagine the courage and endurance of early aviators like Oscar. He had flown hunched up in his open-cockpit plane with no protection from the weather – at times blasted by freezing air and drenched by rain – as he weaved his way through turbulence, lightning, storms and swirling clouds, over mountains and across deserts and oceans. The stress and fatigue, coupled with lack of sleep and food, must have taken him to the limits of endurance. And what did he do when he wanted to go to the toilet? On some stretches Oscar had spent up to nine hours in the air in the tiny cramped cockpit. How did he empty his bladder and bowels in that confined space?

In the last few years of his life, I asked him several times, but I never could get an answer, just a grin. Perhaps he used a bottle and pages of a newspaper, which is what the crew on Kingsford Smith and Ulm's 1928 flight resorted to. Or a small bucket, which Charles Lindberg used on this 1927 flight. He was to later say that the greatest difficulty flying to Australia was to get a meal and the greatest danger of death was starvation. 'The next time I take a long-distance flight', he said, 'I am taking a cargo of fruit.'[55]

CHAPTER 5

Honour and glory business

Most aviators rested on arrival in Australia, but not Oscar. His plan was to fly across Australia to Sydney. And if all went well, he would then fly over the Tasman Sea, becoming the first aviator to fly from England to New Zealand.

In Wyndham, Oscar spent the night at the Blazing Stump Hotel. He was very tired after his long and anxious day and went to bed soon after having dinner. The following day *The Sun* published this delightful anecdote:

'Bill,' said the landlord of the Blazing Stump Hotel, at Elephant Head, 'don't let the bloke in No. 10 sleep after seven. He wants to go to Alice Springs.'

'There ain't no bloke in No. 10,' said the Boots.

'Oh yes,' answered the Boss, 'he came in late last night in a Blue Sedan Moth. There it is, out on the plain.'

'Where from?' asked Bill, faintly interested.

'Oh! Atamboea or Bima or somewhere out there,' said the landlord. 'Anyway he wants to git on the track.'

'Orright,' said Bill.[56]

Oscar got up much earlier than seven, because he left Wyndham at 5:15 am. Stanley Brown, the pilot he had met the day before, was flying back to Perth and accompanied him to Hall's Creek, 223 miles south of Wyndham. Oscar was determined to take the shortest route to Sydney. Even though aviation experts said it would be wiser and safer to fly from Wyndham down the west coast of Western Australia to Perth, he decided to fly via Alice Springs. No aviator had made this crossing before – over the heart of Australia across the Great Sandy Desert and hundreds of miles of desolate country. It was considered more treacherous than the adjoining Tanami Desert, where the previous year, Keith Anderson and Bobby Hitchcock died while searching for Kingsford Smith and his crew. Before they left, Brown told Oscar he was 'stark staring mad' to attempt to fly across the central saltpan desert to Alice Springs.

Oscar recalled:

He was quite right too, because it was an absolute nightmare. I mean it was a suicide trip really. And I was damned lucky to get to Alice Springs, I can tell you. It was a long day, 12 hours and 5 minutes. And, one of the biggest jokes, it shows you what a novice I was and how lucky I was, I suppose, or how green I was. I hadn't even any water aboard, you see, leaving Wyndham to go across this damned desert. This pilot said: 'You're mad anyway but for God's sake take some water! So he dug up half a dozen empty beer bottles from somewhere and we filled them with water. I put them into the front cockpit. I put them there in case I was forced down. Well from then on, before I got anywhere near to Alice Springs, I was burnt to a cinder. There was hardly any visibility as I was flying through a red dust storm practically the whole way, and I had to stick my head over the side to see anything. I was burnt and gasping for water and all my damned water was in the front cockpit – I couldn't even reach it!

They were expecting him at Alice Springs, and bonfires had been lit to guide him to the airstrip, where he landed at 7:20 pm. It was reported that he was very sunburnt and looked very tired after his 850 miles, 'but he soon freshened up.' An Ernie Allchurch met him when he stepped off the plane, and later recalled the incident:

> He [Oscar] said, 'I don't suppose you're any relation to Harold Allchurch, of Timaru, NZ?' I said, 'He's my brother.' That shows you how small the world is. I don't think enough credit was given to Oscar Garden for his amazing flight. I've heard of some good ones, but this chap took the bun. He had a very Scotch accent, and he was a fine character.[57]

Oscar left Alice Springs at 5.20 am the next day and made a stop to refuel at Maree before continuing to Broken Hill, where a crowd of about 300 were waiting to witness his arrival. At 3:30 pm the plane was noticed in the west, but it appeared that Oscar had lost his way, for instead of coming towards the aerodrome it headed northwards and was soon a speck in the distance. Mr Jolly, an insurance agent from Queensland, sent his plane up, piloted by a Captain Shaw who chased Oscar down. They touched down at 3.43 pm. A crowd had gathered at the aerodrome early in the afternoon to await his arrival. 'With smiles wreathing his young face, tanned by the sun of many lands … he was immediately mobbed by a crowd of hero-worshippers.'[58] Oscar told the reporters he had been informed at Maree that there was no aerodrome at Broken Hill and that he should land at the racecourse. Regardless, he said the flight was 'a piece of cake after the day before'. Now that he was in Australia, Oscar changed his story and claimed he had 'not been out to break records but to get to here in one piece'.[59]

He was congratulated by the mayor and rushed off to a civic reception, followed by a dinner party in his honour at the Grand Hotel. It was said that he endeared himself to all who met him because of his most unassuming manner, and he gave clear evidence that he was a man of action more than words, showing a dislike for the limelight. He was handed a cheque with an accompanying letter signed by R. Dennis, the mayor: 'On the occasion of your being the first world-famed airman to land at Broken Hill as a "port of call" from England, the citizens of Broken Hill, in their desire to express their great admiration of your wonderful effort would ask you to accept this very small recognition of what they consider to be an achievement equal to the best to date.'[60] Mr Jolly said he considered the flight of Mr Garden more meritorious than that of Squadron-Leader Bert Hinkler, who had about 17 years of flying experience behind him.

At Broken Hill Oscar sent a telegram to Captain Frederick William Haig, Aviation Manager for Vacuum Oil Company: 'Arriving Sydney 3 o'clock.' On 7 November, he flew non-stop to Sydney against a head wind, a trip of eight hours and five minutes, and arrived there a few minutes before 3.00 pm. Three mustard-coloured planes from the Mascot Aero Club flew out to meet him, and he made a perfect three-pointer in his blue *Kia Ora,* landing at Mascot Aerodrome and slipping down smoothly between the mustard-coloured Club planes. A crowd of about 2000 people was waiting for his arrival, although Oscar would have been happy if no one had been there. In contrast, about 75,000 people greeted Amy Johnson on 5 June 1930 after her flight from England. A fleet of 17 planes met Kingsford Smith in his *Southern Cross Junior* a few miles from Sydney and escorted it to Mascot on 22 October 1930. Thousands watched the plane fly over the city, and a crowd of about 20,000 had assembled at Mascot to welcome him. Both Johnson and Kingsford Smith were flying celebrities, and both loved the public adulation.

Not Oscar. He found the welcome for him at Sydney overwhelming and would have preferred to slip in unnoticed. Waiting in the small crowd was Captain Frederick Haig, Aviation Manager for Vacuum Oil Company, who pressed forward to welcome him. 'Well, that's a job well done,' Oscar said to Haig. One newspaper reported that Oscar had a blistered nose and was wearing 'an old smeared mauve shirt and an old coat dusted by

Oscar on arrival at Mascot Aerodrome, Sydney, 7 November 1930, after his solo flight from England to Australia.

Oscar standing beside his plane *Kia Ora* after landing at Mascot Aerodrome, on 7 November 1930. NATIONAL LIBRARY OF AUSTRALIA.

thousands of miles of tropic flying'. Several newspapers reported that a young, tall lady with a green coat dashed forward and shook hands. She had evidently been persistently calling out 'Oscar, Oscar' from the crowd. It was his mysterious girlfriend, Betty Whye, from when he was living in Sydney in the late 1920s, and he 'turned a delighted grin on her'.[61] Several photos of Oscar on the shoulders of some men leaning over to shake her hand appeared in several newspapers.[62] The newspapers called her a friend of his from Auckland, but Oscar had never lived in Auckland or even visited the city.

I became quite curious about this girlfriend who kept popping up and finally managed to find out that her name was Elizabeth Mary Grace Whye and that she was also known as Betty.[63] Her family lived in Otahuhu, a suburb in South Auckland that is right next to Papakura, where Oscar spent the last 14 years of his life. Betty's father was born in

Oscar being greeted by his friend Miss Betty Whye who he knew when he was living in Sydney. It is likely that she was his girlfriend but he never made any mention of her. NATIONAL LIBRARY OF AUSTRALIA.

Oscar holding a bunch of flowers at the reception held for him at Mascot Aero Club on 7 November 1930. QUEENSLAND MUSEUM.

Onlookers looking at *Kia Ora* outside the de Havilland hanger at Mascot Aerodrome.

Brewarrinna, New South Wales, and shipping records show Betty and her younger sister Josephine sailing to Sydney and back again frequently over a number of years, presumably to visit relatives. Betty eventually married John Gilbert Logan Hooper in Auckland on 7 January 1939, and they had one son, Warwick Hooper (1944–1974), who never married. I have no knowledge of whether she had any further contact with Oscar after she welcomed him at Mascot.

Oscar was carried shoulder high into the clubhouse where he was presented with an illuminated address (now in my possession) from Alderman David Allen Alexander, the mayor of Mascot, which reads:

On behalf of the municipality of Mascot, I extend a hearty welcome to you on your return to Australia and safe landing at Mascot Aerodrome after your flight from England and congratulate you upon the indomitable pluck and persistence shown by you throughout the flight.

After speeches by Haig and the president of the Aero Club, Captain Geoffrey Hughes, who congratulated him on the completion of a hazardous and remarkable flight devoid entirely of ostentation, everyone waited for Oscar's response. When none seemed forthcoming, and they began clamouring for a speech, he nervously said, 'I did not expect this. Even yet I do not know what this is all about, for I have not done anything extraordinary. I thank you for your kindness in welcoming me. You can take my picture all day, but really, I haven't got anything to say. I thank you very much for your welcome. I'm staying here now I've arrived, but that's all I can say.'[64]

Oscar later described his recollections: 'At this big reception at Mascot, Haig had this quizzical look for here's me holding a big bunch of flowers looking like a sissy, I'm burnt to a cinder with a silly grin on my face.' He said Fred [Haig] was 'looking at me out of the corner of his eye wondering what on earth he's struck! I was like a kid you see, a complete novice.'

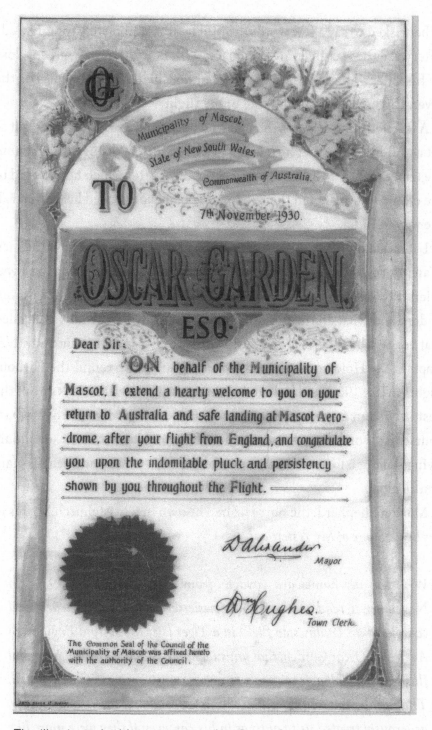

The illuminated address presented to Oscar Garden by Alderman David Allen Alexander, the mayor of Mascot.

When asked to say a few words, he said he was 'completely tongue-tied'. Afterwards he was given afternoon tea, with Betty, the girl in green, close by his side.[65] He makes no mention of her in all the interviews or the several articles he himself wrote of the flight.

A few hours later he was interviewed on station 2BL and said he felt as 'fit as a fiddle', and that he had experienced little weariness throughout the trip, except for the first two or three days, after which he got used to the cramped position in the cockpit. He had experienced headwinds all the way to India.

Later that night he was entertained by a number of well-known airmen at an informal dinner at the Wentworth Hotel. His reply to the toast was brief: 'I thank you for the splendid welcome afforded me. But I do not understand what all the fuss is about.'[66] Local airmen 'readily conceded that he was a born aviator, and ranks with Hinkler and Kingsford Smith'.[67] Captain Les Holden, who had taken Oscar up for two round-the-harbour flights in late 1929, said he had done extraordinary well. 'He is one of the best. It was an amazing performance. He just jogs along on a compass course. It's wonderful.'[68] Oscar had now accumulated 228.40 solo hours flying – enough to obtain a commercial licence – which had been his main aim all along.

Marion Shepherd, the nurse he had known in Christchurch, writes in her book *Some of My Yesterdays*:

While on my homeward voyage [from North Ireland in 1930] in November, I read in the radio newsletter that Oscar Garden had completed an 18-day solo flight in a Tiger [sic] Moth from England to Australia. Oscar Garden, that unusual name. Surely, I knew it. My mind flashed back half a dozen years to my nursing training in Christchurch. That exuberant young man, who after convalescence from surgery, generously treated us to outings in his car, even if they were more like harem-scarum escapades. So his adventurous spirit was taking him

around the world. I was yet to know how this was to steady into a clear
burning flame of vision for the future of New Zealand aviation.[69]

Although he had received telegrams at Wyndham, more now poured in
from Australia, New Zealand, Isle of Man and Scotland. One from Philip
Game, the Governor of New South Wales, said, 'I would like to avail myself
of this opportunity of offering you my most cordial congratulations on
your flight. From what I have read in the press your adventure was full
of incidents that called for an unusual display of initiative and courage.
I rejoice with you in your great accomplishment.' The Australian controller
of civil aviation, Colonel Brinsmead, sent the following telegram: 'Heartiest
congratulations success attending your flight from England to and through
Australia. This very fine achievement deserves commendation highest
terms. Trust have pleasure meeting you due course.'

In his telegram, the Governor-General of New Zealand, Lord Bledisloe,
said, 'I send you warmest congratulations on your courage and successful
flight, which has created intense admiration throughout New Zealand.'
New Zealand's acting Prime Minister, Ethelbert Alfred Ransom, wrote,
'[The] Government of New Zealand wish to congratulate you on your
wonderful achievement.'

In the Isle of Man, Douglas Secondary School flew the Union Jack
above the school in his honour, and the business of the House of Keys
was suspended for the day. The following cable was sent: 'Members of the
House of Keys desire to express to you the warmest congratulations on
successful termination of great flight and performance of feat, hitherto
unaccomplished by any Manxman.'[70]

In the middle of all this unexpected fuss and attention (which he found
quite unnerving) Oscar remembered to send a telegram to London to
Selfridges: 'Your department sells good aeroplanes!' A representative of
Selfridges who used the pseudonym Callisthenes had a long-running
column in *The Times*. His column, titled 'An aeroplane which we sold',

The Sydney Mail, 11 May 1932. NATIONAL LIBRARY OF AUSTRALIA.

finished with, 'We are proud that the little machine served him so well. Our reward is in that knowledge and in a laconic cablegram from Australia: "Your department sells good aeroplanes".'

Even though he broke no records, and the crowds that greeted him were nothing like those that gathered for Kingsford Smith or Amy Johnson, Oscar's epic flight put him in the band of men and women who changed the history of the world by pioneering flight. It was described as 'an intrepid piece of airmanship ranking with the achievements of such names as Kingsford Smith, Bert Hinkler, Amy Johnson, CWA [Charles William Anderson] Scott[71] and others who were making aviation history and blazing trails.[72] But what set Oscar apart was that he was one of the few survivors.

During the next five years, Hinkler, Ulm and Kingsford Smith would all die after crashing their planes. Other early aviators who had flown from England to Australia met a similar fate, including Flight Officer Froude Ridler Matthews, who had left a month before Oscar. He died in May 1939 in a mid-air collision during blind-flying practice near Gravesend, England. Amy Johnson died a year later, in early January 1941. She was flying from Scotland to an airfield in Oxfordshire when she became lost and ran out of fuel. She bailed out into the bitterly cold water of the Thames Estuary and her body was never found. Evidence suggests she may have been chopped up by the propeller blades of the ship sent to rescue her.[73] And Captain Les Holden, the person who first inspired Oscar to fly, died in an aeroplane crash near Lismore, New South Wales, on 18 September 1932.

One survivor of those early years was Francis Chichester. In 1931 he made the first east–west flight across the Tasman Sea using a biplane fitted with floats. Later that year he was badly injured in a crash when he was making an attempt to fly around the world in a seaplane. He served as an air-navigation expert during World War II, and afterwards took up ocean sailing. He died in 1972. Mrs Victor Bruce, who had accompanied Oscar in stages of his flight, continued flying for many years. At age 81, after a brief refresher course, she 'looped the loop' in a De Havilland Chipmunk. She died on 21 May 1990 at age 94.

The day after his arrival at Sydney, Oscar went shopping. He was short of money and had no suitable clothes – he claimed he lost one and half stone (almost 10kg) on the flight due to continuous exertion and lack of meals – and Haig bought him some new clothing, including a few suits. Haig also gave him a crash course in public speaking. He told him to always start with a joke. The rest of the day was spent relaxing – his first break since leaving Croydon – and he was taken around Sydney's beaches and went speed boating on Rose Bay.

On Sunday 9 November, Haig and Oscar left for Wangaratta, Victoria. Haig flew in a separate Moth owned by Vacuum Oil Company and named *Plume* (after the company's logo). They stopped on the way at Wagga. Oscar was the first international aviator to visit the Wagga aerodrome. Their next stop was Albury, where a large crowd was waiting, and an hour later they flew on to Wangaratta, arriving at 4.40 pm. Oscar was welcomed and congratulated by the acting mayor and given a civic reception that evening.

They left for Melbourne the next day, arriving at Essendon Aerodrome at 10.00 am. About 100 people were there to welcome him, including many New Zealanders. At a civic reception, Mr J Stuart Crow, a director of Vacuum Oil Co Pty Ltd, presented him with a mounted model of a stuffed kiwi and a large kiwi egg (as the kiwi is New Zealand's national bird). He said both Australia and New Zealand were proud of his achievement since Oscar was an amateur, with little experience who had in a modest way made his own arrangements for his hazardous adventure, relying entirely on his own very limited resources. Colonel Brinsmead, Controller of Civil Aviation, said the flight had been most extraordinary, particularly as the machine Garden used was an ordinary plane that had not been specially adapted. Bob Firth, New Zealand Government's representative in Melbourne, said Oscar Garden was their greatest flier to date.

On Tuesday 11 November, Oscar and Haig attended the Armistice Day ceremony at Parliament House, and afterwards had luncheon with the New Zealand Association. They returned to Sydney on Thursday, stopping for lunch at Canberra, where they were entertained at a cabinet luncheon at Parliament House and welcomed by the Acting Prime Minister, James Fenton. The flight had some scary moments. *The Evening Post* reported that 'during the journey Garden sometimes fell or shot upwards hundreds of feet due to air pockets',[74] and at Canberra Oscar had another narrow escape. On landing, a heavy gust of wind struck the plane at an angle and the machine tipped over on a wing, balanced for a few seconds before falling back on its wheels undamaged.

By then, Oscar had given up on his original plan of flying to New Zealand as he realised *Kia Ora* did not have the range to fly over the Tasman Sea. Its range was only 800 miles, whereas the distance to New Zealand is almost 1400 miles. Defence circles had regarded this idea as 'little short of suicide', although no authority in Australia had the power to prevent such a flight.[75] The *New Zealand Herald* had said steps needed to be taken to dissuade him from making the venture:

> To make an attempt to fly the Tasman in such a small machine would be more spectacular than useful, even supposing its fuel capacity could be increased sufficiently to invest the venture with a reasonable margin of safety. Merely spectacular flights can now do little to advance aviation.[76]

Haig suggested he and Oscar sail over to New Zealand and do an 'aerial lecture tour'. As Terry Gwynne-Jones (author of *Farther and Faster: Aviation's Adventuring Years*) points out, the early aviators may have pioneered the world's future air routes, but their greatest contribution 'was creating and maintaining public interest and instilling confidence in the capabilities of the airplane'.[77] People still travelled mainly by ship

Crowd welcoming Oscar in Wellington on 25 November 1930 after he had sailed over from Sydney. PHOTO GIVEN TO ME BY JAK GUYOMAR.

Crowd waiting for the arrival of Oscar at Wigram Aerodrome, Christchurch, 29 November 1930.

Date.	Aircraft. Type.	Markings.	Pilot.	Journey.	Time in Air. Hrs.	Mins.	Remarks.
				Brought forward..	241	30	
Nov. 28th	60M	G-AASA	Self.			15	Test flight.
29d	"	"	"		3	15	W'ton - Ch. Ch.
2nd Dec	"	"	"		3	40	Ch. Ch. - Dunedin
3d	"	"	"		1	15	Dunedin - Timaru
3d	"	"	"		3	35	Tim - Blenheim
9d	"	"	"		2	45	Blen - W'ton.
13d	"	"	"		2	5	W'ton - Wanganui
11d	"	"	"			55	Wang - Hawera.
				Carried forward..	258	45	

Date.	Aircraft. Type.	Markings.	Pilot.	Journey.	Time in Air. Hrs.	Mins.	Remarks.
				Brought forward..	258	45	
12d	GAASA	60M	Self.			40	Hawera - N.Ply.
13d	"	"	"		2	0	N.Ply. - Auckld.
15d	"	"	"			30	Auck. Hobson
16d	"	"	"			30	Hobs. - Auck.
17d	"	"	"		2	30	Auck. Rotorua
18d	"	"	"			50	Rotorua.
19d	"	"	"		1	45	Rot - Gisborne
20d	"	"	"		2	0	Gis - Hastings
				Carried forward..	269	10	

Pages of logbook of Oscar Garden, showing some of the towns he visited in New Zealand during November and December 1930.

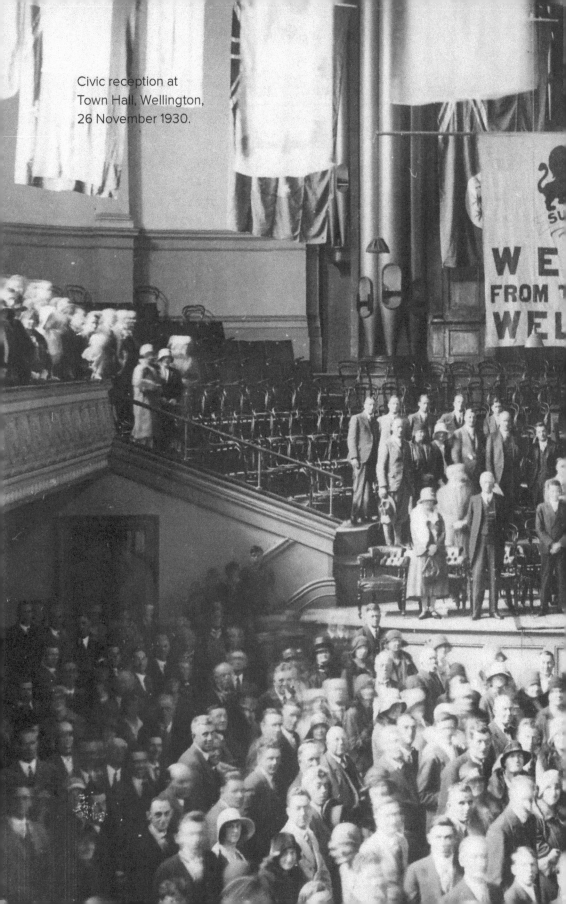

Civic reception at
Town Hall, Wellington,
26 November 1930.

or train, and they needed to be convinced that flying could be a mode of transport.

Oscar told the *Otago Daily Times*, 'I have ambitious schemes in mind, but I am not prepared to disclose them at this juncture. In the meantime, I am impatient to return to New Zealand. That means home, friends and everything a fellow values.' He added that he was bringing his 'faithful old bus *Kia Ora*', and hope to 'amble over the map from Auckland to the Bluff'.[78]

Oscar and Haig sailed across to Wellington on the *Ulimaroa*, shipping their planes, *Plume* and *Kia Ora*, with them. Even before the tour began, people were arguing over which town should see Oscar first. Timaru, Christchurch and Dunedin made special claim, since between 1921 and 1928 Oscar had lived in each place. Mr W Angland, the mayor of Timaru, argued, 'Garden is a Timaru boy. It is not a case of money, but of principle. We have a right to have him first. The Vacuum Oil Company [who was sponsoring fuel for the tour] should have no right to dictate to us for the benefit of advertising.' While aboard the *Ulimaroa* Oscar sent a radio message to the mayor accepting 'his invitation to fly first to his hometown'.[79] He did not keep his word on this: Timaru was one of the last towns to be visited on their tour of the South Island.

The pair arrived in Wellington on Tuesday afternoon, 25 November, and there was a large crowd at the wharf to meet them. They were welcomed by the Wellington Harbour Board, Wing Commander S Grant-Dalton (the Director of Air Services) and members of the Aero Club. As Oscar walked down the gangway, he was given a tumultuous welcome. There were cheers, clapping and the waving of flags from the crowd, and a brass band played, 'See the conquering hero comes'. He was welcomed at a reception in one of the Harbour Board sheds. The chairman of the Harbour Board, JW McEwan, said in his speech that as the Australian government had given knighthoods to Keith and Ross Smith for their 1919 flight from England to Australia, which took them 27 days, Oscar Garden should 'be awarded a similar honour', as his flight of 18 days had cut their time by almost one third. To this Oscar replied, 'This welcome has just about taken my breath away. There were two places I was very pleased to see, they were Alice Springs and Wyndham, but I was certainly glad to see Wellington this morning.'[80]

A procession headed by the Tramways Band then took place through the streets to the Town Hall for a Mayoral reception. *Kia Ora*, mounted on a lorry, was drawn behind the car carrying Oscar. He was given a standing ovation as he walked into the packed Town Hall with Mayor George Troup. Following them were Mrs Troup, the Honourable John Cobbe (the Minister of Defence), John Stannage (the New Zealand wireless operator who flew with Kingsford Smith on his trans-Atlantic flight), and other dignitaries including TE Corkill, president of the Manx Society of New Zealand.

Troup had invited all citizens of Wellington to attend the reception and employers were requested to allow employees time off work to attend. He welcomed Oscar home and expressed the appreciation of the people of Wellington of his success as an airman after he had 'left unheralded, unknown, unsung, on his lone trip across the world'. Troup said that when Oscar's lack of experience and all the circumstances connected with the flight were considered, the achievement was a splendid one, and he therefore should be acclaimed as one of the most illustrious flyers who had visited New Zealand. Cobbe congratulated Oscar on the success of 'his plucky, lonely flight, which would stimulate aviation in the Dominion greatly'. Martin Luckie, a senior city councillor, proclaimed, 'As there was a Lindbergh of America, so we now have our Garden of New Zealand.' Corkill said he hoped his voice reminded him of the Isle of Man, where Oscar had once gone to school, and presented him with a pair of greenstone and gold cufflinks. In response, Oscar said that he had only been following in others' footsteps but hoped the flight would 'give a fillip to aviation in the Dominion'.

The following day, the wireless telephone service to Australia was launched. At the opening ceremony, Oscar spoke to Kingsford Smith.

'Hullo Smithy,' said Garden.

'Hullo Kid, how are you Oscar? I did not expect to hear you so soon again.'

'I hear you very clearly. We had a very nice trip. I think it is a very great honour for me to speak to Australia and especially to you,' replied Garden. 'By the way,' he added, 'I met Stannage here. He sends his regards and hopes to be at your wedding.'

'Oh thanks. How is everyone in New Zealand?'

'Oh very well,' replied Garden. 'We heard on the boat coming over that you were going to do the Pacific flight again. Is that true?'

'You can wash that out. I don't know anything about that. You can tell them that the only flight I contemplate is a matrimonial flight,' replied Smithy.

'Anyway, best of luck Smithy.'

'Good luck; Goodbye.'[81]

The next day Oscar was entertained by members of the Cabinet at a morning tea at Parliament House, followed by a luncheon at the Optimists' Club. Here he gave a speech in which he said, 'I must have been born an optimist', although he added that his instructor had not been quite as optimistic. On Friday, the Wellington Aero Club put on a banquet.

On Saturday, Haig and Oscar set out to tour the South Island. Many New Zealanders travelled considerable distances to catch a glimpse of the famous aviator and his little Moth *Kia Ora*.[82] Ralph Watson was a youngster at the time. Like so many small school boys of the time, his imagination was fuelled and fired by that almost intangible challenge and sense of adventure the early mechanical age spawned. Brought up and schooled within a mile of the Nelson Aerodrome, he developed an abiding interest in aircraft made even keener by the aerodrome's proximity. He recalled that when the first trans-continental aviators such as Kingsford

Oscar with Captain Fred Haig, Aviation Manager for Vacuum Oil Company. Haig accompanied Oscar on an aerial tour of New Zealand from 29 November to 23 December 1930. Photograph by Whites Aviation. Ref: WA-2490-G, ALEXANDER TURNBULL LIBRARY, WELLINGTON, NEW ZEALAND.

Smith and Oscar flew in after their epic flights, the school as a whole would rush down to greet them.[83]

On 29 November they flew to Blenheim where they were given a civic welcome and public reception before leaving for Sockburn, Christchurch, where they arrived at 3.15 pm. Six other Moths had flown up to meet them, and they all flew in formation to circle the city before coming down to land. A crowd of about 3000 people had been waiting, but some broke loose of the barriers and swarmed around *Kia Ora* when it landed. The spectators cheered loudly, including Oscar's sisters May and Rose, who were waiting for him. He smiled at the crowd as he jumped from the cockpit and was congratulated by various officials. He was given a reception at the Canterbury Aero Club's hangar, followed by a civic welcome and reception in the Christchurch Square.

The *Christchurch Press* said the first thing that the crowd remarked upon was his youth: 'Though twenty-seven, he looks only a boy. He is of medium height, slim in stature with fair hair and a clear, youthful complexion.'[84] Speaking on behalf of the Progress League, Mr CH Clibborn said:

> It was a great privilege to join in the welcome home to this full-grown man. He must have finished that growth on the way out here and he timed his arrival with set purpose. There is a garden competition in Christchurch today, but we have the best Garden here. We still live in the days of miracles. In Christchurch, we have the best gardens in New Zealand, and here the very best of all – a Garden that has fallen down from the sky.[85]

Oscar replied that he hoped that they had all come out not just to see him, but because of their interest in flying.

He stayed another day in Christchurch and attended a luncheon put on for him by the Canterbury Aero Club. On 2 December he flew to Dunedin, stopping on the way at Ashburton and Oamaru. This was the first time a long-distance aviator had visited Dunedin, and when he arrived there was a civic reception in the Council Chambers of the Town Hall where speeches were made. Oscar gave a long talk about his flight, and some of his adventures, including the landing near Aleppo, where 200 'scared stiff' Arabs brought him hard-boiled eggs when he tried to indicate his thirst, and the crash at Jhansi, where he sat under the wing of the capsized plane all night waiting for daylight, with the rain turning the field into a bog.

That evening he was a guest of the City Council and the Otago Aero Club at a special dinner at the Savoy Hotel, in which songs were sung at intervals throughout. The Orkney and Shetland Islands Club presented Oscar with a mounted gold nugget, and mentioned that his grandfather, Robert Garden, was Orkney's biggest benefactor. I wonder what happened to that nugget! The deputy mayor, J J Clark, said they claimed a personal interest in Oscar because he had resided for a considerable time in their city. (After arriving from England with Rebecca and Violet in 1921, he

Ladies standing in front of *Kia Ora* after its forced landing at Otago
Aerodrome on 4 December 1930. E. A. Phillips photograph, P1968-001/7-0685,
HOCKEN COLLECTIONS, UARE TAOKA O HĀKENA, UNIVERSITY OF OTAGO.

Crowd surrounding Oscar and *Kia Ora* after landing at Otago Aerodrome on
2 December 1930. E.A. Phillips photograph, P1968-001/7-0477,
HOCKEN COLLECTIONS, UARE TAOKA O HĀKENA, UNIVERSITY OF OTAGO.

had first settled in Dunedin. He only spent 6 months there.) Clark said Oscar has 'bought added lustre to Dunedin' and that he 'can be assured that in this little place of the British Empire we must heartily welcome him and place everything possible at his disposal.' His visit, said Clark, would 'do a tremendous amount of good for the cause of aviation in this dominion. It is going to create an air sense ...'[86]

Fred Haig also gave a speech, in which he mentioned an incident the night before. They had been strolling down the town admiring the shops when they had seen a car by the side of the road, and Oscar had said, 'There's a pretty girl who looks to be in difficulty.' They discovered that her car had run out of petrol, so they pushed the car along to two petrol stations, which were closed. When they finally found a place open and had the tank filled, they discovered they had been pushing the car of the mayoress, Mrs RS Black. She was seated next to Oscar at the reception and laughed at Haig's story. She retorted that she was embarrassed to be found in difficulties with her car, but she was thrilled to find that her helpers had been Oscar Garden and Captain Haig. A local newspaper wrote that Oscar, as well as being 'a Raleigh of the air' was also 'a modern Quixote' in helping ladies in distress.[87]

Sir Charles Statham, Speaker of the House of Representatives, also extended his congratulations to 'the intrepid young airman' and said he was pleased to see the title of 'Mr' being dropped: 'It was a tribute to Garden, as it placed him in the same category as men like Kingsford Smith and Hinkler'.[88] Statham said he believed 'aviation would do a great deal to bring about a better understanding between nations.' Sometimes he felt the world was going a bit too fast, and he often thought 'it would be good to revert to the leisurely days of 50 or 100 years ago.'[89]

On 4 December Oscar left the North Taieri aerodrome in the afternoon. About 200 feet from the ground, the engine suddenly stopped with a loud explosion and the plane flattened out. Oscar managed to bank *Kia Ora* quickly, and racing before the wind he glided down over the buildings of the eastern side of the aerodrome, then turned against the wind and made a perfect landing. On inspecting the plane, he discovered that a connecting rod had broken and smashed through the crankshaft, ruining a cylinder and releasing the oil. He later discovered that the connecting rods of the Gipsy Moths had an alarming tendency to fracture, with a number of mid-air emergencies in which the engine stopped with a frightening bang. He reminisced on his good luck, 'to think it could have happened over the Timor Sea.'[90]

With *Kia Ora* requiring repairs, Oscar continued on to Invercargill in a Moth aeroplane ZK-ACE belonging to Otago Aero Club. Accompanied by Haig in *Plume*, they arrived at 6.00 pm, two hours behind schedule.

On 5 December, they left Invercargill and flew to Gore, arriving at 1.45 pm. After a civic reception at the Triangle near Gore High School, they departed for Dunedin. The next day they flew to Timaru. The airmen were met some distance south by two planes of the Canterbury Aero Club and were escorted to Washdyke, a few miles north of Timaru, where they were welcomed by several hundred people. They were then driven to Timaru, and in the presence of several thousand people Oscar was officially welcomed by the Mayor, Mr W Angland. Oscar later flew to Temuka, where that evening he was the guest of the aero club and municipal authorities at a dinner.

Over the next two weeks, Oscar and Fred Haig visited Nelson on the way back to Wellington and from Wellington toured the North Island, visiting all the main towns, including Palmerston North, Wanganui, Hawera, New Plymouth, Auckland, Whangarei, Hamilton, Rotorua and Gisborne. In each town, he was given civic welcomes and dinners. On 23 December, he returned to Wellington and was glad that it had come to an end. He wrote to Rebecca:

This last week has been the first breather I've had since landing at Wyndham on November 4th as I pushed straight on for Sydney, then immediately toured New South Wales and Victoria; then shipped the plane to New Zealand, and I have been touring New Zealand without a moment's spell ever since ... This honour and glory business is a washout, and as I was not looking for it, that made it worse. I was absolutely sick of receptions and speechmaking before it finished.[91]

As in any tour promoting something, whether a book or airmindedness, a person is left to repeat the same stories over and over again. My father would not have been a compelling public speaker, with his quiet, slightly high-pitched voice, although he could always be assured of a laugh with the story of the 20 boiled eggs.

To make it worse, a controversy played out in the *Auckland Star* as to whether his achievements should be honoured at all, as he had been born in Scotland. One reader wrote, 'Let's get this straight. Is a man who was *born* somewhere else but lives or has lived in New Zealand called a New Zealander just because he has distinguished himself?'[92] Another asked the question that if someone committed some mean or despicable crime, would New Zealand be claiming them as their own? 'New Zealand cannot have it both ways.'[93] Another, signing himself 'Anti-Humbug', wrote, 'All honour to a brave man, but let New Zealand encourage her own native-born heirs. There are many [New Zealanders] still waiting recognition.'[94]

Back in Wellington, Fred Haig was making arrangements to sail back to Australia with *Plume*, and Oscar asked him what he thought he should do now. Fred suggested having a crack at the record going back – New Zealand to England – but Oscar pointed out that it was not much point doing it in *Kia Ora*. He would need something faster and with the range to cross the Tasman Sea. Fred said an alternative was to cash in on his publicity and do some joyriding, become a barnstormer. And this is what he did, although he probably didn't realise that the honour and glory business was by no means over.

Oscar being farewelled by two Māori guides from Whakarewarewa thermal pools on 19 December 1930.

Oscar with Guide Tina at Rotorua on 18 December 1930.

CHAPTER 6

Barnstorming

In the early days of aviation, when people still had to be convinced of the value of air travel, barnstormers played a crucial role. These aviators travelled around giving joyrides, and in some countries banded together to put on flying circuses or air shows. Barnstorming is an American term. Some claim it was coined from the fact that pilots would often use farms as a base and people would gather near barns to watch the show or wait for rides. However, author Rinker Buck suggests the name came about because barnstormers frequently landed in farmers' fields and waited out storms in barns.[95]

Regardless, it was common for pilots to fly low over a rural town to grab the attention of locals and then land at a farm where they would negotiate with the owner for the use of one of his fields as a temporary runway. The drone of a small plane overhead, maybe doing a few loop-the-loops on the way, was always cause for much excitement. Crowds would flock to the field and purchase tickets. Occasionally pilots would place advertisements in local newspapers, or journalists would report the news that an aviator or aviators, or in a few cases an aviatrix, had come to town.

Barnstorming was not only entertainment, but also the beginning of civil aviation as joyrides. They often provided civilians with their first experience of flying in a plane. It was hair-raising stuff, as most had never been near a plane before, let alone climbed inside one. During the post-World War I era, barnstorming flourished as airmen returned from the war with not only flying skills but also a need for money. With no federal regulations governing aviation, for a while they were able to enjoy a reckless sort of freedom. Many of aviation's early pioneers, including Charles Kingsford Smith and Charles Lindberg, were barnstormers. And so was Oscar.

On 29 December 1930 he flew to Southbridge, and landed in a paddock close to town that belonged to William McEvedy. There was a large crowd waiting, and people lined up to go on a joyride, but first Oscar was whisked away to be welcomed at the Town Hall and given afternoon tea. He then returned and gave about 24 joyrides. That night a dance was given in his honour. In one of the speeches Mr Jones, MP, speaking in a 'humorous vein', said he had only just heard that evening the reason why Oscar Garden had taken up flying: 'Their guest had developed a habit of travelling so fast that he was becoming a danger to the public. The only thing he could do in such circumstances was to take to the air, where there were no speed restrictions.'[96] No doubt Jones had been told about the speeding fines Oscar had incurred in 1927 when living in the region.

Oscar decided to officially start his joyride business from a strip of land next to Saltwater Creek near Timaru and in preparation had souvenir flight tickets prepared. The rides began on New Year's Day 1931. They lasted about 10 minutes and cost 12 shillings – roughly the equivalent of $60.25 today – which was a huge amount at the time. The country was in the grip of the Great Depression, but clearly those who could afford it were willing to pay for a few minutes of thrills. Flying was still a dangerous thing to do – considering the crashes and fatalities in those early days of aviation – so it is remarkable that over 1000 people were daring enough to go up with Oscar. Even elderly men and women took what they saw was the opportunity of a lifetime. Alex Galbraith sent me a photo of his grandmother, Mary Ann McKenzie, wearing goggles and a flying hat, about to clamber up into the front cockpit of Oscar's plane on 2 January 1931. She was 75 years old at the time. Another photo was of her daughter, Alex's aunt, Corinita Mona McKenzie, aged 31, going for a joyride.

A further set of photos was sent in by Gillian Owens, who discovered by chance that their house in Cave, near Timaru, had been built by Robert Garden, my grandfather. When Gillian went to the local Canterbury Museum to search the history of the house, she stumbled upon a collection of photos of Oscar giving joyrides at Saltwater Creek. Tony Rippen, the curator of Documentary History at the Museum, told me when I contacted him that the photos had been taken by a Daniel Day of Flinders Street, who had been reluctant to identify which person in the photographs was actually Oscar Garden, as they had no other pictures of him.

John Pryce Parry was 16 years old when he went on a flight: 'One day a friend and I saw a man offering flights for five shillings. We hopped on our bikes and raced there. Ever since that day I wanted to fly. We went over the railway, past Caledonian Ground, past Fairview Hall and back.'[97] In 2005, I spoke with Parry by phone. He said Oscar was the reason he became a pilot. He joined the NZ Air Force in 1940 and during the war flew missions over France, Holland and Germany in Lancaster bombers. Parry died in 2011, aged 98.

While Oscar was at Saltwater Creek, 21-year-old Guy Menzies made the first solo flight over the Tasman in *Southern Cross*, the same plane Kingsford Smith had used to break the England-to-Australia record. On 7 January, Menzies had left Sydney in secret because he did not want to be refused permission by authorities. He crash-landed 12 hours later in a swampy paddock at Harihari in Westland on the West Coast of the South Island. Harihari is just south of Westport. where my mother lived at the time. (She was only 13 years old and told me she could not recall this event;

nor could her elder sister, my Aunt Ola. They were also unaware then of an Oscar Garden.) Menzies made his way to Christchurch and on 17 January set out for a two-day tour of the south of the country using a plane borrowed from the Canterbury Aero Club. He first went to Ashburton, then Timaru. At Timaru, Oscar flew out to meet Guy Menzies some distance from town and accompanied him to the aerodrome. A photo of them appeared a few weeks later in the *Otago Witness*.[98]

After Timaru, Oscar spent a week at Waimate before heading down to Oamaru. The *North Otago News* reported on Saturday 7 February:

During the past week the blue and silver 'Kia Ora' plane of Mr Oscar Garden has become a familiar sight to the residents of Oamaru. During the week many have taken the opportunity of going for a flight in the famous machine and in this morning's paper Mr Garden informs readers that he will only be in Oamaru two more days.

Perhaps this alerted the local police, for the following day, a Sunday, Senior Sergeant Scott went to the paddock where Oscar was working. However, Oscar, while admitting that a customer (TO Irvine) had paid 12s 6d for a flight, told Scott that he would continue to make flights until 8.30 pm, as this was the only country in the world in which flying for hire on Sundays was not permitted. Regardless, he and his assistant, Charles Henry Fowler, were charged. It may be hard to imagine now, but at that time in New Zealand Sunday was a sacred day set aside for going to church and for rest. And under Section 18 of New Zealand's Police Offences Act (1927) people were not allowed to work on Sundays at their trade or transact business in view of any public place. Exemptions were given to persons driving motorcars, carriages or cabs and those working in horse stables or on railway trains, tramcars and boats. But not planes.

In an article for the *Central Canterbury News* (25 July 1990), Oscar is quoted as saying:

Souvenir Flight Ticket 1931.

I was the first person to be taken to court for 'carrying a passenger for hire or reward on a Sunday'. I didn't know it was against the law, but I was hauled up to the Oamaru Court, found guilty and fined 10 shillings. I had made a rule not to carry a passenger on Sundays because I had enough of it six days a week, but someone must have twisted my arm fairly hard.

However, he was not the first. I discovered that two other aviators had been charged: William Henry Lett for taking paying passengers at Washdyke (Timaru) on 25 August 1929, and Captain Trevor Watts White at the Taieri airfield (Dunedin) on 14 December 1930. Both were convicted without penalty. White only avoided a penalty because the magistrate regarded it as a test case and had agreed to an appeal being lodged in the Supreme Court. Oscar's hearing at Oamaru Court was not until 11 March, but before then he was charged a second time, something he failed to mention for the *Central Canterbury News* story. From Oamaru, Oscar had flown down to Gore, the far south of the South Island, where he began to offer rides from a paddock owned by Mr Noble.

Even though the first fatal air service accident in New Zealand had occurred the previous week – a Dominion Airlines Limited de Soutter monoplane crashed at Wairoa killing its three occupants – this did not seem to dampen people's enthusiasm for going for joyrides. One person who went for a ride was Mary Brotherston (nee McDonald). Her son Peter Brotherston emailed me after reading my article in the *Christchurch Press*[99] and sent me the two photos with a note: 'I really don't need to keep them anymore; they are probably of more relevance to you.'

Hello Mary, I was fascinated to read your article in the Christchurch Press about your father's historic flight from England. While reading it my memory was jogged about two photos that I have in my collection handed down by my Mother. Mum worked in the Balfour area of Southland [Balfour is a small town about 30 miles from Gore] somewhere between 1926 and 1933. I remember her telling us children about going for a ride in an aeroplane that came to the area during a NZ tour. On the back of the photo of the plane with the roundels on it she has written 'Osker Gardeners [sic] plane I had ride in at Balfour', on the one of the Gipsy Moth is written 'plane we took day we came to see Oska Gardener [sic]'. My mother wasn't the best speller in the family so it's not hard to assume that it was your father in the photos.

On 15 February 1931, Oscar and Fowler were charged by a Constable Symons for conducting business on a Sunday. Oscar's logbooks show that over a period of seven hours he took 40 people for joyrides – the most he ever took up in a single day. On February 24, the case was heard at the Gore Police Court. *The Southland Times* reported on the hearing and described it as a case of unusual interest involving 'a well-known airman, Oscar Garden'. *The Matura Ensign* reported: 'Oscar Garden, who jumped into fame overnight by flying solo from England to Australia was charged with working at his trade on a Sunday.' His charge in the criminal records register of the Gore District Court reads:

On 15 February 1931, at Gore, being the proprietor of an aeroplane plying for hire, and being the pilot thereof, did work at his trade or calling, to wit, the piloting of the said aeroplane, within view of a public place on a Sunday.

At the hearing, Constable Symons said flights had been in progress all afternoon and he saw Fowler assisting Garden, booking flights and collecting the money. He had asked Oscar for his pilot's licence, but Oscar claimed he had left it in a suitcase in his hotel. Solicitor Mr Ronald Bannerman – a former World War I fighter ace – appeared for Oscar (who was down at Invercargill) and pleaded not guilty. Bannerman said he was quite prepared to admit that Garden was carrying passengers for hire but argued the defendant should not be found guilty as a point of law was involved. A similar case had recently been heard in Dunedin, and an appeal lodged held that aviators were justified in flying on Sundays. Bannerman pointed out that New Zealand was the only country in the world where flying was not allowed on Sundays. He argued that in fact it was not against the law, as an aeroplane came within the definition of a carriage: 'A Moth plane could have its wings folded and then could taxi along the road indefinitely under its own power.'

This was true. Moth planes were designed in England in the 1920s by a Captain de Havilland. He had other interests besides aviation, which included insects, notably butterflies and moths! Just as moths fold their

Date.	Aircraft.		Pilot.	Journey.	Time in Air.		Remarks.
	Type.	Markings.			Hrs.	Mins.	
				Brought forward...	397	40	
Jan 31							
31st	DH60M	G-AASA	Self.	Temuka-Timaru	2	25	Taxi & joyride
Feb. 1st	"	"	"	Timaru - "	2	15	joyriding
" 2nd	"	"	"	" - Oamaru		55	"
" 3rd	"	"	"	Oamaru (Joyride)	2	30	"
" 5th	"	"	"	" "	5	0	" "
" 6th	"	"	"	" "	2	0	" "
" 7th	"	"	"	" "	4	30	"
" 8th	"	"	"	" "	4	55	"
				Carried forward...	422	10	

Date.	Aircraft.		Pilot.	Journey.	Time in Air.		Remarks.
	Type.	Markings.			Hrs.	Mins.	
Feb. 9th	DH60M	GAASA	Self.	Brought forward...	422	10	
	"	"	"	Oamaru (joy)	2	35	joyriding
" 10th	"	"	"	" - Dunedin	2	15	Taxi job.
" 11th	"	"	"	(joy)	1	0	" "
" 12th	"	"	"	Herriot - Gore		45	" "
" 13th	"	"	"	Gore (joy)	3	0	joyriding
" 14th	"	"	"	" "	5	45	"
" 15th	"	"	"	" "	7	15	"
" 16th	"	"	"	Mataura (joy)	3	30	"
				Carried forward...	448	5	

Pages of logbook of Oscar Garden, showing the two dates he got charged for giving joyrides on a Sunday: 8th February at Oamaru and 15th February at Gore.

wings back along their bodies when at rest, de Havilland arranged for his DH.60 to do the same so that it could be towed on the road behind a car, and kept in an ordinary garage. In the Dunedin case the solicitor had put forward the arguments that 'a carriage included anything in which men or goods were carried' and 'there was part of an aeroplane known as the cab and a cab was [sic] a modified form of carriage.' Bannerman further argued that flying was not Garden's ordinary trade, as his actual trade was garage proprietor, but Senior Sergeant Packer said it would be difficult and expensive to obtain this evidence. It was fortunate that this evidence was not sought because Oscar had sold his Christchurch garage three years earlier, and he had no intention of returning to work in the motor industry. His whole purpose of flying from England to Australia was to accumulate enough hours for a commercial pilot's licence. The magistrate, Mr HJ Dixon SM, decided to adjourn the case until the judgment in Captain White's appeal case at Dunedin was given.

I doubt whether Oscar was overly concerned about the outcomes of both cases, Gore or Oamaru, as he was too busy making money. These were the Depression years, and he would have realised he was on to a good thing and should make the most of it while it lasted. Then he received a challenge he could not resist. While he was down in Invercargill giving joyrides, a local by the name of Geoff Todd bet him £5 that he could not land his plane on Stewart Island. This island, also called Rakiura, which means 'The Island of the Glowing Sky'– a reference to the sunsets the island is famous for – lies off the far southern tip of the South Island across the wind-tossed Foveaux Straight. New Zealand's third largest island, it has about 400 residents and is considered an ornithologist's dream, with tuis, parakeets, bellbirds and even kiwis.

Owing to the rough nature of the terrain and the absence of a suitable landing strip, no aviator had dared to do this before, although a few had flown over it. The first aerial crossing to the island had been made on 13 January 1921 by a Captain Buckley and two passengers in a De Havilland

DH.9. The following day *The Southland Times* reported that when they reached the island, the aviators saw a beautiful sight below: 'The numerous inlets seemed like a large cloth on which were laid a collection of glistening jewels – the bays and inlets in which the place abounds.'

Being a betting man, Oscar accepted Todd's challenge. On Friday February 27, he and Todd set out from Invercargill at midday to make the half-hour journey. The people on the island, the majority of whom lived at Halfmoon Bay, had been notified to expect the plane at about 1 pm down at Horseshoe Bay. In 2006 I spoke to the late Beryl Nielson, who was 93 years of age. At the time of Oscar's visit, she was living on the island and worked at Bragg's general store. She remembers how excited most of the people were on the day, although she admits she wasn't very interested at that age (she was 19 at the time). In any case, she had to stay and look after the shop and did not witness the event. Most of the other residents did, however. Along with the county chairman and members of the council, they were taken by surprise when they heard the drone of the plane at 12.30 pm and rushed along the 3-mile track to the bay. On the beach, meanwhile, a small crowd of people was already waiting, including the teachers and children from the local school. Several of the children were evidently so frightened at the sight of an aircraft approaching they ran and hid in the bush.

I spent weeks trying to track down someone who might have been there on that day and just as I was about to give up, I was given the name of the late John Tolsen, then 89, who was at a nursing home in Christchurch. After a brief and muffled conversation by phone I decided to write him a letter and received a long one in reply. He had been a 15-year-old lad when Oscar visited the island:

We had seen a few planes fly over but never one on the ground. We children had about 3 miles to walk to school and that morning when we got there we were told 'No school' as Oscar Garden's plane was landing on the beach that morning.

However, John and several of his friends had to first deliver a box of fruit sent to his mother on the weekly ferry, a steam tug. 'We had just got to Horseshoe Bay when the plane came in to land in front of us. No mucking about. He never flew over the village first.' But as Oscar and Todd were coming in to land, they realised they did not have a straight run. As the name Horseshoe suggests, the beach was curved with a definite camber and, in addition, a strong nor-westerly was blowing. Combined, these factors made it difficult to land safely.

Oscar decided to take off again without stopping. But one of the wheels got caught in a lump of bull kelp (seaweed), which slewed the plane and made it run out into the bay. Todd climbed out of his seat, but as he perched on the front of the plane it suddenly tipped up and he was thrown into the water.

John said his group had run out to help and managed to bring the tail of the plane down. Soon, he said, there were more helpers, including some women and girls, who waded in after tucking their skirts into their knickers. Oscar, by now out of the plane, produced the rope to tow the plane out of the tide and up onto the beach. 'Oscar was shaking the wing of the plane as if it was its fault, together with some under-his-breath mutterings. Everyone knew what he meant.' Luckily, the plane didn't appear to be damaged by its upending in the water, but as a precaution the oil was drained and replaced with motor-car oil.

It was decided to hold a civic reception there on the beach itself, and the school children were given the rest of the day off. Oscar and Todd were entertained to tea 'in a real picnic fashion', and the children who were still hiding in the bush emerged when they saw the lolly-scramble, cakes, tea and lemonade. Most of the residents had never had a close view of a plane before and covered the Gipsy Moth with their autographs.

Historic though the landing was, it wasn't the day's only event of note. That morning a Māori woman, Ruth Ryan, had given birth to triplets, the first triplets to be born on the island. In a speech the chairman of

Stewart Island County Council Mr RC Hicks, said that 'to console the airman for this unusual competition in interest', Ruth had told him prior to the birth that one of the children would be named Oscar. However, the newest residents turned out to be all girls and were subsequently named Ruth, Rona and Elizabeth – although Oscarina and Gardenia were considered.[100] The visitors departed shortly after 4.00 pm, having received 'three hearty cheers and being wished "God-speed" on their return journey'. It was reported that the plane took off perfectly and was soon a speck in the distance.

Seven years afterwards, Robin Hyde wrote that Stewart Island's biggest day was when 'Oscar Garden's aeroplane arrived – and stuck its nose in the sad sea waves a few yards from shore – and almost at the same minute, triplets were born.'[101] She recalled that all the men were away fishing, so the Stewart Island women formed a line, waded out into the sea, and brought the plane to shore.

This first landing has entered the Island's folklore as 'The Challenge'. Even today, tour guide, Sam, who drives a vehicle he calls Billy Bus, always mentions Oscar to the tourists. Photos of the event – *Kia Ora* in a nose-dive; Oscar and Geoff Todd alongside the plane after it had been hauled onto the beach; and of the island residents gathered around the plane – adorn the walls of the South Seas Hotel. No one in the family knew of these photos until a neighbour of my mother visited the island. The neighbour had not known anything of the Stewart Island landing and was astonished to see photos of Oscar on the wall. She took photos of the framed photos so she could give copies to my mother, but on the tour with Sam, she piped up, 'We knew Oscar. He was our neighbour!'

In his letter to me, John Tolsen describes the day as a red-letter day and ends by noting that Mrs Elizabeth Murray, a widow from Horseshoe Bay, retrieved the towrope that had been left behind, and this is now in the island's Rakiura Museum.

I tracked down William (Bill) Todd who lives at Invercargill. He wrote:

Top: Stewart Island residents next to *Kia Ora* on the beach at Horseshoe Bay after they had helped to tow it in to the beach. Most of the men on the island were out fishing.

Above: Oscar talking to Geoff Todd from Invercargill who had accompanied him on the first flight to Stewart Island. Todd had bet Oscar £5 that he could not land his plane on the island.

Left: The first landing on Stewart Island. A collision with a pile of bull kelp on the beach turned a wheel and spun the plane into the tide.

Yes, I am the son of Geoff Todd, who put up The Challenge. As far as the occasion is concerned, my father did talk about it, but I didn't listen. I understand that they ended up in the water by having to deviate from the beach.

Bill Todd and I left it too late to talk about this historic event with our fathers. After my article on this historical event was published,[102] an email arrived from Bill's sister:

My name is Alison Hazlett, daughter of Geoff Todd. I really enjoyed the two-page article in The Southland Times this morning re the landing of the first plane on Stewart Island. Of course, our family know the story well. My husband Bill and I have a holiday house on the Island at Golden Bay, and have the photo of Oscar's plane on our wall. Over the years there has been much discussion over their adventure.

A few days later, another email from Alison:

More excitement last Tuesday. After the article in The Southland Times, some pilot with a vintage plane contacted brother Bill, and suggested a re-enactment of the first flight to Stewart Island. It all happened last Tuesday, a thrill for Bill, clutching Father's helmet!! They didn't land the aircraft as the wind wasn't good, but had a great flight round, another photo in The Southland Times last Wednesday.

With £5 pocketed, Oscar continued on his way back up the South Island. A few weeks later, on 11 March, his charge for flying at Oamaru was heard. He was up at Nelson giving joyrides, and Mr C Zimmerman appeared on his behalf. Like Bannerman, Zimmerman said that the facts were admitted but the defence was on legal grounds as it appeared under Section 18 of the Act that all vehicles and conveyances were exempted.

129

However, the magistrate, Mr Bundle SM, said it was a matter for the Legislature to grant exemptions if it saw fit. Bundle pointed out that when the Act had been modified in 1927, only cars had been included (along with the already exempt cabs and carriages), yet this was a time when aeroplanes were a recognised method of travel. It would have been easy for the Legislature to make them a specific exemption, but it had not.

As with the Gore charge, this case was also adjourned pending the appeal to White's conviction. When White's appeal was cancelled in the Oamaru Court on 25 March, Oscar received a conviction and a fine of 40 shillings with costs of 10 shillings – a lot more than he recalled in the *Canterbury News* interview. Did this make him the first (maybe only) aviator in the world to be convicted with a penalty for Sunday flying?

His assistant, Charles Henry Fowler, was also convicted 'for aiding and abetting Garden' and fined 20 shillings with costs of 10 shillings. In a radio interview in 1990, Oscar recalled that Fowler had approached him at Timaru and asked if he could help out with the joyriding. He didn't expect to be paid, just the odd trip and living expenses. I've always wondered who paid Fowler's fine.

Contrary to his claim that he needed a break by Sunday, Oscar's logbooks show he flew on every Sunday (bar one) from 1 January to 17 April 1931, clocking up over 1000 joyrides plus a number of taxi jobs. As New Zealand aviation historian Errol Martyn pointed out, 'Looking at the number of hours he logged on joyriding, he must have made a handsome amount of dosh – certainly more than sufficient to cover the odd fine here and there!' Oscar claimed he made a few hundred pounds. That's about $70,000 today.

Oscar's Gore charge was dismissed on 21 April 1931. I could find no other cases of aviators being charged and fined for Sunday flying. In Wanganui in July 1931 a magistrate, Mr JH Salmon, dismissed a judgment against Captain Leslie H Brake, saying, 'It would not be doing violence to Section 18 of the Act' if he 'extended the meaning of the word "carriage" to include an aeroplane used for the carriage of passengers, mails and luggage.'

Barnstormers usually performed a range of stunts with their planes, including daring spins and dives, loop-the-loop and barrel roll manoeuvres. Oscar didn't. Fowler told Oscar he lost count of the number of times people wanted to loop-the-loop, or do some aerobatics. But Oscar claimed he wasn't 'game to try any aerobatics. I'm just a plain straightforward flyer. I don't want to frighten anybody.'

Oscar decided at the end of his joyriding venture (by which time his total solo flying hours were only 556.50 hours) that it was time to 'learn how to fly'.

Now that may sound very silly, but you see, all I'd learnt from Mr Bunning at Norwich was to take a plane off the ground, keep it straight and level, do a mild turn, and come back and land. And I'd learnt a lot on the flight from England to Australia but I was still a very, very long way from really knowing how to fly an aeroplane.

He decided to go to a flying school where he could refine his skills of instrument flying and learn some aerobatics. He said he had had so many frights on his 18-day flight from England to Australia. One of the major problems in the early days of aviation was flying blind in the clouds; there were no visual or navigational aids to see where the ground, or sea, was. He had read in the *Aeroplane* magazine of a new flying school, Air Service Training Limited, located in Hamble, England, that had begun training pilots in the use of basic instruments such as Reid & Sigrist turn-indicators. These were still primitive compared to later devices such as the autopilot but were a vast improvement on a compass.

For the time being, Oscar seemed to have lost interest in breaking records. However, no doubt he would have heard that just weeks before, on 10 April 1931, Charles Scott flying a DH.60 Moth, had broken Kingsford

Smith's England–Australia solo flight record. Scott took 9 days 4 hours and 11 minutes to reach Darwin.

Before he sailed back to England, Oscar sold his beloved *Kia Ora* to Tom Mullan, the part-owner of Mullan and Noy Engineers of Hamilton. The last entry in his logs is dated 29 April 1931: '*Delivered good old G-AASA to new owner. Hope he treats it well. Kia Ora.*' The plane continued to have a colourful history for 15 more years.[103]

CHAPTER 7

Africa and the Middle East

On his way to England, Oscar sailed to Canada to attend an aviation conference at Winnipeg, which discussed flights across the Northern Atlantic, and then went to America to look at some aircraft factories. He sailed from New York on the *Caronia* and evidently, as soon as he disembarked in Southampton on 30 June 1931, enrolled in a course at the new Air Service Training Limited in Hamble. While waiting for the course to begin, on Tuesday 8 July he sailed across to the Isle of Man on the steamer *Ben-my-Chree* to visit Rebecca and Violet, who were visiting Rebecca's family. Oscar's visit was also reported as 'unheralded'. He simply telegraphed Rebecca that he was on the steamer. A public reception had been mooted, but it seems Oscar would have none of it. Apart from Rebecca and Violet, friends and relatives, he was met by TR Radcliffe, member of the House of Keys for Douglas. There was firing of a gun from the grounds of Fort Anne on Douglas Head.[104]

The next day he was the guest at a luncheon at the Douglas Rotary Club, before being congratulated at a meeting of the Douglas Town Council. The press described him as the modest Manx flying hero who has brought a measure of credit and fame to the Island because of his

Rebecca meeting her son Oscar Garden after he sailed across to the Isle of Man in July 1931. TR Radcliffe, member of the House of Keys, the lower house of the parliament, is on the right.

Oscar being congratulated by the Speaker of the House of Keys, Isle of Man, one of the oldest parliaments in the world, while other members look on.

sensational flight from England to Australia: 'Manxmen all over the world were proud of Mr Garden.'[105] They noted his retiring and bashful manner and his dislike of welcomes and public functions. One reporter said he was brown and bronzed and looks the picture of health. He only spent a few days at Douglas before sailing back to Liverpool.

On 16 July, he began the nine-hour flying course. Group Captain Barton was in charge, and the two instructors were Flight Lieutenant Jenkins and Flight Lieutenant Pope. The planes used were Avro Tutors, which Oscar said were 'marvellous for that sort of thing'. The course cost £108 pounds (worth about £6309 today). Oscar later recalled that only at the end of the course did he feel he had 'learnt something about flying'. 'It was pretty expensive!' he said. 'But I reckoned it was worth it.' One of the tests involved a triangular flight of 70 miles in an Avro Tutor, during which he had to sit in the back cockpit, which was hooded so he could only see the controls and not outside. His instructor sat in the front cockpit so as to be able to trace on a map the actual track followed and to avoid a collision. Jenkins wrote in his report that Oscar Garden looped the loop with great accuracy and was able to emerge from a spin 1.5 seconds faster on instruments than in an open cockpit.

Oscar won the course's first competition for blind flying and received a trophy of a solid silver model of an Avro Tutor with a hooded cockpit. In 1973, he gave this to the Royal New Zealand Aero Club. Since 1975 it has been competed for annually as the Oscar Garden Trophy. I remember it perched on the mantelpieces in the lounges of our various homes in Tauranga and Papakura. We were never allowed to touch it. My mother says it is a miracle my father didn't sell it, as he usually sold anything of value.

After this course, Oscar had no plans of what to do next until someone put him in touch with John Tranum, the famous Dutch-born parachutist. Tranum was an aerialist – a daredevil artist – who had just finished touring England as part of Captain CD Barnard's flying circus, the first to be held in the country. Tranum and Oscar decided to set up a company called Skyworks Ltd and go to South Africa to put on that country's first flying circus.[106] The plan was to tour for about six months, and their aim was to 'promote, assist and encourage aerial navigation in all its forms'.

Oscar said they had a 'hook up' with Spartan Aircraft Company, which was based at Hamble, and shipped three three-seater Simmonds Spartans[107] to South Africa. The planes, which had plywood fuselage and wooden wings, were registered in Oscar's name as G-ABRB, G-ABRA and G-ABPZ. Tranum and Oscar engaged the services of several ex-war pilots, who had also been part of Barnard's tour: Captain ED Ayre, Captain JR King, Captain ED Cummings and CE Riley. Ayre had his own plane, a de Souteur. These pilots had years of experience – between two and four thousand flying hours – in contrast to the 580 hours Oscar had accumulated. King, for example, had begun flying in 1910, when Oscar was only 6 years old. Oscar and Tranum decided to go to Cape Town ahead of the rest of the group so they could act as publicity men for the tour. They sailed from Southampton on the *Warwick Castle* on 9 October, and the others followed on 20 October.

Meanwhile, Oscar's peers were still intent on breaking the records between Australia and England and vice versa. Scottish aviator Jim Mollison broke Charles Scott's Australia to England record in August 1931 with a flight of just under nine days. (Interestingly, Mollison had set out from Wyndham instead of Darwin.) Mrs Victor Bruce and Oscar were among the first to welcome him at Croydon. Kingsford Smith decided to attack this record, and left Melbourne on 21 September. His bid was unsuccessful. He did not reach England until 7 October, two days before Oscar left for South Africa. Oscar and Jean Batten were the first to rush out and greet him on his arrival at Heston Aerodrome at 5.30 pm. Other aviators joined them, including Jim Mollison and Mrs Victor Bruce, with Jim (the holder of the existing record) shouting 'Bad luck, old man.'[108]

Kingsford Smith was shattered. He looked thin and ill on arrival. On

RECORD OF FLIGHTS. Solo 556·50.

Date.	Aircraft. Type.	Markings.	Pilot.	Journey.	Time in Air. Hrs.	Mins.	Remarks.
	AVRO TUTOR	G-ABIR	Flt. Lt. JENKINS	Brought forward...	579	40	Blind flying
28/7/31					1	10	tests.
				[signature] CHIEF INSTRUCTOR. AIR SERVICE TRAINING LIMITED, HAMBLE. DATE:- 28/7/31			
15/11/31	HERMES SPARTAN	G-ABRB	SELF	Local. Capetown		35	Landings
2/1/32	"	ABRA	"	Benoni - Jo. Burg.		25	
13/1/32	"	ABRB	"	Local. Kimberley		25	Joyriding
				Carried forward...	582	15	

RECORD OF FLIGHTS. S. AFRICA.

Date.	Aircraft. Type.	Markings.	Pilot.	Journey.	Time in Air. Hrs.	Mins.	Remarks.
	HERMES SPARTAN			Brought forward...	582	15	
16/1/32	"	ABRA	SELF	Local Bfontein		45	
4/2/32	"	ABRB	"	" C. Town.		40	Joyriding
30/10/31	"	ABRA.	"	" Witbank		25	Formation
13/2/32	"	ABPZ	"	Local C. Town.		35	Wing walking
20/2/32	"	ABRB	"	" "	1	25	Joyriding
27/2/32	"	"	"	" "	1	5	"
3/3/32	"	"	"	" "		30	"
6/3/32	"	ABPZ	"	" "		30	Test flight.
				Carried forward...	588	10	

Pages of logbook of Oscar Garden. The test for blind flying was 28 July 1931, for which he received a trophy – a silver model of an Avro Tutor. His first flight in the Hermes Spartan that he used in the Flying Circus in South Africa was on 15 November 1931.

Oscar on the right of Charles Kingsford Smith, Jim Mollison on the left. Taken at the clubroom at Heston Aerodrome after Smithy's arrival from Australia on 7 October 1931.

the flight he had had several panic attacks – assailed by waves of fear and nausea and vomiting over the side of the plane – and had resorted to 'medicinal swigs of alcohol'. (His paralysing panic attacks, especially over water as he had a phobia of drowning, beset him in almost all his flights.) He was instructed to have a medical examination the next day and RAF doctors concluded that he was suffering a nervous disorder. However, according to his biographer, Ian Mackersey, it is more likely that Kingsford Smith was an alcoholic, his experiences in World War I having left him psychologically damaged and with some degree of post-traumatic stress disorder. On his long flights, alcohol-withdrawal would also have aggravated his panic attacks.[109] Interestingly, Mollison was known as an alcoholic playboy; he became chronically dependent on alcohol on his long-distance flights.

In November 1931, the England to Australia record was cut by Cecil Arthur Butler. Butler was an Australian engineer and pilot, and newspapers delighted in reporting that he wore carpet slippers (as Oscar had done) while flying the small aircraft. This record was slashed by Charles Scott, who left Lympne on 19 April 1932 and reached Darwin on April 28; his flight of 8 days, 20 hours and 47 minutes shaved about 6 hours off Butler's record.

Rebecca and Violet had meanwhile sailed back to New Zealand, arriving in Wellington on 14 October 1931. Rebecca contacted newspapers, which reported the return of the mother and sister of the aviator Oscar Garden. She told them it was unlikely that her son would attempt a flight from England to New Zealand because he had difficulty raising the funds for a suitable machine. Rebecca reported that he had 'a great reception' on the Isle of Man.

Oscar, however, seemed more interested in his new business venture than breaking flying records. It is hard to imagine now, but back in 1931 'the public was not yet educated in the value of air transport.'[110] Hence, flying circuses and air shows were attempts to educate the public. Tranum and Oscar provided a 17-page souvenir program for circus goers. They stated their aim in the introduction to the program:

Airmindedness for the world – and particularly for South Africa. There is absolutely nothing in flying except the sheer exhilaration of roaming well above the clouds into the realms of God's fresh air. But so few people would know it. It is this that the Flying Circus aims to show.

Airmindedness, they claimed, is aided by demonstrations of flying that they would provide. They also wanted to show that lessons gained from the Great War – World War I – revealed that an aeroplane could be used as a fighting weapon, and stunting could be lifesaving rather than a dangerous device. For accomplished pilots, stunting was as safe as straight flying. The program is sprinkled with homilies: 'You'll feel better after a flight', 'Why on Earth?', 'Say it in the air', 'Flying is good for you', 'You will eventually fly', 'Fly and forget'.

Oscar was promoted as 'The Sundowner of the Skies'. The program said he 'was described thus by world press for his delightful habit of "turning up unexpectedly" in any part of the world'. The shows began with joyrides, rates starting at 10 shillings. A formation flight of all machines over the town followed. Then there would be a demonstration of 'crazy flying' by Captain Ayre in which, presumably, he performed aerial antics such as dive-bombing and loop-the-loops. One event was called 'Bombing the Bridal Pair'. Aerialists delighted in dropping bags of flour on the audience. A similar circus in England put on by Alan Cobham had people dressed up as policemen in the crowd – pilots would fly over and empty bags of flour over them. Presumably Tranum and Oscar had arranged for a couple to be dressed up in bridal wear and bombarded with flour. Then there was 'Aerial Marksmanship by Captain Dead Eye Dick'. What was this stunt, and which pilot had a patch over one eye for it? I do not know. William Courtenay had accompanied Barnard's circus in England the previous year as the representative of the *Daily Mail* and wrote:

The spectators at air displays always like a parachuting descent. It remains the one thing which makes one's heart almost stand still for a second, just as the parachutist leaps and one wonders if the airchute will open … I suppose at the back of many people's minds is the morbid fear (or hope) that the 'chute may not open and that a livelier thrill will be provided. But it always did open with a regularity that grew monotonous, so safe is the modern airchute of the type made by Mr Leslie Irvin, which has saved over 1000 lives throughout the world in the last 10 years, which has saved over a hundred lives in the Royal Air Force.[111]

The Irvin parachutes were high-grade silk canopies approved by the Air Ministry. For some years my father had a silk parachute although I do not know where he obtained it. He used to let us play with it when we were children. We would run down the hill with it billowing behind and

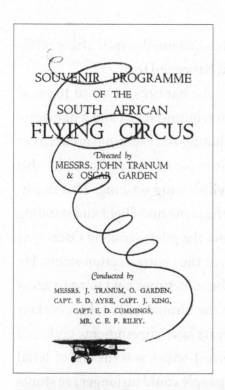

Flying circus show in South Africa in early 1932. Oscar Garden is flying a Simmonds Spartan while John Tranum is wing walking.
PHOTO PROVIDED BY JOHN ILLSLEY, PRETORIA, SOUTH AFRICA.

wrap ourselves in its soft folds, and I often imagined myself lifting off up into the sky. None of us remember what happened to it.

John Tranum was promoted as 'one of the star turns'. He had 10 years' experience as a pilot and had begun parachuting seven and a half years earlier – breaking every record in parachuting and escaping unhurt from 1400 descents. For the circus, apart from parachute descents, he also delighted the crowds with his dare-devilish wing walking. This death-defying stunt involved climbing out of the plane mid-flight and standing on either on the rear fuselage just behind the pilot – usually Oscar – or else on the cowlings with his legs against the centre-section struts. He never wore a safety harness, although he sometimes held reins to assist his balancing acts. Wing walkers were the ultimate risk-takers of their day, and several lost their lives. A few years later governments outlawed wing walking below 1500 feet (457 metres), which was the end of aerial stunting for entertaining the public, as people could no longer see stunts performed above that altitude. Sadly, in 1938, Tranum died in a parachute jump in Copenhagen while trying to beat his own world record for delayed opening descent. His main oxygen tank apparently failed.

Journalist and flier William Courtenay seems to have disliked Tranum:

Parachutists are, as a rule, lazy men. They think that jumping from aeroplanes is a quick and easy way of making money. So it is, but there is no livelihood in it, and upon the whole they are too lazy and short sighted to fit themselves for anything else. Tranum was no exception to the rule. He would carry out his item every day, give a few minutes' wing-walking display, and would do nothing else all day.

However, he also admits that:

He was all the same, really very clever at his job, could nearly always land in the centre of the airfield at the point pre-selected by him …

his wing-walking displays were certainly breathtaking and he was good at devising humorous [sic] situations, such as suddenly running after a machine which was about to take off, clambering on the undercarriage, while a 'bogus' policeman in orthodox uniform (in reality a pilot) would chase him, arrive on the scene too late, and 'arrest' him to march him away handcuffed on his return after the wing-walking exhibition.[112]

Courtenay said he could not see how wing walking assisted in the development of airmindedness, as 'aeroplanes were not made to be walked on in mid-air and one was always taught to treat them with the greatest respect.'

South Africa was one of the countries hardest hit by the Great Depression. Even in its worst years, some people were willing to pay large

Refuelling *Miss Mobiloil* at Wingfield Aerodrome, Cape Town, South Africa in early 1932. Oscar is standing with his back to camera.
PHOTO PROVIDED BY JOHN ILLSLEY, PRETORIA, SOUTH AFRICA.

amounts of money for a few minutes of thrills. Most, however, would simply have watched from the fringes of the airfield to avoid paying entrance fees.

John Illsley, South African aviation historian, claims that thousands attended the flying circus shows and an estimated 15,000 arrived for the first show of the tour in Cape Town on 15 November 1931.[113] The flying circus began at Cape Town and travelled to 64 towns, including Bloemfontein, Cape Town, Witbank, Kimberley, Pretoria, Johannesburg, Port Elizabeth, Kimberley, Graaff-Reinet and Potchefstroom. While Oscar was in Johannesburg, he had a run-in with authorities and was 'flung into jail for a night' because he was 'drinking with some natives at a party.'

During these months Oscar sent his mother money. In a letter dated 29 January 1932 he writes that he is enclosing a draft for £20 and asks if the previous money order for £10 was received. I do not know how much money he gave his mother over the years, but it seems to me he felt obligated to help her financially.

In spite of the initial success, the flying circus folded in early April 1932. It was a financial disaster. At the end of the year, aviator Alan Cobham also brought out his flying show to South Africa, and that was not a success either. According to Illsley, the venture cost Cobham £6000. According to Rebecca, Oscar 'must have lost fully 5000 pounds with the Flying Circus'.[114] As his share, Oscar kept G-ABRB, which he called *Miss Mobiloil*. The G-ABPZ was sold to the Air Taxi Company at Wingfield, Cape Town and became ZS-ADP – the first plane the company operated.[115] The third, G-ABRA, was shipped back to England and sold to someone in Kent.[116]

After the circus folded, Oscar realised the South Africa-to-England solo flying record was 'wide open' and decided to have a go at breaking it. The record the other way, England to South Africa, had been broken the previous month by Jim Mollison. On 28 March 1928, Mollison took

4 days and 17.5 hours to reach Cape Town. There had only been two successful solo flights from South Africa to England, remarkably both by women. One was accomplished by Lady Sophie Mary Heath, who took just over three months (12 February – 17 May 1928) in an Avro Avian III. When Heath arrived at Croydon, she announced, 'Flying is so safe. A woman can fly across Africa wearing a Parisian frock and keeping her nose powdered all the way.' She made the trip with a Bible, a shotgun, a couple of tennis rackets, six tea gowns and a fur coat. On the way, she crossed paths with Lady Mary Bailey at Khartoum, who was flying her de Havilland DH.60 Moth in the other direction. When Bailey reached Cape Town, she flew back to London, the round trip spanning from 21 September 1928 to 16 January 1929. About this time on 22 May 1932, Amelia Earhart became an international hero when she became the first woman to fly solo across the Atlantic. She took almost 15 hours, more than halving Lindbergh's 33.5-hour flight, undertaken in 1927.

Oscar planned to fly from Cape Town to London, over the route Bulawayo, Salisbury, Mpika, Lake Victoria, Juba, Khartoum, Cairo and Southern France. He arranged for a special Fairey metal propeller to be shipped out from London, as this, he determined, would increase the speed of *Miss Mobiloil* by about 12 miles an hour.

His first start was made secretly, but he had engine trouble and had to return to Cape Town. Thereafter he was busy day and night preparing for the flight, getting little sleep. He wrote to Rebecca that he tried to keep his 'plans for another attempt secret' but the *Johannesburg Star* had 'found out about it and told South Africa.'[117] As usual, Rebecca passed the letter on to the New Zealand press. After a test flight on 19 April 1932, he left Wynberg – near Cape Town – just after midnight and flew to Bulawayo, Southern Rhodesia, with a stop at Kimberley. The total flight took 14 hours and 15 mins. The next day he flew for 16 hours and 5 minutes to Abercorn (now called Mbala) in what was then Northern Rhodesia (now Zambia), with a stop at Broken Hill (now called Kabwe). His logbooks show he had a three-day break, so presumably he was doing some repairs to the plane. The *Cape Argus* reported on 27 April 1932 that he 'had a slight accident when landing at Abercorn'. On 25 April, he was in the air again, but only for two hours and 20 minutes. He stopped at Mbeya in Tanganyika (now Tanzania) with a note in his logs: 'nursing motor'. On 28 April, he flew to Iringa in 2 hours and 5 minutes. There he made a forced landing. The only note in his logs is 'full stop!' The engine crankshaft had broken with the propeller shearing the bolts; Oscar had made the mistake of assuming the old bolts would suit the new propeller. The plane was trucked to Dar es Salaam, and Oscar went on to Mombasa, Kenya, where he boarded a ship back to England, arriving in Southampton on 24 June 1932. While on board he wrote to Rebecca:

Am on my way home by boat. Was flying home and broke the engine crankshaft right out in [sic] the 'blue' in the middle of 'darkest' Africa. Was missing nearly a week before I got to civilization. Had a pretty rotten time and am absolutely broke now. Had to borrow some more money from Grandma [Margaret Jolly Garden] to pay my fare home. Have got the wings and the engine on board, so if I can borrow some more money from her will get them repaired and take a boat back to East Africa (Kenya) and get it flying again. It just seems as if one darned thing after another goes wrong. Guess I'll have to get a job somewhere.

Missing for nearly a week! He actually crashed in Iringa, a town (now a city), the capital of the Southern Highlands of Tanzania, and locals were soon there to help him. There are photos of the crash with the nose of the plane wedged into a tree.

He asked Rebecca to contact Beau Shiel to see what the prospects were for joyriding in New Zealand the next summer. 'I hate writing anybody just now as the bottom seems to have dropped right out of everything as far as I'm concerned and the Lord only knows what I'm going to do next.'

Oscar's crash in Iringa, Tanzania, East Africa on 28 April 1932.
PHOTOS PROVIDED BY JOHN ILLSLEY, PRETORIA, SOUTH AFRICA.

Date.	Aircraft.		Pilot.	Journey.	Time in Air.		Remarks.
	Type.	Markings.			Hrs.	Mins.	
	HERMES SPARTAN			Brought forward...	662	40	
19/4/32	"	ABRB	SELF	C'Town (Local)		40	test flight new prog.
20/4/32	"	"	"	" - Bulawayo	14	15	stop Kimberly
21/4/32	"	"	"	Bul.- Abercorn	16	5	" B. Hill
25/4/32	"	"	"	Abercorn-Mbeya	2	30	nursing motor
28/4/32	"	"	"	Mbeya - Iringa	2	5	full stop!
12/11/32	"	VR-TAJ	"	Daresalaan		30	test flights
"	"	"	"	"	2	5	joyriding
13/11/32	"	"	"	"	8	40	Daresalaan
				Carried forward...	709	20	

Page of logbook of Oscar Garden. In an attempt to break the South Africa to England record, he crashed *Miss Mobiloil* at Iringa on 28 April 1932.

On 26 August 1932, a London newspaper reported that he was back in England and looking for a job. He would like to return to New Zealand but was chiefly concerned with a regular position. The article headline was, 'Roaming airman is tired of roving life.'[118]

When the New Zealand aviatrix Jean Batten heard that Oscar was back in London, she contacted him to 'pick his brains for route information', because she planned to fly from England to Australia. Almost 60 years later, the late Ian Mackersey interviewed Oscar for the book he was writing on Batten. Oscar told him:

I remember I took her to the pictures. I can't recall the occasion very clearly now but she was a very serious, very quiet, shy girl. I think she wanted to get hold of my maps but I had to explain they weren't actually good enough. I remember taking her home on the underground and standing on the doorstep and kissing her good night. It was just a peck on the cheek.[119]

Peck on the cheek! I never once saw my father kiss anyone, not even Mum, not even a peck. Batten was able to borrow some maps from Kingsford Smith, who gave her two pieces of advice: 'Don't attempt to break men's records, and don't fly at night.' She said 'she made a point of ignoring them both.'[120]

By the time Oscar arrived back in Kenya in September 1932 with the repaired wings and engine, he had changed his mind about trying to break any flying records. 'Blow this record business, I'll get back to the old caper I had in New Zealand and earn a few bob joyriding.'

In November *Miss Mobiloil* was re-registered in Tanganyika as VR-TAJ, and he spent 10 days giving joyrides at Dar es Salaam, Tanzania. He picked up a young Greek by the name of Vlakos, who offered to give Oscar help with the plane for a lift up to Cairo. They went to Zanzibar, where no joyriding had been done before. From there they gradually worked their way up through East Africa. I could find no detailed records or accounts of Oscar's time during this period, except for the occasional terse entries in his logbooks such as 'nasty trip', 'dead air for joyriding', 'remarkable

Oscar standing in front of *Miss Mobiloil*, a Hermes Spartan VR-TAJ, Omdurman, Sudan, January 1933.

Date.	Aircraft.		Pilot.	Journey.	Time in Air.		Remarks.
	Type.	Markings.			Hrs.	Mins.	
	HERMES-SPARTAN.	VR-TAJ	Self.	Brought forward...	742	5	
8/12/32	"	"	"	Tabora (local)		10	Joyride!
9/12/32	"	"	"	Tabora-Shinyanga	1	55	Day of storm.
10/12/32	"	"	"	Shinyanga. Mwanza (local)	1	50	some aerodrome! ate tail
11/12/32	"	"	"	Mwanza	1	20	joyriding
12/12/32	"	"	"	"		15	"
13/12/32	"	"	"	Mwanza - Entebbe	3	35	perfect flying
14/12/32	"	"	"	Entebbe - Masindi	2	—	b- aerodrome at Masindi
15/12/32	"	"	"	Masindi - Nimule	2	40	Murchison Falls thousands of elephant!
				Carried forward...	755	50	

RECORD OF FLIGHTS. SUDAN.

Date.	Aircraft.		Pilot.	Journey.	Time in Air.		Remarks.
	Type.	Markings.			Hrs.	Mins.	
16/12/32	HERMES SPARTAN	VR-TAJ	SELF	Brought forward...	755	50	
"	"	"	"	Nimule - Juba	1	20	Still down hill
18/12/32	"	"	"	Juba		10	Test flight. O.K.
19/12/32	"	"	"	"		10	joyride
20/12/32	"	"	"	"		30	"
21/12/32	"	"	"	Juba - Malakal	5	5	Refuel Boor
22/12/32	"	"	"	Malakal - Khartoum	6	25	" Kosti
29/12/32	"	"	"	Khartoum		30	Test flight
8/1/33	"	"	"	"	1	10	joyriding ideal weather
				Carried forward...	771	0	

Pages of logbook of Oscar Garden. With *Miss Mobiloil* repaired, Oscar worked his way up through East Africa to Khartoum, Sudan, giving joyrides.

up and down currents 3000 ft. in 2 mins', 'thousands of elephants' (at Murchisan Falls), 'narrow margin' and so on. And in one interview he says he had 'all sorts of excitement and experiences'. Although many people view barnstorming as a romantic period in aviation, it wasn't like that for the pilots. Their nomadic existence meant that it could be difficult for them to find fuel or the right parts for their planes, or find somewhere to sleep – they often slept under the wings of their planes. They could go for days without attracting enough people to make a profit.

Oscar reached Khartoum, the capital of Sudan, in late December 1932 to find he had to wait several weeks for a permit from the local British governor. At that time Sudan was under British colonial rule, and it did not gain independence until 1956. When the permit came through it stipulated that he could only do restricted joyrides in Khartoum and Wad Medani (about 85 miles southeast of Khartoum) and was not allowed to take up any native Sudanese. Oscar would have baulked at such a restriction, as he loathed apartheid. However, he stayed for six weeks and managed to take up a few hundred Europeans (many were Greek businessmen) before he flew on to Cairo. There he found that a small

Flyer for the joyrides my father put on in Palestine.

Oscar (back seat) about to take 73-year-old Mr Dizengoff (the first mayor of Tel Aviv) for his first ride in an aeroplane.

airline called Misr Airwork – owned by the government in association with England's Airwork Company at Heston – had been established in May 1932 to promote the spirit of aviation among Egyptian youth.

Oscar claimed this airline had a 'stranglehold on stuff there', so he said goodbye to Vlakos and decided to try his luck in Palestine.

Arriving in Palestine in March 1933, he found 'good flying country' and managed to procure the use of an old orchard near Lydda (the Lydda airport was built in 1936 by the British Government, and in 1974 its name was changed to Ben-Gurion Airport). Fliers promoting his joyrides again contain slogans such as 'Flying is good for you!' and 'You will eventually fly!'. People were urged to look out for the red, blue and silver Hermes-Spartan aeroplane piloted by Mr Oscar Garden.

Oscar became friendly with many younger Jews and they worked out that if they each contributed £5 this would help him set up Palestine's first aero-club. The Jews were very excited. They were willing to sell their bike or take out a loan to fulfil their dream of flying a real airplane. They were encouraged by the mayor of Tel Aviv, Meir Dizengoff, who had gone on a joyride with Oscar – his first flight. Rebecca Garden even wrote to Dizengoff to see if he could help with the aero-club; in his reply, dated 27 October 1933, he wrote:

I can assure you that I am only too pleased to do what I can for your 'boy'. I liked him the moment I saw him and was not in the least afraid to entrust myself in his care when he took me and our Town Clerk in his plane and gave us the opportunity of seeing our little Tel Aviv from the air. He did the job well and neatly, so much so that I am doing all I can to help him find a suitable flying field in Tel Aviv and together to endow Tel Aviv with its own air service. Your 'boy' is a nice and gentle fellow and deserves getting on. What can I do to help him I will not stint, and perhaps before long he will be in a position to bring you over when I shall be pleased to meet you.

However, in order to set up a club, Oscar also needed permission from the Colonial Office back in England, as the British had gained control of Palestine after World War I. His logbooks note: 'At last! Real birth of aviation in Palestine? Here's hoping!'

While waiting, Oscar continued to give joyrides throughout Palestine and Egypt. During this time, a man called F Brookes joined him. Oscar had met him back in England after the Australian flight, and he was keen on flying. Since then, Brookes had lost his job as a policeman, and upon hearing of the aero club venture he wrote to Oscar and asked if he could come out and give him a hand, saying, 'If you make money, you can pay me; if you don't it doesn't matter.' I managed to find some photographs of people having joyrides.[121] These are in the possession of Itai Meshulam, who now lives in Sydney, and are of his grandparents, Avraham and Zipora Fellman, and Avraham's sister, Rivka Hayutman, and her husband, Herzel.

RECORD OF FLIGHTS. *PALESTINE.*

Date.	Aircraft. Type.	Aircraft. Markings.	Pilot.	Journey.	Time in Air. Hrs.	Time in Air. Mins.	Remarks.
	HERMES-SPARTAN	VR-TAJ	Self.	Brought forward...	811	50	.
26/3/33	"	"	"	Haifa (local	1	10	Joyriding
27/3/33	"	"	"	" - Ramleh		40	perfect
31/3/33	"	"	"	Ramleh-Jericho		20	very bumpy
1/4/33	"	"	"	Jericho (local)		30	joyriding 1400' below sea level
3/4/33	"	"	"	" "	1	10	"Dead "Sea
5/4/33	"	"	"	" "		35	very rough.
6/4/33	"	"	"	Jericho-Tiberias & local	1	15	River Jordan
7/4/33	"	"	"	Tiberias (local)	2	0	Sea of Galilee
				Carried forward...	819	30	

RECORD OF FLIGHTS. *PALESTINE.*

Date.	Aircraft. Type.	Aircraft. Markings.	Pilot.	Journey.	Time in Air. Hrs.	Time in Air. Mins.	Remarks.
	HERMES-SPARTAN	VR-TAJ	Self.	Brought forward...	819	30	extremely bumpy peculiar currents.
11/4/33	"	"	"	Tiberias (local)		15	
12/4/33	"	"	"	Tiberias (local)	1	40	from 1200' below to 9000' above (mt. Hermon)
"	"	"	"	Tiberias-Ramleh	1	5	1st 2-crosscountry passenger
1/5/33	"	"	"	Ramleh (local)		40	advertising
26/5/33	"	"	"	Ramleh-Yazur.		10	At last! landing.
27/5/33	"	"	"	Yazur (local)	2	50	Real birth of aviation in
28/5/33	"	"	"	" "	3	55	Palestine? Here's hoping!
1/6/33	"	"	"	" - Haifa return	1	40	Dibeck ads?
				Carried forward...	831	45	

Pages of logbook of Oscar Garden. Joyrides in Palestine. Note his remarks for 27 & 28 February: 'At last! Real birth of aviation in Palestine? Here's hoping!' This refers to his plan of setting up Palestine's first-aero-club; the permit was refused.

At the end of seven months the joyriding was drying up and Oscar said he was going broke. Although confident that he would get the permit to establish the aero club, it was refused. He was dumbfounded. He recalled the letter saying something along the lines of 'We are sorry, but if we give you permission to form an aero-club to train Jews to fly, then the Arabs will want to learn, and we can't allow that.' That was the last straw, he said. His logbooks for *Miss Mobiloil* end on 12 December 1933 with 'Shalome! Another chapter closed.' He now had accumulated 892.50 flying hours.

During 1933, flying records continued to be broken, and one famous aviator died in an attempt. The year began with the devastating news that Bert Hinkler had disappeared. On 7 January Hinkler left England in his Puss Moth in an attempt to break the flying record to Australia, but his plane crashed on the northern slopes of Pratomagno in the Apennines, Italy. The plane and Hinkler's body were not discovered until 27 April when the mountain snow was melting. This tragedy did not put off Jean Batten or Kingsford Smith, who both tried to break the record. In April 1933, Batten failed in her first attempt to fly from England to Australia. She crashed twice near Karachi, the second time writing off her aeroplane. Kingsford Smith had more luck later in the year and reclaimed his record. He landed in Australia on 11 October, and his flight of 7 days 4.5 hours cut Scott's time by around 40 hours. For the first time, he decided not to make landfall at Darwin but to land in Wyndham – following in Oscar's footsteps.

Surprisingly, Oscar still had his eye on an elusive record. While in Palestine, he became interested in an air race that was to take place in 1934 – the Centenary Air Race, from London to Melbourne. He had sent Rebecca every cutting he could find on it, and told her that if he could get the financial backing, he might enter it, but he would continue on to New Zealand, for 'it was one of his ambitions to be the first pilot to fly solo from England to New Zealand.'[122] He had also told Rebecca he might just sell the plane and return to Australia.

As Brookes wanted to accumulate some flying hours, Oscar agreed to let him fly *Miss Mobiloil* back to England while he went by boat. His dream of participating in the Air Race was dashed when Brookes crashed the plane on 21 January 1934, in the Libyan Desert in North Africa. After the plane had been repaired, Oscar sold it to a W Mackay, who was the pilot when the plane crashed again on 26 May 1934 at Ladysmith, South Africa. A passenger, Mr Higgins, was killed. There seems to be no record of the plane after this crash; it is likely that it was scrapped.

CHAPTER 8

Trapped in England

S hortly after arriving back in England, Oscar became very ill with malaria and went to stay with an aunt in Edinburgh for a month to recuperate. On 21 July 1934 he landed a job with Scottish Motor Traction (SMT), which had extensive interests in Scotland's road transport industry. Oscar's work was to give charter rides and also joyrides around St Andrews, Edinburgh, in a four-seater DH.83 Fox Moth.

Jean Batten, meanwhile, was determined to fly to Australia. She made two more attempts in 1934. Only two newspapers reported her departure from Lympne on 21 April 1934 with the headline 'Try Again Girl'. She had had a secret toilet installed in her Gipsy Moth, discreetly designed by Sir Geoffrey de Havilland himself. The engineers were instructed not to discuss the contraption with anybody. Batten also had special zippers fitted to her flying suits so with some contortions she could empty her bladder and bowels during flights.

In France she landed in heavy rain and, disregarding advice not to continue, made the mistake of not topping up all her fuel tanks. She crashed near Rome, seriously damaging her Moth, but luckily escaped with bruising, a badly cut lip, and shock. She returned to England.

Oscar standing in front of a Highland Airways plane in Kirkwall in 1934.

Oscar's Aunt Mary and Uncle George McKay about to fly from Inverness to Kirkwall, Orkney, in a DH.84 Dragon.

Date.	Aircraft. Type.	Aircraft. Markings.	Pilot.	Journey.	Time in Air. Hrs.	Time in Air. Mins.	Remarks.
				Brought forward...	955	35	
4·8·34	DH 83	GACEC	SELF	St Andrews Dundee local.	2	30.	
5·8·34	"	"	"	St Andrews.	4	45	
6·8·34	"	"	"	"	1	25	
7·8·34	"	"	"	"	1		
"	"	G-ACEJ	"	"	2	40	
8·8·34	"	G-ACEC	"	"		30	
7·8·34	DH 60	G-ACHL	"			30	
7·8·34	DH 83	G-ACEC	"		1	50	
				Carried forward...	970	25	

Date.	Aircraft. Type.	Aircraft. Markings.	Pilot.	Journey.	Time in Air. Hrs.	Time in Air. Mins.	Remarks.
				Brought forward...	970	25	
10·8·34	DH 83	GACEC	SELF	Lunch. Ren. St And & local.	3	45	
11·8·34	"	"	"	Macmerry Dundee	1	0	
12·8·34	"	"	"	Macmerry St Andrews		35	
28·8·34	DH 84	GACGK.	"	Inverness.		25	Landings.
29·8·34	"	"	"	"		25	"
1·9·34	"	"	"	"		35	"
2·9·34	"	"	"	"		30	"
15·3·35	SPARTAN CRUISER	GACYL	"	Eastleigh		30	"
				Carried forward...	977	50	

Pages of logbook of Oscar Garden showing some of his flights for Scottish Motor Traction and Highland Airways Limited. The last entry shows his first flight with United Airways Limited on 15 March 1935.

In May 1934, on her second attempt, she finally succeeded. Although she did not break the record, her trip of 14 days beat both Oscar's and Amy Johnson's times.

Oscar was sacked from SMT because of a forced landing that he insisted was not his fault. On 12 August 1934 he was at West Sands, St Andrews, giving pleasure rides. It was a Sunday afternoon and to avoid people standing on the beach he kept nearer to the water than usual. The wheels of the plane touched the water and the plane tipped nose first into the soft sand and turned upside down. His two passengers escaped with minor cuts and bruises and said it was 'a thrilling experience'.

At the end of August Oscar procured a job with Highland Airways Limited, established in 1933 by Ted Fresson to provide air services between the Scottish mainland and Orkney and Shetland. Oscar began flying an eight-seater DH.84 Dragon, but his log books only show four entries of practice landings at Inverness. It is not known why he left Highland Airways.

Then he 'struck a really bad patch'. He said he was 'completely broke, out of work, and near starvation in London'.

There were no jobs for me around and that winter was extremely grim. I'd met up with a man in London, who used to work for me in Sydney when I had the motor garage and he had a job as a chauffeur. He was on a wage of three pounds per week. We shared a basement flat; the rent was seven shillings and six pence a week, I survived the winter. I was pawning a few things and what have you and altogether a very bad time.

The air race that Oscar had been interested in took place on 20 October 1934. It is considered the most important air race that has ever taken place, because as well as attracting more publicity and worldwide organisation than any other air race before or since, it stood to encourage the extension of an established air route for both air mail and passengers to Australia.

Two teams participated: Charles Scott and Campbell Black, and Jim Mollison and his wife Amy Mollison, nee Johnson. (Amy Johnson had married Jim Mollison in July 1932. Although they were dubbed *The Flying Sweethearts* by the press and the public, the marriage was an unhappy one and they divorced in 1938.) Scott and Black touched down in Darwin after 52 hours and 33 minutes. The previous record had been 162 hours. This record remains unbeaten today by any other piston-powered aircraft. In December 1934, another of Oscar's aviation peers died. Charles Ulm was lost at sea between San Francisco and Hawaii; the aeroplane and its crew were never found. Ulm was only 36 years old.

From the time of Oscar's return to England he was intent on finding work in New Zealand or Australia. He wrote to his mother, 'I am not so keen on a flying job in NZ but if nothing turns up in Aussie, guess I'll be better off there than staying another winter here.' Why was he so keen to settle in Australia? What was it about this country that appealed to him? He never told me, but when I came to Australia in 1976 to do a Buddhist meditation retreat in Queensland, I had the strongest sense that this place felt like 'home'. I loved the climate, the beaches, the laid-back Aussie spirit, their openness. Compared to New Zealand, there was a lightness here. Maybe my father felt more at home in Australia, as I did.

Or was it the aviation prospects – compared to New Zealand – that appealed? Qantas, one of the oldest airlines in the world, was founded in 1920. Initially it operated taxi and joyride flights, as well as airmail services. In 1934, Qantas Empire Airways was formed by combining the interests of Qantas and Britain's Imperial Airways. In 1935, it took over the Darwin–Singapore sector of the Royal Mail route. There were also other airlines, including West Australian Airways and Hollyman's Airways, which had begun to fly routes throughout south-eastern Australia, including from Melbourne to Sydney via Canberra.

In contrast, the first major airline in New Zealand – Union Airways of New Zealand – only began services in 1936 and operated between

Palmerston North and Dunedin via Blenheim and Christchurch. It wasn't until 1939 that the company began extending services north to Auckland.

Meanwhile back in Christchurch Rebecca was writing rambling letters to various New Zealand officials, including John G Cobbe, the Minister for Defence, who had spoken at Oscar's 1930 reception at the Wellington Town Hall. She detailed all the bad luck her son had had 'through no fault of his own' and how he was stranded in London, penniless and borrowing money from an old chauffeur of ours.

I am so worried about my son. We used to be in much better circumstances – the boy has never known want – and it makes it so much harder. Can you help us in any way, or help my boy? I am all alone here save for a married daughter – I miss Oscar so much – my youngest daughter Violet I guess you have seen at the Chateau – in the office. She is very happy there. If a position was available for him, we could cable him and I know he would try and get a boat he could. He is so longing to get home. I would of [sic] sent his last letter but I sent it to Violet at the Chateau and the last one I sent Mr Sullivan the mayor.

(In the late 1920s, Violet left Christchurch to work as a receptionist at the world-famous Hermitage Hotel on Mt Cook, and in the 1930s worked at another world-renown hotel – the Chateau in the Tongariro National Park in the North Island.)

Cobbe replied to her the following day:

I was sorry to read in your letter of yesterday of the unfortunate position your son, Oscar, is placed in England. It must be all very distressing to you, your family, and to your son who achieved such a fine record of aviation. I do not exactly know at the moment what I can do to secure the assistance he needs. I have started a series of enquiries on his behalf and it would be pleasing to me if something could be done to help him in the way of employment. I will advise you when the reports on my enquiries have been completed.

Rebecca replied thanking him for his kindness:

... and do hope you can find my dear laddie a decent post. My heart has been nearly broken thinking of him – and how helpless I am to help him. May God reward you. Your letter has been the first bright spark of HOPE. Again, thanking you.

Cobbe referred her letters to the Defence Department to see if they could help.

On 23 March 1935, a New Zealand newspaper reported (based on what Rebecca had advised them) that Oscar had started a job in Paris but had become seriously ill and returned to England to convalesce. He intended to return to New Zealand to seek employment.[123] I don't know what this job was or what illness he had. However, I suspect that his time in Paris was where he was introduced to gambling. Mum used to say he learnt to gamble in Monte Carlo. 'He was always going to recoup his losses the next week!' There is no casino grander and more famous than the Casino de Monte Carlo in Monaco on the French Riviera. Built in the 1850s, the ornate gambling house has featured in multiple James Bond movies. There is no record of Oscar having visited France earlier, so it had to have been during these months or at some time over the next five years.

But Rebecca's news was old. Oscar decided against returning to New Zealand because in February he managed to procure a job with the newly established airline company, United Airways Ltd, backed by a glowing reference from the chairman of directors of Vacuum Oil Company in London. The company was formed to provide air services between London, Blackpool, Carlisle, the Isle of Man and Dublin. The fleet of

Inauguration of United Airways, 30 April 1935. Oscar flew a Spartan Cruiser from the Isle of Man to London.

aircraft consisted of de Havilland DH.89 Rapides, a twin-engine biplane for up to eight passengers, red and silver Spartan Cruisers, three-engine monoplanes which can take up to 10 passengers, as well as an Armstrong-Whitworth Argosy, a huge triple-engine biplane which could seat 28 passengers and would be used for joyrides.

Oscar was put in charge of United Airways flying operations at the Hall Caine Manx Aerodrome at Ramsey on the Isle of Man. The aerodrome had just been established on 45 acres of land that had been levelled and drained, and a small hangar erected, together with a wooden hut to accommodate the office staff and passengers. Oscar was paid £5 a week, and his first flight was on 15 March in a Spartan Cruiser taking passengers to Cowes. On 26 April 1935, he obtained his certificate in radiotelephony, which gave him the licence to operate wireless telephony apparatus on board British aircraft for the purpose of sending and receiving spoken messages. He also had to sign a declaration that he would preserve the secrecy of correspondence.

He was also part of United Airways' official inauguration ceremony which took place at Stanley Park Aerodrome at Blackpool, Lancashire, on

RECORD OF FLIGHTS.

Date.	Aircraft. Type.	Markings.	Pilot.	Journey.	Hrs.	Mins.	Remarks.
	SPARTAN CRUISER			Brought forward...	1059	35	
23/5/35	"	G-ACYL	SELF	R-B-R-Black.	2	5	
"	"	SM	"	Blackpool-Ram.		45	
24/5/35	"	SM	"	R-Car-R	1	25	
25/8/35	"	SM	"	R-B-R-B-Ram.	2	45	
26/5/35	"	"	"	R-B-R-B-Ram.	2	45	
"	"	ZM	"	Blackpool(local)		30	
"	"	DX	"	wireless test(Bl.)		10	
27/5/35	"	SM	"	R-C-Ramsay	1	25	
				Carried forward...	1071	25	

RECORD OF FLIGHTS.

Date.	Aircraft. Type.	Markings.	Pilot.	Journey.	Hrs.	Mins.	Remarks.
	SPARTAN CRUISER			Brought forward...	1071	25	
28/5/35	"	G-ACSM	SELF	R-B-R-B-Ramsey	2	45	
"	DRAGON RAPIDE		"	Blackpool		35	landings
29/5/35	CRUISER	G-ACDX	"	R-B-Ramsay	1	30	
"	"	SM	"	R-B-R-B-Ram	2	45	
30/5/35	"	DX	"	R-Carlisle-R.	1	25	
31/5/35	"	DX	"	R-B-R-Black.	2	10	
"	"	SM	"	B-R-B-Ramsay	2	5	
1/6/35	"	YL	"	Ramsay-Black.		45	
				Carried forward...	1085	15	

Pages of logbook of Oscar Garden, showing his flights in a Spartan Cruiser and a Dragon Rapide for the Blackpool-Ramsay-Belfast run for United Airways.

30 April 1935. '[O]ne of the greatest days in the history of civil aviation in Blackpool,' wrote the *West Lancashire Evening Gazette*, 'with new highways of the air opened today.' Aeroplanes carrying various dignitaries converged on Heston Aerodrome, leaving from Heston, Carlisle and the Isle of Man. Oscar took off from the Hall Caine Aerodrome (Isle of Man) in a Spartan Cruiser with Alderman JH Skillicorn, the Mayor, and Mr PM Shimmin, the Town Clerk of Douglas, as passengers. The mayor described Oscar Garden as 'a splendid pilot and a splendid fellow. Everyone thoroughly enjoyed the trip. There were no bumps whatsoever. It was more comfortable than sitting in a saloon car riding in the country.'[124]

From the Isle of Man, United Airways was soon operating four services a day to Blackpool (with connections through to London) and daily services to Carlisle as well as to Glasgow and Renfrew in Scotland. Oscar then graduated to flying de Havilland DH.89 Dragon Rapides. On 30 September 1935, United Airways, along with a number of other companies, merged to form British Airways Limited.[125]

In November 1935, Oscar wrote to Rebecca that he was doing the Blackpool–Ramsey–Belfast service as well as the mail service each morning from the Isle of Man to Liverpool. 'It's no joke flying in this country on a service in winter. I hardly know whether to hang on to this job or try Aussie. My present job should be worth £1000 (about £60,810.00 today) a year in about two years' time and it's a question if I could get the same in Aussie.' During that year his two other sisters, Violet and Rose, were both married. He makes no mention of these events in letters to his mother, except to point out in a letter in June 1936 that Violet had written to thank him for the cocktail set he sent for a wedding present, although, he said, he hadn't sent it. It was a relative on the Isle of Man. Presumably he did not send her a present.

On 28 January 1935, Rose married James Dunn, whose parents lived in Wellington. Their daughter Margaret was born in 1937 and son Roger in

Publicity photo for British Airways taken at Liverpool in 1936. Oscar with a 93-year-old passenger who evidently had over 40 grandchildren.

1940. Rose and James, however, separated shortly after Roger's birth and, after waiting the minimum time, were divorced in 1948. It was difficult to obtain a divorce in New Zealand in the 1940s, and one of the partners had to be in the wrong – there had to be grounds such as adultery or five years' desertion (no-fault divorce was introduced in 1980). Rose was to spend the rest of her life alone, and in 1973 she moved from Wellington to Auckland where she spent the last 16 years of her life. Here she was close to her daughter Margaret and her four grandchildren. Gillian MacColl, her granddaughter, said she was much happier up in Auckland with family close by. In October 1935, Violet married Arnold Clark in Christchurch. Their marriage was not to last either; they separated in 1947 but were never divorced. Violet spent the rest of her life in Christchurch, except for a few years in Mount Maunganui, Bay of Plenty, in the late 1940s.

In other events of 1935, Kingsford Smith and his co-pilot, Tommy Pethybridge, died on 10 November. They were flying *Lady Southern Cross*, a Lockheed Altair, in an attempt to beat the England-to-Australia record set by Scott and Black in October 1934. They had passed over Calcutta, Akyab and Rangoon – the same route Oscar had taken in October 1930 – and then disappeared. Despite the RAF's search of the entire Rangoon–Singapore route, no trace of the Altair was found for 18 months. In May 1937, its starboard undercarriage leg was found by Burmese fishermen on the rocky shore of Aye Island, off the south coast of Burma, about 140 miles south-east of Rangoon. Perhaps Smithy had flown into the top of the jungle-covered island and the plane plunged into the sea. Oscar must have been shaken by the deaths of both Ulm and Kingsford Smith. While not close friends with either of them, he had fraternised with them in Sydney and in London. The early aviators, even though they competed against each other, were kindred spirits. They were joined together by the shared experienced of flying solo to Australia.

On 17 February 1936, British Airways Limited started a service from London to Malmö, Sweden, stopping at Amsterdam, Hamburg and

Copenhagen, and in March was awarded the contract for a mail delivery service on this route. In July 1936, Oscar was transferred to Heston to do a conversion course for the four-engined De Havilland 86s, after which he was put on the new service to Sweden, which soon included flights to Stockholm and back – a journey of over 2000 miles by air. The planes were adapted to carry only nine passengers, as the main purpose of these flights were the mail runs. Before the Second World War, the carriage of mail was of greater importance than the carriage of passengers.

In a letter to Rebecca dated 17 July 1936, he says he has moved from Glasgow to Surrey and describes how hard his job is. He says he leaves London at 9.00 am and reaches Stockholm by 6.10 pm. Then he leaves Stockholm at 8.00 am the next morning and arrives back in England about 5.00 pm. 'All my time off is spent in taking it easy or I couldn't stand the pace. Stockholm is a really beautiful place and the people are wonderful. It's like dropping into Aussie or NZ after being in England.' Again, he writes that he would like to get a good flying job in Aussie and asks if things are improving there. 'Not interested in NZ for flying … don't think I'll ever settle here. The people talk and think a different language.' He adds that he still owes his grandmother £600 (about £39,150 in today's currency) and it will be more than a year before he can save. Why will it be more than a year before he can save? Did he have other debts? What was he spending his money on? Had the gambling addiction he had when I knew him taken hold of him then? And why the pressing need to repay his very wealthy grandmother?

In October 1936, Jean Batten became the first person to fly from England to New Zealand. I always wondered how my father felt about this. Being an emotionally devoid Scotsman, private thoughts and feelings were never shared or spoken about. That trip had been his dream for years. And now beaten by a woman! Jean Batten is considered New Zealand's greatest aviator. Even though she gained her pilot's licence in 1930, her first long-distance flight – from England-to-Australia – did

Date.	Aircraft.		Engines.		Journey.	
	Type.	Markings.	Type.	H.P.	From.	To.
						Brought forwa
4/7 27/6/36	FOKKER F12	G-ADZI			Gatwick	(local)
6/7/36	DH86	G-ADEA			"	"
28/6/36	DH89	G-ADAH			Renfrew-Ardo-Fyfe-Ardo-Re	
4/7/36	F12	G-ADZI			Gatwick	(local)
6/7/36	DH86	G-ADEA			"	"
10/7/36	"	" YG			" - Stockholm etc.	
11/		" YJ			"	"
14/ "					"	"
15 16/7/36	DH89	" AE			Gatwick-Lympne-Gatwick	
						Carried forwa

Date.	Aircraft.		Engines.		Journey.	
	Type.	Markings.	Type.	H.P.	From.	To.
						Brought forw
25.4.37.	DH86	G-ADMY.			Cro. - Paris - etc.	
26/27.4.37	JU52	G-AERU			" - Han - etc.	
29.4.37	DH86	" DMY			" - Paris. - "	
5.5.37.	ELECTRA	" EPP			Cro - Hesta - Gatwick - Cr	
" "	JU52	" ERU			" - Col - Hanovy.	
14.5.37	"	"			" "	" etc
19.8.37 20/	"	"			" / "	" - "
25/27	"	"			" ~	" - "
						Carried forwa

Pages of logbook of Oscar Garden, when he was flying for British Airways.
The flight on 10 July 1936 was his first to Stockholm, where he met his first
wife, Greta Norlén. In 1937 he began the night airmail service first on the
DH.86s and then the more suitable JU52s.

FLIGHTS.

Time of Departure.		Time of Arrival.		Time in Air.		Pilot. See Instructions (5) & (6) on flyleaf of this book.	Remarks.
Hrs.	Mins.	Hrs.	Mins.	Hrs.	Mins.		
...	...			1771	5		
				2	45	FLOWER DAY	
				1	10	PUGH	
				4	30	SELF	
					55	SELF	
					45	SELF	
				15	50	PUGH & SELF	
				16	35	,, ,,	
0	30	12	00	1	30	PUGH —	night
...	...			1815	5		

FLIGHTS.

Time of Departure.		Time of Arrival.		Time in Air.		Pilot. See Instructions (5) & (6) on flyleaf of this book.	Remarks.
Hrs.	Mins.	Hrs.	Mins.	Hrs.	Mins.		
...	...			2648	25		NIGHT SERVICE
				3	45	SELF	,, ,,
				7	5	,,	night service .
				3	35		,, ,, ,,
				3	10	L.B & SELF	,, ,,
				3	55	SELF	(lightning) ,, ,,
				7	20	,,	,, ,, ,,
				7	15	,,	,, ,, ,,
				8	0	,,	,, ,, ,,
...	...			2692	30		

not take place until 1934, but over the next few years she broke a number of records. On the England to New Zealand flight, she also broke the England-to-Australia solo record, with a time of 5 days and 21 hours. In 1937 she broke the Australia to England solo record in a flight of 5 days, 18 hours and 15 minutes and became the first person to hold both England to Australia and Australia to England solo records at the same time. For these record-breaking flights she flew a Percival Vega Gull – a four-seater cabin monoplane with a cruising speed of 170 mph. In contrast, the plane Oscar used was an open cockpit Gipsy Moth which had a speed of 85 mph. Jean Batten gave up flying in the late thirties and went into seclusion.

In January 1937 Oscar was transferred to the night airmail service from Gatwick to Hanover via Cologne, and completed the conversion course for the Fokkers. In mid-1937, he began the London to Berlin night and freight service, which lasted for seven months. The DH.86s were unsuitable for night flying, so British Airways decided to purchase a mixed fleet of foreign airliners. Junkers JU52s were purchased, along with the Lockhead Electra 10As that Oscar was also trained on. For a while his flying became quite varied, doing night-runs to Stockholm, then Paris, and also day-runs.

On 24 June 1937, he wrote to Rebecca that he had received a very discouraging letter from Fred Haig concerning prospects in Australia, but Fred had heard they wanted some pilots in NZ. Oscar reiterated he was not so 'keen on a flying job in NZ', but went on to say, 'If nothing turned up in Aussie by the autumn, guess I'll be better off there than staying another winter here.'

Meanwhile, Rebecca was still writing letters to officials in New Zealand, even the Prime Minister, Michael Savage:

I have been listening in to your speech at St James Theatre. I am now so very deaf that I rarely go to a meeting as I cannot hear but with the

Oscar with his first wife Greta Norlén, who he married in November 1937. Photo taken soon after their marriage.

headphones, I heard every word. And I did indeed enjoy it – and I just want to send you my hearty congratulations on your safe return home. I also wish to thank you for your letter from London. I shall keep it as a souvenir. It rejoiced my heart to see you raise your voice almost alone at the Conference on the wage question. The faithful in our walk of life has generally to walk mostly alone – But you will yet be repaid. You are now I am sure, as you look upon the happy unknown faces. May God grant you many years yet to work for our Adopted Country. I wonder if you came across Oscar at all in England. His last letter to me I enclose.

I don't know what to make of these strange letters, sprinkled with God-talk, something Oscar never includes. Oscar was not happy. On 24 August, he wrote to Rebecca:

Well, I am still here because I can get nothing definite yet from Aussie or NZ. What on earth are you writing to the NZ Government? I certainly want no job in the Air Force and promises of help after arrival are quite useless. I want a job guaranteed before I leave this one and writing from this end seems useless, so unless you can contact something out there, looks as if I'm stuck here which I don't like ... I dread the thought of another winter in this wretched climate, but what can I do?

On 11 December 1937, Oscar married Greta Norlén, in the registry office at Epsom, Surrey. He had met Greta in Stockholm while doing night-flights; she was a receptionist at the hotel he stayed at. In the letters he wrote to Rebecca he never mentions meeting her or his marriage. Why? Mum told me that my father alleged Greta had used 'the oldest trick in the book' and that he would never forgive her for writing a letter to British Airways claiming she was pregnant and 'forcing' him to marry her. But perhaps she was pregnant. Margareta has a photo her Swedish cousin sent to her mother with the words, 'The heartiest congratulations to Aunt Greta the 29 September 1938.' Did she have a baby and then lose it? Neither Margareta nor I could get to the bottom of this apparent mystery.

Oscar's grandmother, Margaret Jolly, died in May 1938 at her home in Kirkwall. At the time of her death her total estate was worth £50,626 (about £2,877,000.00 today). She had revised her will several times over the years. The bulk of her estate was left to her five remaining children – four had died: Edith in 1913, Robert in 1925, William in 1933, and

Barbara Bain in 1934. In the 1933 version, her grandchildren were to receive £1000; in the 1936 alteration, her 28 surviving grandchildren were to receive £100, except for Oscar as his £100 was 'under deduction of whatever sum he may be indebted to me at the time of my death'. According to the inventory accompanying the will, he was in debt of £652 (about £37,050.00 today). He would have not received anything.

He and five other pilots had been taken off for six months to sit for a first-class navigator's licence at a school at Gatwick. Oscar had left school at 13 so it was quite a challenge but he was one of two who passed the course. He was back in service by July 1938 and his last flight for British Airways was in November 1938. Oscar had decided to switch over to Imperial Airways and learn to fly flying boats (planes that could take off from any reasonably calm body of water such as harbours, lakes or rivers) because of the proposed new service between New Zealand and Australia.

In the mid-1930s there had been talk of a new service between New Zealand and Australia that would use flying boats to cross the Tasman Sea, but Oscar made no mention of this in his letters to Rebecca. He had made it clear to her that he was after something 'definite' and 'guaranteed'. And this new service was to take years to get off the ground.

In 1935 Colonel Norris Falla, chairman of the New Zealand Union Steamship Company Ltd (of which Union Airways NZ was a part), had first approached Imperial Airways suggesting a joint company operation. Imperial Airways was an early British commercial air transport company that began using flying boats for some of its routes. In 1928, it introduced the Short S8 Calcutta flying boat (manufactured by Short Brothers) for the Mediterranean-to-Karachi leg of its mail and passenger service to India. At that time, there were few airfields capable of coping with large planes, whereas flying boats were ideal as they could take off from the water. The luxurious Short Empire series was then developed and the S23 – which could carry 24 day-passengers, or 16 in a sleeping berth layout – was launched in July 1936. Imperial Airways opened the

Southampton–Sydney route on 26 June 1938. This took 10 days (via Marseilles, Basra, Alexandria, Karachi, Calcutta, Bangkok and Singapore) compared to 40 days by ship.

It was Britain's wish that Imperial Airways operate the new link over the Tasman. Australia and New Zealand both opposed this, even though New Zealand lacked the funds to do it alone and Australia had no particular interest in the service at all.[126] After a conference in Wellington between 29 September and 1 October 1936, attended by representatives from the three countries, it was declared that a joint company to operate a trans-Tasman service would be formed. Despite the declaration, attempts to resolve matters of detail led to an impasse. There were even objections from residents of Rose Bay, Sydney, whose 'most extraordinary outcry'[127] over the prospect of a flying boat-base in their suburb was condemned:

The storm in a teacup over Rose Bay as an airmail base would be as ridiculous as it is trivial if it were not that it is holding up preparations for the commencement of the new Empire air service next year ... Already we have had enough dilly-dallying with the Empire air service, and there should be no more avoidable delays. The Commonwealth Government should make up its mind and get on with the job... It is a matter of parish-pump politics against the broad vision of national and imperial progress. Which is to come first, Rose or the Empire?[128]

In contrast, over in New Zealand, not only Auckland but also Nelson, Blenheim, Christchurch, Wellington and even Invercargill put forward claims as to their suitability as a terminus for a flying boat service. However, Auckland was the ideal place for a marine airport as it was within a few minutes from the heart of the city and, in preparation, a breakwater and workshops were built at Mechanics Bay, on Auckland's waterfront. The bay itself was deeply dredged, weighty flying boat moorings were put in position and a U-shaped pontoon was built for passengers to step onto once the flying boat had been towed in, tail first.

In July 1937, an agreement was finally reached for the service to be operated by a company Tasman Empire Airways Limited (TEAL) with each government represented by directors from Imperial Airways, Qantas Empire Airways and Union Airways NZ. The decision was greeted with pessimism by Christchurch's Press:

The pettifogging obstinacy of the Australian and New Zealand Governments over minor issues has so long delayed the inauguration of an air service across the Tasman that no one will be rash enough to assume that the agreement finally removes all obstacles.[129]

New Zealand's prime minister said he did not know when the air service would commence as decisions, such as determining the type of machine to be used, had not been made. Nevertheless, the Empire flying boat S23 *Centaurus,* with additional fuel tanks added, conducted an experimental flight across the Tasman on 27 December 1937 under the command of New Zealand-born Captain John Burgess. The crossing took 9 hours and 10 minutes at an average speed of 133 mph.

The wrangling between the three countries came to an end in February 1938 with a final agreement that ownership of TEAL would be split with 20 per cent to the New Zealand Government, 19 per cent to Union Airways, 38 per cent to Imperial Airways and 23 per cent to Qantas Empire Airways.

Colonel Falla and Maurice Clark (the manager of Union Airways) came to London to recruit staff for the airline. Oscar jumped at the opportunity. Burgess was selected as chief pilot and Oscar was appointed next to him in seniority. Clark negotiated with Imperial Airways for Oscar to gain flying boat experience on the S23s, and in November 1938 he studied for the first-class navigation licence, a mandatory qualification for a command

Oscar Garden in his uniform as a pilot for Imperial Airways. Photographed in London in 1940 by the Imperial Airways press department. Ref: 1/2-181964-F, ALEXANDER TURNBULL LIBRARY, WELLINGTON, NEW ZEALAND.

role in their flying boat fleet. His first flight was on 17 November 1938, and in December he was appointed first officer.

Oscar wrote to Rebecca in a letter dated 15 October, which she shared with the New Zealand press, that he had now started with Imperial Airways and was back in Training School for another examination. He tells her he expected it will take five or six months to complete this training and then he hopes to be 'heading to the Tasman'. He was over at the factory the previous week looking at the flying boats that will be used and tells her they are 'a very fine job for it' and that they will weigh 25 tons when loaded. 'Makes you think, doesn't it, 25 tons getting through the air at 200 miles per hour. I think that in another five years boats will be flying which will weigh 100 tons.'[130] He makes no mention of his new wife.

Oscar became acting captain in August 1939 and in January 1940 was appointed captain. He flew what was called the Horseshoe Route, a route which circled the Indian Ocean in a semi-circle. It covered Cairo, Basra, Karachi and Singapore, with many stops in between, before terminating in Australia. Oscar recalled doing a night landing on a lake near Santa Lucia. Christopher Griffiths was his first officer. When they got up in the morning, the lake had about a quarter of an inch sheet of ice on it, and he told Griffiths to get up on the wing and open up and turn these engines over by hand, in order to be able to crank them.

Hell of a job, you see, they were frozen. Poor old Griff, he had to get up and wind them all up and then we had a go at starting them. Fortunately, they took off. Then the next problem was, well, what's going to happen when I start trying to get through this ice – it wasn't a very thick skin, you know, on those boats. And then we took it very carefully, and just moved gradually, and oh, the noise, coming up from below, cracking.

The first two flying boats ordered by TEAL – ZK-AMA *Ao-tea-roa* (subsequently unhyphenated) and ZK-AMC *Awarua* – were delivered to Imperial Airways in April 1939 and the third – ZK-AMB *Australia* – on 6 July 1939.[131] These Empire flying boats, the S30s, had been developed for the Atlantic crossing and were a 19-passenger long-range version of the S23 Burgess had test flown to New Zealand. The three planes were used and tested on long-range flight trials prior to their intended delivery to New Zealand. The first to go to New Zealand was *Aotearoa*, piloted by Burgess. It left Southampton on 18 August 1939, and landed on Auckland's Waitemata Harbour on 28 August 1939, five days before the outbreak of World War II.

RECORD O

| Date. | Aircraft. | | Engines. | | Journey. | |
	Type.	Markings.	Type.	H.P.	From.	To.
						Brought forw
17·11·38	CALCUTTA	G-AATZ	JUPITER	550	HYTHE	LOCAL
18·11·38	"	"	"	"	"	"
19·11·38	"	"	"	"	"	"
21·11·38	"	"	"	"	"	"
"	SHORT "C" Class	VH- G-ABF	PEGASUS	900	"	"
4 12·38	"	G-AETY	"	"	"	"
6·12·38	"	"	"	"	"	"
9·12·38	"	G-AEUA	"	"	"	"
						Carried forwa

RECORD O

| Date. | Aircraft. | | Engines. | | Journey. | |
	Type.	Markings.	Type.	H.P.	From.	To.
						Brought forw
14-9-39	S23	G-AEUA	PEGASUS	900	Bangkok	Singapore
19-9-39	"	G-AETY	"	"	Singapore	"
20-9-39	"	"	"	"	"	Bangkok
21-9-39	"	"	"	"	Bangkok	Calcutta
22-9-39	"	"	"	"	Calcutta	Karachi
27-9-39	"	G-ADUV	"	"	Karachi	Basra
28-9-39	"	"	"	"	Basra	Alex
29-9-39 201	"	"	"	"	Alex	Marseilles
						Carried forw

Pages of logbook of Oscar Garden. He began the conversion course to fly the flying boats for Imperial Airways on 17 November 1938. In 1939 he was flying what was called the Horseshoe Route, covering Cairo, Basra, Karachi and Singapore.

FLIGHTS.

Time of Departure.		Time of Arrival.		Time in Air.		Pilot. See Instructions (5) & (6) on flyleaf of this book.	Remarks.
	Mins.	Hrs.	Mins.	Hrs.	Mins.		
...	...			...3654	30		
					15	BURGESS	CONVERSION COURSE
				1	45	" & SELF	" "
				2	40 55	" "	" "
				4	25	" "	" "
					25	BURGESS	TEST.
				1	55 04	" BROWN	"
				1	15	GURNEY	NIGHT LANDINGS. " "
				—	35	LYNCH-BLOSSE & SELF	
...	...			...3668	44		

FLIGHTS.

Time of Departure.		Time of Arrival.		Time in Air.		Pilot. See Instructions (5) & (6) on flyleaf of this book.	Remarks.
rs.	Mins.	Hrs.	Mins.	Hrs.	Mins.		
...	...			...4609	00		
				7	09	SELF	SERVICE
					25	"	TEST
				6	35	"	SERVICE
				7	46	"	
				11	45	"	
				10	37	" "	
				9	20	"	
				13	15	"	
...	...			4675	52		

It appeared that the proposed Tasman service was doomed, at least until peace returned. Disaster had already struck *Australia*. On 9 August 1939, after a few weeks of service, it was badly damaged at Basra when it ran aground on a submerged sandbank while taxiing at high speed. Some repairs were done there, and in February 1940 Oscar was sent out to fly the plane back. At Hythe, an astonished team of engineers found it hard to believe the boat had survived the return flight. Oscar said it was a wreck. Following repairs *Australia* was not delivered to New Zealand. It re-entered service with Imperial Airways and was renamed *Clare*.

Months of uncertainty followed regarding the delivery of *Awarua* (which means 'Twin Rivers' in Māori). Oscar wrote to Rebecca in September 1939, 'Am sorry not to be going through to NZ with all this war business. I suppose this war will hold things up for a while.' He points out that she is in a better place this time than she was for the last war, stuck in Manchester. 'I am afraid it is going to be much bigger thing than most people realise. Burgess was very lucky to get away when he did.' In another letter dated 24 October 1939, he writes, 'I am still on the boats flying on the Empire routes but know nothing about the Tasman service on a/c [account] of the war. Just have to wait and see. Well, the war seems at a standstill as far as France is concerned at present. It is a very peculiar situation.' Again, he makes no mention of Greta, who by then is pregnant. Was this because he didn't think the marriage would last? That he had thoughts of separation?

At a war conference in London in December 1939, New Zealand's Deputy Prime Minister Peter Fraser argued the importance of the Tasman link as it would be their only hope of maintaining regular wartime contact with Australia and the outside world. Even though he pressed for the release of *Awarua*, he was not immediately successful. Oscar wrote to Rebecca in late January 1940, 'No definite news about the Tasman service although I may still be going out.'

CHAPTER 9

The Boss

With little notice, on 15 March 1940, *Awarua* slipped moorings at Hythe. It was a bitterly cold day. Wartime livery of stripes of red, white and blue had been painted vertically on the plane's tail fin and horizontally on each corner of her hull. Captain Oscar Garden and First Officer Christopher Griffiths were at the controls. Behind them were Radio Officer Paddy Cussans and Flight Engineer Geoffrey Wells.

There were six passengers on board, including the wives of Griffiths and Wells. Greta, who was seven months pregnant at the time, was not with them. Her seat had been booked, but a few weeks earlier on Oscar's return from a trip on the Empire route she said she had changed her mind and wanted to return to Sweden for the birth.[132] According to Margareta, it is likely that they had actually decided to separate. Three passengers were carried on an Imperial Airways schedule only as far as Singapore, where the crew changed into TEAL uniforms. Three passengers, including Mrs Griffiths and Mrs Wells, as well as an Anne Harrison, continued on to Auckland. Anne was flying to New Zealand for her wedding (she would become Mrs Anne Squires) and had been offered the seat three days

Oscar Garden being being greeted in Auckland in April 1940 by his mother Rebecca and sister Violet after delivery flight of Awarua for TEAL.
Whites Aviation Photograph, Ref: WA-11261-G, ALEXANDER TURNBULL LIBRARY, WELLINGTON, NEW ZEALAND.

Crew of *Awarua*: From left Geoffrey Wells (engineer), Mrs Wells, Captain Oscar Garden, Paddy Cussans (radio operator), Miss Anne Harrison, Christopher Griffiths (first officer), Mrs Rosemary Griffiths. Photograph by Stewart & White, Auckland. Ref: 1/2-181961-F, ALEXANDER TURNBULL LIBRARY WELLINGTON, NEW ZEALAND.

before the plane left. It was to be the last civilian flight over France for the duration of the war.

As well as stops for refuelling, there were overnight stops at Marseilles, Brindisi, Haifa, Basra, Karachi, Calcutta, Singapore, Darwin, Brisbane and Sydney. The flight was not without dramas. They were delayed at Calcutta when they discovered a magneto drive shaft had sheared. They were able to replace it with the drive shaft fitted to the spare engine carried in the aft hold.

Awarua reached Brisbane at 5.30 pm on 27 March, after a one-day flight from Darwin. Incoming flying boats usually took two days but 'Captain Garden decided to leave at the crack of dawn and make the trip to Brisbane in one day.'[133] The local paper, the *Courier Mail*, described *Awarua* as a giant flying boat of 22 tons, about three tons heavier than the Empire boats that were at that time calling regularly at Brisbane. 'Fifteen double-decker buses could shelter under her wings. The cubic capacity of the hull is four times that of a double-decker bus.' It was reported that the commander, Captain Oscar Garden, said that 'the ship had behaved splendidly during the trip.'

On the way to Sydney, the port outer engine developed an oil leak due to a six-inch crack in the oil tank. In addition to repairing this, they were delayed in Sydney as a mark of respect to New Zealand's Prime Minister, Michael Joseph Savage, who had died on 27 March.

The *Awarua* finally departed Rose Bay before dawn on 3 April 1940. They flew into a headwind for most of the flight and reached New Zealand after 9 hours and 14 minutes. The delivery flight had taken 21 days. *Awarua* circled Auckland's Waitemata Harbour and made a circuit of the city before a graceful descent and 'feathering sheets of spray into the air from her floats'.[134] They touched down at 4 minutes past 3.00 pm. A welcoming party of about 50 were there to meet them, including Rebecca and Violet. Because Anne Harrison was the first fare-paying passenger from England to New Zealand, Oscar rang Maurice Clark and

RECORD O

Date.	Aircraft.		Engines.		Journey.	
	Type.	Markings.	Type.	H.P.	From.	To.
						Brought forw
17/18-2-40	S30	G-AFCZ	PERSEUS	890	BASRA	ALEX
20-2-40	"	"	"	"	ALEX	ROME
21-2-40	"	"	"	"	ROME	HYTHE
6-3-40	"	ZK-AMC	"	"	HYTHE	"
7-3-40	"	"	"	"	"	"
15-3-40	"	"	"	"	"	MARSEILL
16-3-40	"	"	"	"	MARSEILLE	BRINDISI
17-3-40	"	"	"	"	BRINDISI	ALEXANDR
						Carried forwa

RECORD O

Date.	Aircraft.		Engines.		Journey.	
	Type.	Markings.	Type.	H.P.	From.	To.
						Brought fo
3/3-4-40	S30	ZK-AMC	PERSEUS	890	SYDNEY	AUCKLA
2-4-40	"	"	"	"	"	SYDNE
4-5-40	"	"	"	"	AUCKLAND	AUCKLA
6-5-40	"	"	"	"	"	SYDNE
9-5-40	"	"	"	"	SYDNEY	AUCKLAN
20-5-40	"	"	"	"	AUCKLAND	HOBSONVI
						Carried for

Pages of logbook of Oscar Garden, showing the delivery flight of *Awarua*, which left Hythe on 15 March and arrived in Auckland on 3 April 1940.

FLIGHTS.

Time of Departure.		Time of Arrival.		Time in Air.		Pilot. See Instructions (5) & (6) on flyleaf of this book.	Remarks.
Hrs.	Mins.	Hrs.	Mins.	Hrs.	Mins.		
...	...	...		4892	47		
				9	37	SELF	
				8	19	”	R/F Australia.
				8	41	”	
				1	32	”	TEST
				1	14	”	” 48.000.
				6	51	”	D/F "Awarna".
				5	30		
				7	14		
...	...	...		4941	45		

FLIGHTS.

Time of Departure.		Time of Arrival.		Time in Air.		Pilot. See Instructions (5) & (6) on flyleaf of this book.	Remarks.
Hrs.	Mins.	Hrs.	Mins.	Hrs.	Mins.		
2nd.	(3rd			5013	43		
7	50	03	04	9	14	SELF	DELIVERY.
					59.	”	TEST.
						LOG BOOK CHECKED. 23/4/1940 Init.	
4	55	05	33		38	”	TEST
26	04	46	10	20		”	SERVICE AW2
7	57	02	27	08	30	”	” AE2
2	21	23	10		49	LOG BOOK CHECKED.	
...	...			5044	13	24/5/1940 Init.	

Captained by Oscar Garden, Tasman Empire Airways Limited's Short S.30 flying boat *Awarua* ZK-AMC arrives in Auckland in April 1940 after a delivery flight from wartime Britain.

said, 'This passenger's here, but we haven't got her fare sorted out.' It was £160 from England to Sydney. Clark said to add on £25 to cross the Tasman and call it a day.

With *Awarua's* arrival, TEAL could now be formally established. On 26 April 1940 it was registered in Wellington as a limited liability company. The first regular trans-Tasman service took place on 30 April 1940. *Aotearoa*, commanded by Captain Burgess, took nine hours, and on board were 10 passengers and 40,000 letters. 'We have all looked forward to this very moment for a long time,' said Frederick Jones, New Zealand's Minister of Aviation, at a ceremony prior to the departure. TEAL director Wilmot Hudson Fysh was a passenger and said, 'Rarely has a service been started with such difficulty, but which is also fraught with such possibilities, as the one today inaugurated.'[135] The return flight to Auckland was on 2 May, and Oscar's first flight from Auckland to Sydney was four days later. It took 10 hours and 20 minutes. In August

1940, TEAL increased the frequency of its service to three times a fortnight, and by the end of the war it was four times a week. For most of the war the two flying boats were New Zealand's only regular means of communication with the world, carrying priority passengers to Australia, and, importantly, international airmail.

The Empire flying boats were beautiful to look at:

With their pleasingly flared chines and uncluttered aerodynamic hulls, they were creatures of considerable beauty. Afloat at their moorings, and with their towering flush-riveted sides and ship like portholes and hatches, they evoked the luxury and the exotic sense of theatre of a Cunard liner.[136]

The flying boats were in effect 'flying hotels', a luxurious way to travel. Passengers would dress in their finery – women in hats and furs, men in suits and neckties, and children their Sunday best. The aircraft had two decks, including a promenade where passengers could look at the views. As the flying boats cruised at just 150 miles per hour and were seldom as high as 5000 feet above the ground, passengers experienced what it was like to 'sail the skies'. Short Brothers claimed, 'We don't build aircraft that float, we build ships that fly.'[137] As in ships, there was space for passengers to play quoits or get in golf putting practice, and up the front a smoking cabin where they could have a cigarette.

There was also a wide range of quality food brought on board in large vacuum jars; even after several hours in the air the steward could still bring out piping hot meals. Breakfast could include tomato juice, grapefruit and other fresh fruit, hot cereals and cream, scrambled eggs, grilled pork sausages and tomatoes, as well as cold meats, toast and rolls. Lunch could be oysters on the shell, cream of tomato soup, cold turkey and ham, veal and ham pie, cold beef and Russian salad, fresh fruit salads and cream.[138]

However, few could afford a flight, as the cost of a one-way ticket was £20, the equivalent of 30 days' pay on an average income. In the early years, passengers were on a priority system, and they had to have a good reason to be granted a seat. Each received a certificate to show they had flown the Tasman, which the captain had to sign. Oscar said he signed thousands of them, and it was a real pain in the neck. If the weather was good 14 to 18 passengers were taken, but if there was a forecast of excess wind, passengers were offloaded at the last moment.

For the pilots, however, there was little time to enjoy the mystique of flight. They had to worry about engine problems and faulty oil coolers, not to mention flying what pilots considered to be one of the worst crossings in the world due to its unpredictable weather. Oscar believed that flying boats were never designed for flying such a distance over water. He thought they were 'temperamental beasts', but he loved their leather seats. He reckoned they were 'the finest aeroplane seats ever built. They were padded, boy oh boy'.[139]

In the long run we had a lot of trouble with them [the planes]. They couldn't cope with some of the temperatures we struck, especially in summer at the Australian end. The first few years we had a lot of headaches and some pretty good frights when the engine slows down across the Tasman. I've had the daylights frightened out of me. This was a kind of guinea-pig stuff. It took over three years to get the bugs out and the worst part of all, especially on this over-water job, for which this kind of boat was not really originally designed, was that we couldn't turn off the propellers. So, when we had to shut an engine down, halfway across the Tasman, it wasn't a bit funny, you know, with the load we were carrying. We had very little margin. In fact, once or twice I gave up the ghost, but we were lucky enough and got out of it.

Evidently Oscar complained to Albert Earnest Rudder, the

deputy-chairman of TEAL, 'We are just guineas pigs. We are being used to try out something new … these Perseus engines have never been properly tested.'[140] The autopilot on the S.30 caused some anxious moments because it was a new, untried piece of equipment made by the English firm Smiths. In its first few months of use, it would suddenly pull the aircraft into a straight dive. They had to unhook it and pull the aircraft back up. It took an engineer from Smiths several months to sort out the problem. Oscar said he could not understand why they did not use the American Sperry autopilot used in the S.23s.

There were no pressurised cabins, which meant they could not take the aircraft above 10,000 feet to escape bad weather, but had to fly through storms and squalls. The Tasman Sea below them could be 'a dirty stretch of water, breeding a vicious type of storm' as described by Francis Chichester.[141] They often encountered pretty rough weather when they left Sydney:

Nine times out of 10 we would strike trouble about 300 miles from the Australian coast – it almost looked like line squall stuff – I've had the daylights frightened out of me. Get down below them and you'd find yourself in amongst some waterspouts and all sorts of capers. One trip we had left an awful storm behind us, one of those southerly busters and when I got clear of that I looked down at the Tasman and you couldn't see any clear water colour. All I could see was a sheet of white. We were at about 10,000 feet and going like a bat out of hell, perhaps 200 miles an hour, with an incredible wind behind us and there was a wind just about as strong going the other way on the surface. It was incredible. I had never seen anything like it. I told the steward to go down and tell the passengers to have a look at the white caps on the water and they were absolutely amazed.

Passengers were jostled about by heavy turbulence and deafened by drumming rain if the plane flew through a squall. Maurice McGreal, who Oscar employed as a pilot in 1944, recalls: 'The torrential rain in these fronts found entry through every joint and crevice of the cockpit windows, and the captain would sit hunched with his raincoat draped over his shoulders as the rain came in.' It could also get cold and in the first few years the heating system was not efficient and failed to work above 5000 feet. Oscar would tell the steward to ask passengers if they'd prefer to either have a smooth ride up higher and be cold or fly lower and have a pretty rough trip but be warmer. 'That was a real mid-air election. Invariably we'd stay up high.' Supplies of woollen rugs and foot-warmers would be provided. In the first few years they would leave Sydney in the dark at 4.00 am. Oscar thought that was unnecessary, as they had ample time to get into Auckland in daylight. After he took over as chief pilot, he said he talked the powers-that-be into leaving at 6.00 am.

McGreal wrote:

Soon after take-off the second officer would climb from the right-hand seat and spread the big chart of the Tasman on the navigation table, take a few sharp pencils, his parallel rule and Douglas protractor and push the drift recorder through the hole in the side of the aircraft. He was ready for the day's work.

Navigation was all dead reckoning and 'drift crawling' supported by sun lines and bearings from long-range shore stations ... the radio officer would bang away on his Morse key to a group of three shore stations, then hold the key down. After a minute or so back they would come with good plottable bearings ...

On other occasions, he would rotate the big loop aerial that sat above the upper fuselage, its operating wheel almost as big as my car's steering wheel, and with careful skill he would take a bearing on a shore transmitter ...[142]

Oscar with his mother Rebecca, wife Greta and daughter Margareta at Auckland on 5 February 1941. Photograph: Whites Aviation Ltd. Ref: WA-11292-G. ALEXANDER TURNBULL LIBRARY, WELLINGTON, NEW ZEALAND.

Because of the war, the pilots had to rely on very sketchy reports, and there was a clampdown on shipping reports. There were also long periods of radio silence, especially once Japan became involved. They would receive brief messages after leaving Auckland, and then cross-check with the station at Lord Howe Island to pinpoint their position. Oscar said, 'We really got into trouble just through lack of weather information. One trip was the longest flight, a real horror trip, 12 hours and 8 minutes. On reaching Rose Bay the engineer said I had about 10 minutes' fuel left.' When the manager of their Sydney hotel saw the crew on arrival, he took them straight to the bar.

There were some lighter moments. In the first year, on a trip to Sydney, there were three chiefs of defence aboard: navy, army and air force. They flew into a bad frontal condition off Sydney, and Oscar thought he would give the chiefs a fright. He decided to carve his way through huge cumulus clouds at about 10,000 feet:

It was like going into a great big cabin, a cave – oh boy, oh boy! Lightning started, sheet lightning, and then we struck hail and these blokes were up front, you see, I got them up to have a look and I think they were getting lighter by the minute. Actually, I was getting lighter too, so I turned tail and went down, got right down near the water and we got just about as bad a fright then – that's when we got real line squall effects stuff. And I thought afterwards, well how damn silly, the three chiefs of the defence forces, the whole lot could have been bumped off in one crack.

The loud explosion and blinding flash of a lightning strike was frightening but usually did no harm as the metal hull enclosing the crew and passengers acted as a Faraday Cage (a shield to block electromagnetic fields), protecting them. However, when lightning threatened, they had to earth everything and wind in the 200-foot-long trailing aerial. On one occasion, about 400 miles from Sydney, they flew into a fierce front with lightning flashes and Doug Reid, a new radio operator, forgot to wind in the aerial. Oscar said there was 'an almighty flash' and they were struck by lightning, which in an instant went up the back of his seat and burnt all the hair off the back of his head, as well as scorching the back of the seat. Griffiths, the first officer, liberally doused him with a fire extinguisher. It took a few weeks for Oscar's hair to grow back. They replaced the seat.

On one flight the steward came up and said there was a man smoking a cigar which he refused to put out. Oscar sent his co-pilot, but he had no success. Oscar was reluctant to do anything because of the poor weather conditions, but he was so angry he grabbed a fire extinguisher on the way down, pointed it at the man, and said, 'If you don't put that cigar out you will get this right in your face.' The cigar went out immediately.

While most airlines at the time allowed the smoking of cigarettes, cigars and pipes, only cigarettes were allowed on flying boats, and smoking was confined to the smoking cabin. The likely explanation for the banning of cigars and pipes was that they produced large volumes of smoke for a long period and made the cabins difficult to ventilate.[143] There were always exceptions. In 1942, during a perilous 18-hour flight across the Atlantic on a BOAC-operated Clipper B314, Sir Winston Churchill puffed away on a cigar for most of the trip and even convinced the pilot to give him the controls of RMA *Berwick* while he was smoking. The Prime Minister was returning from America after lobbying President Roosevelt to fight in Europe.[144]

Not long after the TEAL service began, the New Zealand air force – which had no long-range aircraft – decided to use the flying boats for reconnaissance work. On 8 September 1940, Oscar received a temporary Royal New Zealand Air Force (RNZAF) commission as a flight lieutenant (with seniority backdated to 1 September 1937). His first mission was a few weeks later. On 27 November 1940, the New Zealand Shipping Company's *Rangitane* was about 300 miles east of New Zealand when it was attacked by three German raiders: *Kulmerland, Komet* and *Orion*. En route to Britain, *Rangitane* was laden with dairy goods, frozen meat and wool, and was carrying more than 300 crew and passengers, including women and children. When the *Rangitane's* captain sent a distress signal to New Zealand, the Germans opened fire. Seven passengers and eight crew members died.[145] The remaining 297 passengers and crew were transferred to the German ships by lifeboats and the *Rangitane* was sunk. The *Aotearoa* went out and arrived at the scene at about 2:30 pm but found only an oil slick and debris, and there was no sight of the raiders.

Oscar had arrived back from Sydney in *Awarua* to see everyone rushing around like 'scalded cats'. He was told he was off on a reconnaissance flight to search for the raiders as soon as the plane was refuelled and armed up. Oscar had time for a cup of tea and a sandwich, and to put on his RNZAF uniform before they took off. A Lewis gun had been placed

RECORD OF

Date.	Aircraft.		Engines.		Journey.	
	Type.	Markings.	Type.	H.P.	From.	To.
						Brought forwa
14-11-40	S30	ZK-AMA	PERSEUS	890	AUCKLAND	SYDNEY
18-11-40	"	"	"	"	SYDNEY	AUCKLAND
27-11-40	"	AMC	"	"	AUCKLAND	AUCKLAN
28-11-40	"	AMA	"	"	"	SYDNEY
1-12-40	"	"	"	"	SYDNEY	AUCKLAN
4-12-40	"	AMC	"	—	HOBSONVILLE	"
7-12-40	"	"	"	—	AUCKLAND	SYDNEY
8-12-40	"	"	"	"	SYDNEY	AUCKLA
						Carried forwa

RECORD O

Date.	Aircraft.		Engines.		Journey.	
	Type.	Markings.	Type.	H.P.	From.	To.
						Brought forw
20-1-41	S30	ZK-AMC	PERSEUS	890	AUCKLAND	HOBSONV
23-1-41	"	AMA	"	"	"	AUCKLAN
16-1-41	"	"	"	"	"	SYDNEY
17-1-41	"	"	"	—	SYDNEY	AUCKLAN
3-2-41	"	AMC	"	"	AUCKLAND	SYDNEY
4-2-41	"	"	"	"	SYDNEY	AUCKLA
28-2-41	"	AMA	"	"	AUCKLAND	SYDNE
2-3-41	"	"	—	—	SYDNEY	AUCKLA
						Carried forw

Pages of logbook of Oscar Garden showing the search for the German raider on 27 November 1940; and the flight to Sydney and return on 4 February 1941 in order to collect his wife, Greta Norlén, and his baby daughter, Margareta.

196

FLIGHTS.

Time of Departure.		Time of Arrival.		Time in Air.		Pilot. See Instructions (5) & (6) on flyleaf of this book.	Remarks.
Hrs.	Mins.	Hrs.	Mins.	Hrs.	Mins.		
...	...	...	...	5337	14		
17	58	03	32	9	34	SELF	AW 36 _Raider search_
18	04	02	38	8	34	"	AE 36
02	12	11	37	9	25	LOG BOOK CHECKED.	SPECIAL FLIGHT
18	00	03	04	9	04	2/11/19.40 Init	AW 39
18	15	03	43	9	28	Controller of Civil Aviation.	AE 39
03	33	04	08		35		TEST
18	00	03	26	9	26		AW 41
20	45	05	26	8	41		AE 41
...	...	...	...	5402	01		

FLIGHTS.

Time of Departure.		Time of Arrival.		Time in Air.		Pilot. See Instructions (5) & (6) on flyleaf of this book.	Remarks.
Hrs.	Mins.	Hrs.	Mins.	Hrs.	Mins.		
...	...	...	...	5456	13		
21	48	22	16		28	SELF	FERRY
23	05	06	36	7	31	"	SPECIAL FLIGHT
17	53	02	32	8	39	"	AW 49
18	14	03	00	8	46	"	AE 49
17	59	04	02	10	03	"	AW 53
18	00	02	04	8	04	"	AE 53
18	04	03	26	9	22	"	AW 58
18	07	03	23	9	16	"	AE 58
...	...	...	...	5506	22		

where the astrodome used to go and two 500-pound bombs slung under each wing in a makeshift fashion. Two 'odd bods' (according to Oscar) from the RNZAF base at Hobsonville accompanied them. He said he was afraid they might shoot the tail off because there wasn't anything for them to stand on to get up to the Lewis gun. 'I never figured out how we were supposed to use the bombs because all they had was two trip wires inside the flight deck that you were supposed to pull when the pilot told them to.'

After leaving, they opened the sealed directions, which said the speed of the raider was 10 knots. Oscar asked the air force men if they thought 10 was a bit slow for a raider as he thought the speed would be more like 15. They agreed, and so he worked out a course at 15. After five hours and 40 minutes of flying, and with poor visibility due to fading light and a thick haze, Oscar decided to turn back. Being in the left-hand seat, he naturally banked to port. Had his co-pilot in the right-hand-seat taken the controls they would have seen the *Orion*, which was on full alert at the unexpected sound of an aircraft.

In the report that came out after the war, it was stated that the crew of the *Orion* were standing by with a Dornier seaplane armed with four machine guns ready to launch if Oscar broke radio silence. Oscar said it was the closest he came to being 'bumped off'.

It was a damned good thing because if we had seen them, there was nothing in cooee that could have done anything. We would have been out of fuel in a few hours, and couldn't have shadowed them for very long. And you can bet your life, if they knew they'd been spotted, they would've taken off on another tack, and they would have gone further and further away.

If they had bombed the *Orion*, they might have killed the prisoners battened down in the holds. (The prisoners were put ashore at an island called Emirau off New Guinea and six days later, were picked up by the Australian ship SS *Nellore* and taken to Townsville.)

In early January 1941, yet another of Oscar's former record-breaking colleagues – Amy Johnson – was killed. Johnson was delivering a twin-engined Oxford trainer from Scotland to an airfield in Oxfordshire when she got lost, ran out of fuel, and bailed out. Her parachute opened but, unfortunately, she landed in the bitterly cold water of the Thames Estuary and died before she could be rescued.

Oscar had a special cargo on a trip back from Sydney on 4 February 1941. His daughter, Margareta, had been born in Sweden on 14 May 1940, but by the end of the year the Nazis arrived in neighbouring Scandinavian countries. Greta decided to flee to New Zealand, making the perilous five-week journey of 15,000 miles via Russia, Iran and the East. Oscar met them in Sydney and piloted the *Awarua* to Auckland. Their arrival was reported widely in newspapers and, according to one report, Margareta was 'a picture of health ... dressed in an exquisite blue crepe de chine frock and a matching sun bonnet'.[146] For a while they lived in Rota Street, Parnell, before moving to a house at Cliff View Road, Green Bay.

In 1943, John Burgess left TEAL to take up a position with British Overseas Airways Corporation (BOAC) in Baltimore, USA. BOAC had been formed in April 1940 when British Airways Ltd merged with Imperial Airways Ltd. On the recommendation of Burgess, Oscar took over as chief pilot of TEAL as well as operations manager. He became responsible for training a corps of young pilots, many returning from the war.

Over the next few years, there were two records that Oscar kept breaking: the time it took *Awarua* and *Aotearoa* to cross the Tasman from east to west, and the time from west to east. Newspapers would report the records for both directions. Sydney to Auckland was a quicker crossing due to tail winds. It took Kingsford Smith and Ulm 14 hours and 25 minutes when they made the first east-bound crossing in 1928. Oscar must have felt delighted when in June 1940 his journey in *Awarua* from

Sydney to Auckland took 7 hours and 37 minutes, a record! In December 1941 he made the crossing in 5 hours and 56 minutes. He broke the Auckland-to-Sydney record on 9 July 1940 with a flight of 8 hours and 13 minutes. While Burgess took it back on 4 October 1940, Oscar broke it again on 10 August 1943 with a flight of 7 hours and 8 minutes.

Oscar also made the one thousandth flight across the Tasman on 18 June 1944. A *New Zealand Herald* reporter aboard wrote:

Roaring out along a flare-path in the half-light at Rose Bay, Sydney Harbour, yesterday morning, the Aotearoa was quickly airborne, and shortly after the twinkling lights of the city had been left behind the passengers were regaled with a breakfast voted by them as better than any they had received in a Sydney hotel. Most of them dozed and read as the aircraft flew steadily on as though in a groove above masses of white clouds.[147]

The reporter added that 'Aotearoa was commanded by one of the most capable airline pilots in the world, Captain Oscar Garden.'

Oscar and Greta separated in early 1944. Their relationship had been a tempestuous one. Margareta says she remembers the screaming and crying of her mother. Evidently, Oscar hated Greta playing the piano and singing, and walking around the house naked. Margareta told me, 'OG was supposed to have been a heavy drinker, possibly a womaniser – in the sense that women were hugely attracted to him, as a pilot. And of course, he was a dreadful gambler, which you will know about.' She said years later Oscar would tell her, 'Your mother was mad, of course, quite mad. I don't know if she ever got better.' And Greta would say to her, 'Your father was quite mad of course, I don't suppose he'll ever be quite right in the head.'

Although I was not aware of it until 2006, my father had a much warmer relationship with Margareta when she was young than with us. He even had an extraordinary nickname for himself, 'Kicknee Picknee'. This letter to Margareta written in pencil in capital letters was sent while flying on a Radio Message form:

FLYING AT 10,800 FEET BETWEEN SYDNEY AND AUCKLAND, ROYAL MAIL AIRCRAFT, AWARUA, 79 WORDS, 10-10-46, 10.40 AM

I AM SENDING YOU A SMALL PARCEL WITH A PASSENGER CALLED MR FAWCETT WHO IS FLYING ACROSS WITH US TODAY. I HOPE YOU LIKE IT BUT DON'T EAT ALL THE HUNDREDS AND THOUSANDS AT ONCE AND GIVE SOME TO THE MĀORI CHILDREN. I WOULD LIKE TO GET A LETTER FROM YOU SOME TIME. HOPING TO SEE YOU SOON.

KICKNEE PICKNEE

Their house was sold in June 1944 and a deed filed in the New Zealand Supreme Court on 11 October 1944 regarding custody, access and maintenance, as well as distribution of certain chattels, including a camphor-wood chest that my father kept. He used it to store all his aviation paraphernalia: photographs, newspaper cuttings and logbooks. I remember it in our various lounge rooms; we were not allowed to open it. At some stage, he must have sold it.

Oscar also told us of the fright of two men having heart attacks mid-flight – one was very serious – and how lucky they were that on each occasion there was a doctor on board. This gave him the idea of hiring stewardesses with nursing experience, although it took two years of arguing with TEAL directors to get permission. When they agreed in 1945, there were about 1300 applicants for the positions of six stewardesses. Oscar was sitting in the passenger lounge at the terminal in Mechanics Bay waiting to interview them when he told Eric Mullane, the chief in charge of the stewards, 'I've got a curly one here. Where are these girls going to stay when we get to Sydney? Are they going to stay at

TEAL flying boats Aotearoa ZK-AMA, Awarua ZK-AMC and New Zealand KZ-AME at Mechanics Bay, Auckland. Photograph by Whites Aviation Ltd. Ref: WA-04920-G, ALEXANDER TURNBULL LIBRARY, WELLINGTON, NEW ZEALAND.

Passengers and crew disembarking from the TEAL Short S.25 Sandringham flying boat ZK-AME at Mechanics Bay, Auckland. Photograph by Whites Aviation Ltd, Ref: WA-04215-G, ALEXANDER TURNBULL LIBRARY, WELLINGTON, NEW ZEALAND.

the same hotel as the stewards?' He explained to Ellis that the stewards were 'quite good blokes … but they were ex-ship stewards and boy they were a different kettle of fish to these girls we were engaging'. Mullane suggested it would be better if the girls stayed at the same hotel as the crew, while the stewards stayed in Kings Cross.

Oscar was flying *Awarua* to Sydney on 14 August 1945 when news came over the radio that the Japanese had surrendered. On his order, the crew and passengers 'spliced the main-brace' (a nautical term meaning to celebrate with a drink) and the aircraft was taken for a rapid circuit of the city so passengers could see the revelling crowds.[148] The following day, VJ Day, Oscar returned to Auckland, a city also alive with celebration.

Late that night Oscar drove out to Carrington Mental Hospital in Mt Albert with his engineer, Bert Carlyon, to drop off Bert's girlfriend, who was a nurse. (The Carrington Mental Hospital was originally called the

The first six flight stewardesses appointed to Tasman Empire Airways Limited (TEAL). From left Betty Morton, Val Beckett, Launa Magnus, Judy Everand, Joyce Paterson, Pat Woolley. Photograph taken by Whites Aviation, August 1946. Ref: WA-03093-F, ALEXANDER TURNBULL LIBRARY, WELLINGTON, NEW ZEALAND.

Whau Lunatic Asylum when it opened in 1865.) While waiting in the car for Bert, some nurses, who had been out celebrating, crossed in front of the car to go to their quarters. Oscar turned the car lights on when he saw them and turned them off. Then he turned them on again and stared at one of them who had long, wavy auburn hair. The woman, whose name was Helen Varie Aroha Lovell, had to shield her face from the bright light. She thought, 'What a silly bugger.' Helen was, of course, my mother.

The following day Oscar visited the hospital and asked the resident hairdresser who this woman might be (he described her hair). The hairdresser said that must be Helen. And so it was. The hairdresser contacted Oscar and said she thought she had tracked down the woman he was interested in. They arranged to all meet together (the hairdresser, the chief pilot, his engineer and the nurse) at midnight during Helen's one-hour break in her night shift.

My mother recalled:

Bert and the hairdresser were sitting in the back and they were giggling and laughing their heads off while Oscar looked me over and said things such as 'good strong legs'. He even pinched my arm to see how strong I was. I felt I was a horse on parade and should wave my tail. Or I was being examined for some position. I thought what a balmy, unusual, fascinating man. The next day he invited me over to his place. His mother was visiting and she seemed a dear old funny thing. Bert was also there, and he and Oscar were painting the flat or something.

From then on, Oscar would often come to visit my mother at midnight during her one-hour break. He would ring up at odd hours, even from Sydney, to arrange a meeting. He would fly from Sydney after long and sometimes rough flights and weather, and she would go outside and sit in his car to talk. Often, they would hear the screaming of patients of Ward 3. There was only straw in that room. They couldn't put anything else

My mother, Helen Lovell (on the left), with a friend, Christina Spear, outside the Carrington Mental Hospital in Mt Albert about the time she met Oscar in August 1945.

there because the patients would tear it apart or try to hang themselves. Occasionally, they would drive up to Mt Eden, where he had bought a house, and sit there. He would often take a bottle of whisky. He was very popular for bringing back cheap whisky from Sydney because of the war restrictions. They discussed the children they wanted; my mother wanted four, but Oscar only wanted three. She recalled him going on and on about what was happening at TEAL, but she didn't take much notice. Sometimes he would fly in low over the mental hospital and nurses would run out and wave, jumping up and down and shouting out at him.

My mother said that when she first met Oscar, she had never heard of him or realised how famous he was. She said that wherever he went people flocked around, and ladies fawned all over him. Papers called him 'the debonair Oscar Garden'. There was often something in the paper about him. I think he both loved and hated the fame, going from one extreme to another. In the beginning, if I was reading a newspaper, he'd pipe up 'Is there anything about me?' She recalled that they took a barge to Devonport one day and he was told by an attendant to move the car. He retorted, 'Don't you know who I am?' My mother said she felt so embarrassed. Jean Batten said the same thing as Oscar when in 1990 she tried to board a boat to Green Island on Australia's Great Barrier Reef but it was full. 'Don't you know who I am?' she asked. When they said they didn't, she retorted, 'I'm Jean Batten.'[149] This inflated sense of self-importance can often be the price of fame. People become addicted to being recognised and lauded – adulation is the ultimate addiction.

Because the divorce from Greta had not come through, my mother had to lurk around in the background trying to be invisible. Between 1945 and 1947 Oscar was always flitting backwards and forwards, and she sometimes wouldn't see him for weeks at a time. He was busy and so was she, getting her nursing medal. Rebecca often stayed at his unit for long periods, doing his housework and washing.

In 1946 the New Zealand government, under pressure from Britain, decided to replace the S30s with four Sandringham IVs, overriding a preference amongst TEAL's senior personnel for land-based DC-4s. Oscar was furious. He regarded the Sandringhams as 'obsolete'. 'The decision was a very bad move. They had a contract practically signed up for DC-4s from the Americans [there were no suitable British aircraft available] and we'd have been home and hosed if we'd got those.' He considered the DC-4s to be 'an excellent aircraft, probably the best available at the time, with which to expand the Tasman service and at the same time develop the southern route [to the South Island]'.[150] Maurice McGreal, a pilot Oscar had employed, told me that Oscar, more than anyone, knew the 'significant operational limitations' of flying boats.

In May 1946 Geoffrey Roberts was appointed general manager of TEAL, a position Oscar had applied for but was unsuccessful.[151] Roberts had been commander of the New Zealand Air Task Force in the Pacific during the war. Noel Holmes writes in his biography of Roberts, 'When it came to hiring executives something like an old-boy network often existed between managers or personnel managers of companies sharing similar interests.'[152] According to McGreal, the fact that Geoffrey Roberts would now be Oscar's 'master' would have been a hard lump for Oscar to swallow. He had been the 'Man at the Top' for three years, and he did not appear to accept the reality that the policy of government overrode all else with regards to the question of the flying boat versus the land planes he had lined up. McGreal told me that when the newspapers announced Roberts' appointment there was a lot of 'shock and horror [in the company] because Oscar had become "Captain Tasman Airways" to the pilots'.

In January 1947, Oscar watched from his office at Mechanics Bay as the first Sandringham landed. When it had been pulled back into the pontoon and only a few loaders were working about it, he strode quickly down the ramp and went aboard. Climbing the ladder to the flight deck, he looked about for a few minutes, sniffed and made a few succinct remarks that were, according to McGreal, unprintable, turned and walked ashore.[153]

On 20 March 1947 Oscar suddenly resigned. According to Mum he resigned to save face. She said he was jealous and resentful of Roberts because he had been in the air force. 'Nothing on earth would have made him stay as a deputy to Roberts. He thought he was brainless and reckoned he had had some mishaps.' Mum told me she attended the farewell function on 6 May 1947 but had to stay at the back of the room, as Oscar was still married. She told me that she was shocked to overhear someone say about Oscar, 'He's the best administrator but I hate his guts.' She added, 'I can imagine him giving orders with his sharp staccato voice.' However, there were no indications that Roberts disliked Oscar, and he was full of praise for him in his speech:

> [Oscar Garden] had been largely responsible for building the organisation into the successful undertaking it was today. His record both as a pilot and as an administrative officer had been outstanding and his services would be missed by the company. All those with whom he worked and also the travelling public had formed a deep affection for him.[154]

Oscar did not miss them. He walked away with a chip on his shoulder (Mum used to call it a large plank) that would stay there for the rest of his life. However, Roberts was right. In 1943 TEAL had only a handful of men capable of flying increasingly unreliable aircraft. When Oscar resigned, the airline had a corps of young pilots who were to serve it well for many years. Driscoll writes that it was Oscar Garden's ability to 'impart his technical proficiency and experience to the young pilots that marks him as a man of distinction. The measure of his talent lies in the warm appreciation with which they regard him.'[155]

This was evident almost 60 years later when, in 2006, I went to Auckland and interviewed some of the TEAL pilots. One said Oscar had been a hard taskmaster and 'kept them on their toes', but he had been shocked when Oscar left. Roberts was later regarded as the 'Father of Air New Zealand', although the pilots I spoke to thought that title belonged to Oscar. Ronald Puttick said they did not expect Roberts to be given the job as general manager, and not everyone 'had a high regard for him'. Puttick pointed out that Oscar was a top captain and would not have liked anyone issuing orders or criticisms. Frank Bethwaite claims it was clearly a political appointment. He said they called Roberts 'Ferdie' after Ferdinand the Bull, 'an idiot of a pilot'. In contrast, Oscar Garden was held in awe, even reverence. They respected him, looked up to him.

Could it be that Oscar lacked some of the skills to be a good manager, such as good communication and diplomacy? A few remarked that he didn't go out of his way to get to know people closely. He was a loner and kept to himself. Former 'Met' man at Mechanics Bay, Larry Larsen, told me, 'He disappeared into oblivion; I was surprised that he left.' Jim Kennedy said, 'Most of us were shocked when he left TEAL and cut himself off.' Mike Hart, who is writing a book on John Burgess, pointed out that, 'Like a lot of pilots (most probably) Oscar would have had no skills or personal appetite for the political machinations of large businesses, especially those owned by Governments.'[156]

However, Oscar also left because he was bored. He said he was sick of flying back and forth over the same stretch of water. Hart told me, 'Aviation is a difficult Mistress and it might seem dashing and exciting, which it can be, but it is dangerous, completely inconsiderate of a normal life with family or friends and despite the glorious views, you're a travelling shift worker. You live an itinerant life, out of a suitcase, sleeping alone in hotel rooms.'[157]

Awarua and *Aotearoa* were retired that same year after seven years of accident-free flights in which 16 million letters and 13,000 passengers had been carried. *Awarua* was broken up in June 1947. *Aotearoa* was hauled ashore and used as tea-rooms at Tamaki Drive in Mission Bay for a few years, but then was also broken up. The Sandringhams were beset by mechanical problems. They remained in service until 1949 but proved to be underpowered for the Tasman crossing and prone to overheating. A near-disaster occurred on 31 December 1947. One of the Sandringhams – ZK-AME – was forced to make a hazardous 400-mile return trip to Sydney after one of its engines failed during a fierce squall. The captain ordered all the luggage of the passengers and crew, as well as freight, to be jettisoned. The only thing saved was a spool of films recording the royal wedding of Princess Elizabeth and Philip Mountbatten. TEAL purchased four Short Solents to replace the Sandringhams.

By 1950 New Zealand was the only country in the world using flying boats on long-haul routes. Oscar's frustration with the continued use of flying boats is evident in an eight-page letter he wrote to Sidney Holland, New Zealand's opposition leader, in July 1948. He mentions 'the sorry story of the Sandringhams since they commenced service' and 'common sense and practical advice should have been used' before choosing Solent flying boats to replace them. There was no justification for not using American landplanes, he writes, and points out that even BOAC had to buy their planes for the Atlantic service.

His anger about not getting the job as General Manager of TEAL is barely concealed when he writes that 'one question that needs investigation is the method of selection of directors and key men in Air Lines in NZ', adding that 'every successful airline overseas has at its head men with proven ability and practical experience.' Men like Oscar, in other words, not Geoffrey Roberts! He maintains there are many questions worth investigating, and that the only way to do this is through a Royal Commission 'to have the whole field of aviation cleaned up'.

In June 1954, TEAL bought its first landplanes for international flights – Douglas DC-6s – and withdrew the outdated Solents from service, except for *Aranui*, which was retained for use on the Coral Route (from Auckland to Suva, the Cook Islands and Tahiti) until 1966. It is now at

Auckland's Museum of Technology and Transport (MOTAT) and has been restored by the Solent Preservation Society.

According to Maurice McGreal, Roberts turned the tiny airline into something like an air force squadron of which he was commanding officer. He appointed many administrative staff, most of who had come from units Roberts had commanded during the war.[158] The charisma and the air of romance that Oscar had brought to TEAL disappeared. Throughout the 1950s Roberts played a major role in promoting the case for a New Zealand-owned airline. In 1953, New Zealand and Australia became joint owners and in April 1965, New Zealand assumed full ownership. TEAL was renamed Air New Zealand. Roberts resigned as general manager in 1958, but continued as a director and served as chairman for 10 years until his retirement in 1975. In 1973, he received a knighthood for services to aviation.

Between 1930 and 1947 Oscar had amassed approximately 10,000 flying hours. After he left TEAL, he never flew a plane again.

CHAPTER 10

The Tomato Grower

After leaving TEAL, Oscar decided to try something different. He bought a citrus farm in Kerikeri in the Bay of Islands. The idea of growing something and being on the land appealed to him. He saw it as another challenge. My mother used to visit him up there, and when the divorce from Greta came through, they married in August 1948 in a registry office at the nearby seaside town of Russell. No friends or relatives attended.

Oscar didn't tell Rebecca he had married until a week later. Nor did he tell my mother he had placed the farm on the market. She said she was shocked when a real estate agent appeared at the door a few days after they returned from their short honeymoon. This was the beginning of a long nightmare of constantly being on the move due to Oscar's restlessness and instability, although he always had what he thought were valid and sensible reasons. On this occasion he claimed that the bottom had fallen out of the citrus market.

Without discussing it with Mum, Oscar bought a milk bar, with living quarters out the back, at Paeroa, a midway stop for those travelling between Auckland and Tauranga. When he was interviewed about this in 1995, he said it was much to 'Hel's disgust'. Mum, who was there at the time of the interview, piped up, 'Why in God's name?' and Dad replied 'Because I am a lunatic.'

The milk bar venture only lasted a few months and it was during this time that my mother fell pregnant. Oscar sold up and moved further south to Whakatane where he purchased Willowbank Nurseries, which had a shop, house and a nursery on a couple of acres. The house was small and run down. It was meant to be a temporary living space, as the plan was to build a new house. Rats the size of cats came through the holes in the floor, and Oscar kept a spade by the side of their bed to bash them on their heads.

Even though my mother was pregnant, she was still expected to work in the nursery and pick the fruit, including tree tomatoes (tamarillos) and citrus. They tried to employ people to work in the shop and the nursery, but these never lasted long because Oscar would soon find fault with them.

My brother Robert was born on 24 June 1949. A few months later Mum was pregnant again – with me! I was born on 18 June 1950. My mother was loading boxes of oranges onto the back of a truck when she fell off and suddenly went into labour. She said as soon as she reached hospital that I 'rushed out'. This was a story she told repeatedly over the years, always adding 'and Mary hasn't stopped rushing since'.

Mum told me that Oscar didn't show his true colours until they were married. Within weeks she knew she had made a mistake. She said they didn't get on well and she found him very strange. When they first met, she was attracted to him because he was so different. 'Oh boy, did I have to pay for wanting to be with someone different from the usual run of the mill. I was too smart for my own good. Other men were too nice. Oh God, serves me right.' At the beginning, he had even warned her, 'You will have to keep an eye on me as I'm very impetuous.' Mum's sister Aunt Ola said, 'Your father had plenty of intelligence but was damn odd as well. I would have hated to have him. I'd hate all men to be like that.'

It wasn't long after I was born that they moved north to Papatoetoe, a suburb of South Auckland. Within the year Oscar sold up and bought a house in Kumeu, a small town 15 miles north-west of Auckland. Mum became pregnant here with my sister, but even that was not enough to make Oscar settle down. The Kumeu house went on the market, and after it was sold Oscar went on the househunt again. My sister Anna was born in Westport (on the west coast of the South Island) on 23 April 1953. Mum had gone to stay with her parents for a few months while Dad was looking for a house. Mum said that all the time she was in Westport waiting for the birth, Oscar wrote her only one letter:

Dear Hel,
Where's the ink? Nothing much happening here.
Oscar

Eventually Oscar bought a property on Otumoetai Road in Otumoetai, Tauranga, within walking distance of the local primary school. Behind the house was a large glasshouse with tomatoes. My father became a tomato grower for most of the next 21 years. Thankfully, in Tauranga during my childhood years, there was some stability. Tomatoes, for some reason, had a special appeal to Dad, and he excelled at growing them. He was a perfectionist, as he had been with the maintenance of *Kia Ora*.

Tauranga is a beautiful place on the east coast of the North Island, located at the head of a large harbour that extends along the western Bay of Plenty. The name Tauranga comes from Māori and roughly translates to 'sheltered waters'. Perhaps living by the sea was a reminder for Oscar of his childhood years in Tongue. In 1950, Tauranga was a town with a population of only about 14,000.

Interestingly, in the mid-1940s, Rebecca and Violet lived in Mount Maunganui, which back then was a coastal resort town on a peninsular north-east of Tauranga. In 1988 Mount Maunganui became a major

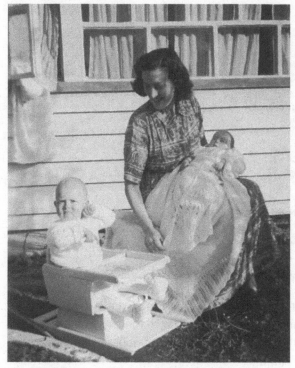

My father holding me.
Whakatane, June 1950.

Mum cradling me;
Robert is in a chair.

Oscar picking tomatoes.

The property Oscar bought in 1958 at Levers Crescent, Otumoetai, Tauranga. It is on the right hand side of the photo with the large glasshouse and a smaller glasshouse at the front. To the left of the house is the small hut in which I lived with my sister Anna.

suburb of Tauranga due to the completion of the Tauranga Harbour Bridge, which connected it to Tauranga's central business district. In 1952 Rebecca moved back to Christchurch, where she bought a house at Redcliffs, across the road from her daughter May. Violet moved back there as well.

Oscar's cousin Robin Barclay, who had studied medicine in Edinburgh, also settled in Tauranga in the early 1950s and became our family doctor. Robin's mother Dora (Oscar's aunt and Robert Garden Sr's youngest daughter) made several trips from Scotland to visit her son and moved to Tauranga in the late 1960s. She stayed there for the rest of her life. Robin died in 1982 aged 55. He was another Garden alcoholic, according to his son Alastair, who now lives in Mt Maunganui. One of my first jobs (apart from jobs for my father), when I was 12, was to go to the Barclay's home to do the ironing.

On 26 November 1954, a year after we moved to Tauranga, Rebecca died. She was 83. Oscar caught a plane down to the funeral – the first time he had been in a plane since leaving TEAL. In her will, Rebecca left £200 to her housekeeper Audrey Coutts and the rest of her estate to Oscar and Violet. She left nothing to the two eldest daughters, May and Rose, who had stayed with her husband Robert when they separated. Mum was not aware that Oscar had received any inheritance until I showed her the copy of Rebecca's will. What did he spend the money on? The horses?

In Tauranga, our lives revolved around tomatoes. Oscar worked seven days a week in his glasshouses or the packing sheds and never went on holidays. Mum also worked long hours helping with the tomatoes, as well as doing the housework and cooking and so forth. We seldom had visitors, and the few that came would usually just have morning tea. My father seemed content being by himself with his tomatoes, away from people. As soon as we were old enough, we were expected to work, as anyone he employed seldom lasted more than a day. I started helping when I was six or seven and would work after school and weekends, as well as on holidays. Margareta also used to help when she came to stay during school holidays. She hated working, going by these diary excerpts:

15 January 1956: Dad expected me to pick tomatoes today. I think he is positively horrid. The way he treats Helen is appalling.

16 January 1956: I picked tomatoes and found it heavy work. I really don't like Daddy that much and I would hate to work for him for any length of time. If mum should die Heaven help me.

17 January 1956: I picked tomatoes all morning and Daddy wouldn't let us go for a swim … Daddy is very unfair and I just find myself hating him.

It was a cold environment to grow up in; there was an absence of music, laughter, conversation and hugs. Not only was Oscar authoritarian, but he was puritanical and even recoiled from human contact. I never saw him kiss or hug my mother or put his arm around her. However, neither do I remember ever hearing them fighting, yelling or screaming. There was none of the volatility that marked his relationship with Margareta's mother Greta. Nor do I recall them not speaking to each other. And yet, years later, Mum told me that they were always falling out and wouldn't speak for days. Even though I never saw him hit her, she said he used to choke her and this was why she had to have part of her thyroid removed. Alys Wicksteed, the daughter of Mary Revfeim, a close friend of Mum's, told me they knew about Dad's violence. When we were living in Otumoetai Road, Mum would visit them at their home (the historic homestead Maungawhare), which was close by. Alys recalled one occasion when Mum arrived very distraught, with Anna in a pushchair. They ended up staying the night, sleeping in an upstairs bedroom. The next morning Dad turned up, Robert and I crying in the back of our small green station wagon. I have no memory of this!

Mary Revfeim went out and had 'a heated exchange' with Dad. Shortly after, we moved house, to the far end of the Otumoetai peninsular. Alys said they always believed Oscar wanted Mum away from Mary Revfeim's bad influence!

Working for Dad, I'd be on edge, fearful I'd make a mistake. Once I accidentally broke a tomato plant and spent the next few days in a state of panic. And I was frightened he would hit me. However, I can only remember him giving me two hidings. The first was when I was about four. I had gone outside with a glass to fill it up with water from an outdoor tap. The glass fell and smashed on the ground; one of the pieces flung up

The wedding of Dad's cousin Robin Barclay to Patricia MacKenzie in February 1957, Tauranga. From left: Margaret McColl (Oscar's niece), Dora Barclay (Oscar's cousin), Mum and Dad. Margaret's husband Guy is standing behind her. Mum looks so beautiful and happy here.

and cut me on the wrist of my right hand, a cut that required stitching. The scar remains visible today. The other time was when I was about six years old. I had chucked an apple core down the side of a shed and he had found it. It still had a bit of flesh on it. I remember him shouting at me, 'What about the poor children starving in Africa?' This was something he often said, as well as 'You should have lived through the Depression.'

On one occasion, Dad came up to Otumoetai Primary School when it was a sports day. The parents were sitting or standing under the trees watching the events. My father noticed a boy out on the field hitting another boy. To my horror he ran out and gave the boy a hiding, walloping him on his bottom. No one, of course, said anything, pretending it didn't happen. Immediately afterwards my father strode back home. I don't think he ever visited any of our schools again.

Remarkably – because she didn't stand up to him about anything else – at some point Mum told Dad not to hit us, something he evidently complained about to other men. We got off lightly compared to other children of that era – in the 1950s corporal punishment was meted out regularly in both homes and schools. Ironically, there was a short period after I began secondary school when Robert began punching Mum and me on our upper arms, leaving bruises. Mum told me to ignore it, that he had to take out his frustration with my father on someone.

Dad was also miserly. He gave my mother just £10 a week to pay for food, household and clothing. Henry, her father, paid her about the same amount and paid for our fares to go on holidays to her hometown of Westport. Yet, although Oscar was frugal, he didn't hesitate to spend money on horseracing. When they lived at Whakatane, he would take off on the weekends to the racing circuits in Thames or Paeroa, but in Tauranga he'd find his way to the nearest TAB.

Mum said:

What a situation. If only I had some money to leave him. He had a cold streak, yet when a bird flew into the side of the glasshouse he would sit there with a saucer of water and some crumbs and stroke it. Wouldn't do this with humans.

Margareta was surprised when I told her in 2005 what a terrible father he had been. 'In what way?' she asked. 'I know he beat Robert, can't now remember why, but he certainly never hit me, or did anything else

Me on my bike outside the Hut, where I slept with my sister Anna. It was about 100 yards away from the main house. Levers Crescent, Otumoetai, Tauranga, 1959.

The Gardens at Otumoetai, December 1960. Robert on the left, me in the centre and Anna on the right.

horrible.' When I shared this with Mum, she became angry: 'What would she know? He was a bastard of a father. And a bastard of a husband. There are things Margareta doesn't know.' Mum said that we were all primed up before her visits. 'Your father drilled us on what or what not to say as he didn't want anything bad getting back to "that woman" [Greta].' Recently Margareta told me she was unaware of much of what went on but years later she had the feeling that Oscar married Helen because 'he was totally unable to provide meals etc. when he had me to stay. 'How mad!' she said.

However, we were lucky that we had another place to escape to in the summer school holiday that gave us some respite from living with Oscar. In the summer school holidays, Mum used to take us down to Westport to stay with her parents. At my grandparents' home, we encountered a different world. It was a safe place. There was no tiptoeing around in fear, hiding under beds waiting for a scolding. Music, laughter and warmth filled their beautiful two-storey house. We would go on family picnics at Carters Beach and Cape Foulwind, and we even went to horse races, something my father never took us to. I adored my nana and loved riding her upright bicycle around the streets and bringing back groceries in the front basket. As I was an early riser, my job was to take her a cup of black tea with a slice of lemon, along with the newspaper.

When I was about eight years old, we moved a few miles away onto acreage at the end of Levers Crescent on the Otumoetai peninsular. There was a large glasshouse on it, and Dad soon built another smaller glasshouse. However, the house had only two bedrooms. About a hundred yards away was a small hut, a narrow wooden building divided into three rooms, separated by curtains. This was for my sister and me. In some ways living in this hut was like being grown up in a house of our own. However, during storms it was terrifying in the hut, and I'd hide under the bed covers listening to the sound of the wind shaking the branches of the large willow tree that hung over the roof.

At the end of my room there was a bench with a sink. Dad would recycle wooden boxes that would need soaking at one end to remove the old labels. That was my job. I would stand the boxes upright in my sink, one by one. I'd come home from school to find rows and rows of boxes stacked in my small bedroom. He would also get me to find things he had lost, even his false teeth, which I found buried in the soil in one of the glasshouses. And he would make me disentangle twine he had inadvertently knotted up. I had nimble fingers and didn't give up. He would say to Mum, 'We'll have to wait for Mary to come home from school.'

We spent most of the time outside, – working or playing, – only going inside the house for meals. At mealtime, my father would sit at the head of the table. We were not allowed to talk and were told to *never* lick our knives. On the odd occasion, he would lick his knife and look at each of us with a big grin on his face. I never thought it was funny. Afterwards we were sent outside, out of Oscar's way, so he could listen to the races on the radio and fill out his racing forms. He would sit in his armchair with a notebook and pencil.

My father was different from all the other fathers I knew. He was much older, for a start. He usually wore baggy khaki work trousers splattered with stains from the tomato plants and a large straw hat with holes in it. If I was in town with him, I would try to walk well behind him so as I could pretend that he was not my father and that we were not together. He was also gruff.

I seldom had friends home to play because I was worried my father would get angry at them. Those who came over would invariably be given a lecture about the state of their bicycles and how they weren't taking care of them. Then my father would proceed to fix them or do the odd repair.

Nonetheless, there was something I admired about him – he had a strong sense of injustice, which he must have inherited from Rebecca. For example, there was a man and overweight son who lived down the road in a shed on an overgrown property. They were shunned by the neighbourhood. who thought they were weird or mad, and they smelt terribly. Despite this Dad used to take them things such as clothing and food, and sometimes he would take me with him. We would ride our bikes to school, but the overweight boy used to walk. My father was the only person in Otumoetai who would pick him up to give him a lift, but he would leave the windows of the car down for hours afterwards to let the smell out. He never seemed to care what people thought of him.

There were also fun times at our new place. We had an idyllic playground at our back door – the Matua Estuary. We would hang our lines over the end of the jetty, swim, float into the channel on large logs and dig out caves in the tall cliffs. And we had beautiful bicycles that my father maintained to perfection. We would cycle all over Tauranga. Mum would pack us a lunch of marmite and chive sandwiches, slices of date loaf, fruit and a glass bottle of lime cordial, which we would stack in the front baskets of our bikes.

During these years, I was vaguely aware of my father's former life as an aviator. There were reminders, such as the Avro Tutor trophy he won in 1931, sitting on the mantel piece, the framed photos of *Awarua* making a graceful descent into Auckland's Waitemata harbour and the carved chest which stored his flying stuff. He certainly never talked to us about his flying adventures, or anything else, for that matter, except to criticise something we had done or bark out orders.

However, in 1960 an article was published in New Zealand's *Whites Aviation* magazine in which Leo White reminisced about old pilots and wrote, 'Oscar Garden ... well, I am stumped, for here is one person I have lost track of in the years which have passed.' Leo subsequently tracked him down. In an article for the next issue, he wrote that my father's only current association with aviation was to glance up at the fast-flying Aero Commander that passed overhead every day on the Auckland – Bay of Plenty service, saying, 'Damned rowdy, but a beautiful little machine'.

A local journalist also became interested. Dennis Burley and his wife, Tiki, lived near us and became friendly with my mother. Dennis's article on Oscar was published in 1964 in the *Bay of Plenty Times*. There were several letters in response. One reader wrote that he and many of his friends found them very interesting. 'They must be of profound importance in aviation history. Surely, they rate New Zealand-wide, even world-wide publication … a weekly series of Mr Garden's whole flying experience from the beginning, as a serial, would be popular with all *Bay of Plenty Times* readers.'

Soon after the article appeared, my father – after a relatively stable period growing tomatoes – became restless. We moved into town to a two-storey house in Second Avenue. By then I was 13 and determined to grow up as quickly as I could. Dad had ostensibly banned me from wearing makeup or going out with boys until I was 21. My bedroom was upstairs, so I hid my makeup and high heels in the garden, and at night I would climb out the upstairs window, scale down the wall and take off. As well as the Down Under coffee lounge in the next street, there was the Inferno coffee lounge on the waterfront, where Tauranga's top rock-and-roll band, The Four Fours, would play. The flame-walled club was the hottest spot in town. Mum just said 'don't let your father catch you!'

Part-way through 1965 – my third year of secondary school – we moved to Papakura, a suburb in South Auckland, as Dad wanted to try his hand at being a real estate agent. Anna was sent to Auckland to attend Epsom Girls Grammar and stay with Aunt Margaret, my mother's eldest sister. Mum told me later she wanted any excuse to get us away from home; she struggled to look after three children as well as having to put up with Oscar. My brother and I went to Papakura High, a co-ed school, which I loved after being at an all-girls school. I wrote to Margareta, saying 'It's absolutely fantastic being here in Papakura. It is miles better than Tauranga, especially the school and the boys – the only thing that counts.'

Dad did not enjoy his stint as a real estate agent, and at the end of the year he sold up and returned to Tauranga – back to Otumoetai and more tomato-growing. For my final year of school, I was sent to Auckland to also board with Aunt Margaret. At Epsom Girls Grammar I was in the same year as former prime minister Helen Clark, but I do not remember her. It was a miserable year and I hated the restrictiveness of once again being at a single-sex school. I wrote to Margareta, 'School is an absolute bore and I just can't wait to get out of this mouldy hole.' I had few friends and made little effort in the subjects I had selected. This was reflected in my leaving certificate in which is written: 'A student of quite good ability … Mary has not revealed as yet either her personality or her capacity though she has been quite co-operative.'

The next year – 1967 – at age 16, I moved to Hamilton and enrolled at Waikato University. I was free at last. I had my own flat, a small motorbike, and began living it up – sex, drugs, drinking and parties. I had boyfriends much older than I was and my main interest was having a good time. Just like Oscar after he left home to get away from the control of puritanical Rebecca. He lived it up in Christchurch, was given fines for speeding and took nurses out for wild rides in his car. The life of the party for a few years.

After two years I was sick of waking up with hangovers and stopped partying. I began doing yoga instead and attended the first yoga class held in Hamilton – yoga was yet to become popular in the West. I loved it. It was a way of soothing my mind. It relaxed me. I also joined the university tramping club and on weekends went exploring the hills and forests in the Waikato region. I put my head down and excelled academically. But eventually – like my father – my past caught up with me. The Black Dog visited. I thought it was the Devil.

By 1970 I had a Bachelor of Education, a Diploma of Teaching, and was one of two students selected to do a prized one-year Master's degree. However, I wasn't coping. I decided to drop out. I can't remember what excuse I gave the Dean, but he was furious and said I wanted the world at my feet. The year previously I had been Waikato University's entrant in the Miss New Zealand University contest in Dunedin. I had inherited my father's good looks, as well as his intelligence and perfectionism. But I felt cursed. I was becoming emotionally shut down and repressed like him. And I had inherited his ghosts, the Garden ghosts, and no doubt some of my mother's as well.

I moved to Auckland and found a teaching job. That didn't help. By the end of the year the Black Dog was a constant companion, and I still thought it was the Devil. I didn't dare tell anyone or ask for help for fear of being carted off to the 'loony bin'. The only way for me to get any relief – albeit short-lived – was to move house, rent another flat. Just like my father, moving constantly. Perhaps he, too, was trying to get some respite from depression. Yoga helped me a little, but at times my depression was so bad I would stay in bed for days, even crawling under the bed itself and curling up there. I seldom went down to Tauranga to visit Mum and Dad.

Even though my father was constantly on the move, he continued to be tracked down by journalists. On 6 November 1970 an article appeared in a British newspaper *Eastern Evening News* titled 'Oscar Garden – where are you?' Wilf Reynolds, the chief flying instructor of the Norwich Aero Club, had been delving into the club's past and wrote 'The whereabouts – or the fate – of one Oscar Garden. He was a member who joined the club in the thirties, learnt to fly – and immediately bought a plane and flew off to Australia! Since then, he has not been heard of. Oscar Garden, where are you now?' It took Wilf 12 months to discover Oscar was still alive. As well as publishing an article about him, the club decided to present him retrospectively with a trophy for 'the most outstanding navigational flight of the year'.

In 1968 Dad had bought a house with glasshouses at Matua Road. This was their fifth house at the end of the Otumoetai peninsular – each around the corner from the other. On a merry-go-round in Otumoetai! What did people think? In 1973, as soon as Oscar was eligible for the age pension, he was on the move again. He sold the property in Matua

Road and bought a house at Katikati, a small town on the northern end of Tauranga harbour. This was the end of his career as a tomato grower.

CHAPTER 11

The Forgotten Aviator

If the years of growing tomatoes and putting up with us three children were challenging for my father, the years after we had all left home were even more miserable. He had few interests, the main one being gambling on horse racing. Surprisingly, given his success with tomato growing, he didn't even keep a vegetable garden. He had little interest in aviation and never bought aviation magazines. If he read something about aviation in the newspaper, he'd invariably disagree with it and make some negative comment. And now that he was no longer working and had nothing to keep his mind occupied, he had more time to brood over, and to feel bitter about, TEAL. 'Those bastards up there', he used to say.

Oscar was a loner and had long cut himself off from former pilots he had flown with. Even though he was trained by John Burgess in England in the late 1930s and was with him for two years at TEAL, they don't seem to have had any contact after Burgess left in 1942. Mike Hart who, as previously mentioned, is writing a book on Burgess, whom he calls 'another forgotten leading light of aviation', points out the parallels between the two men. Burgess stayed at BOAC until 1951, when he suddenly chucked it all in and went sheep farming in New Zealand. Like

Oscar, he never flew a plane again, although Burgess did not have a chip on his shoulder. Mike says that not only does the constant travel and strain of flying take its toll on pilots, but Oscar and Burgess would have worked long hours for fairly mediocre pay. In the 1970s Burgess moved to Australia and died in 1993 at Laurieton, near Port Macquarie, NSW.

After Oscar retired and he had no tomatoes to tie him down, he became more restless. For the next ten years they moved every year and sometimes within nine months. Mum later wrote a list for me of the houses they had lived in. During their 49 years together, they moved more than 23 times, most of them in the first 35 years. For his last 14 years they stayed put in a unit in Papakura. Against this entry Mum scribbled: 'O.G. was too tired to move. He was ready for the crematorium! Me on a reprieve! – a mental institution.' Mum said, 'There was always something wrong. "Soil no good, so let's move." Nothing was ever right for Oscar. On the move all the time.'

In 1974 he bought a unit in Tauranga, but within a few months he decided it had been a bad decision (for some reason), and so he bought the place next door. Mum said that was an easy move as they simply 'chucked stuff over the fence'. My father claimed his motivation to keep buying and selling was to make money. But each move seemed to be a downgrade with a shrinking backyard. The places they lived in were not only drab on the outside, they were drab inside. The décor was always neutral in colour – shades of grey, cream and beige.

In one letter to Margareta, Mum writes of the relief that the sale of their house had fallen through: 'I simply couldn't face the thought of packing, moving out in a fortnight and renting a place in Tauranga for a couple of months before moving on again, with Oscar resting most of the day, not fit enough to do anything.' Mum hated all the moving but went along with it.

It was as if my father was forever on the move to escape his ghosts, the pain of his past that he dragged along with him and inflicted on all of us. But I also believe that underlying his behaviour was a mental illness. Did he have Asperger's? There were his social and communication difficulties: his failure to develop friendships, his awkwardness, his long-winded rants about his medical ailments or reminiscing about his flying days, his insensitivity and disregard of others' feelings, and his aversion to crowds and large gatherings. There was also his acute sensitivity to noise and his need for routines. His lunch had to be ready on the dot of 12.

Or was his incessant need to move house, his impulsiveness and restlessness, symptomatic of manic depression or bipolar disorder, as it is now known? He was a problem gambler, and evidence suggests that those who suffer bipolar disorder often have a gambling addiction. After Dad died, a family member was diagnosed with bipolar I disorder and received treatment. Perhaps they inherited this illness from Dad. Even though I cannot imagine how difficult it was for this family member over many years, the challenges they faced, we were all impacted, especially Mum. I received heartbreaking letters from her, such as this:

> I have a lot of time to think about my time with Oscar, I really do not want to think of him except that XXXX really is showing some of that weird side of him. It could drive me crazy if I had to have a repeat performance.
>
> I sometimes think there is an improvement in XXXX then there is a day when they are really are out of this world talking madly and loudly to themselves. I have a heavy heart when I think of the future if I have one – and also if I haven't [this family member] will have to go into some sort of home.

Although symptoms appeared when our family member was young my parents never sought help; they would have had a real fear that their child would end up somewhere like Carrington Mental Hospital, where Mum had worked and where my parents would sit in the car and listen to the screaming of patients in the straw-filled Ward 3. It is no wonder my parents did not seek medical advice in the case of their child.

My father had had a long history of mental health issues that were never adequately addressed by the long line of medical practitioners who saw him during those years. He also had had pain and headaches over his left eyebrow and in the 1950s had started to have operations on his left frontal sinus. From the 1970s, he became increasingly obsessed by his physical health and began to see numerous specialists, including neurologists, neurosurgeons, otolaryngologists, general surgeons and pain clinic specialists.

In a letter to Margareta dated 6 March 1975, my mother writes:

He is so depressed about himself and thinks his head pains are worse than ever. I get angry when I think of the many doctors and specialists plus private hospitals he has been to and nobody seems to be able to help him. I just don't think they try hard enough nor are they frank or honest. He seemed to enjoy seeing you and the children so he really needs to see more people but he seldom wants to and our friends don't get much of a welcome. It is a pity because he needs more distractions. He needs some interests other than himself.

Regardless of what Dad suffered from, he was definitely odd. In April 1973 I had done away with most of my possessions and taken off to India on a spiritual odyssey. It was a disastrous trip, and in July 1976, after managing to escape the clutches of an abusive yoga teacher in the Himalayas, I returned to New Zealand, my dreams of creating a new life, of becoming spiritually enlightened, shattered. I had flown into Auckland in the morning and caught a bus down to Tauranga, about a four-hour journey. I had had a bad headache for some days and was feeling exhausted. My parents knew I was coming, and I arrived at their small brick unit in the early afternoon. The front door was locked. I knocked on it, and after a while Dad opened it. There was a blank look on his face. He did not smile or say hello. In his tight, high-pitched voice, he said, 'You woke me up. I was having a nap. Your mother is out. You'll have to come back later.'

I can't remember what I did next. Maybe I left my orange backpack on the ground and went for a walk. Maybe I just sat down on the path and waited for Mum. I thought nothing of my father's behaviour at the time. I wasn't angry or upset, which is an indication of how split off from my emotions I had become, even more so after my Indian trip. It is unlikely that when Mum returned, she thought anything of me waiting outside for her. By then, she had also become emotionally frozen and used to my father's peculiar behaviour.

The next day Mum took me to see our doctor, Robin Barclay, Oscar's cousin who in the early 1950s had moved out to Tauranga from Scotland. Tests revealed I had acute hepatitis and was suffering from malnutrition. Even though I was not well, I only stayed a few days with my parents before travelling to Wellington to do a 10-day Buddhist Vipassana meditation retreat. When it was finished, I decided to follow the teacher to Queensland, Australia, to do his next retreat in the bush near Nambour. I remember looking out the window as I was driven up the old Bruce Highway and having the strongest sense that this place was home. After the course I went and lived in West End, Brisbane, for a few months before returning to India. At the end of the 70s I would settle in Queensland. It would become my home. The dream of my father's to settle in Australia became my reality.

Apart from his health and horseracing, the only thing Oscar seemed interested in was reminiscing about his past as an aviator and brooding on the fact that he had been forgotten. Life had lost its meaning for him, as it had also for Jean Batten. Someone who met Batten in 1970 said, 'She just talked about her famous flights. Her entire life seemed to have begun and ended with those years.'[159] As writer Derek Grzelewski points out, 'There were no more goals, no challenges, no way in which to stand in the limelight again. She seemed to live only for her past ... The once supreme navigator had now lost her bearings.'

However, Batten has numerous places in New Zealand named after her, including primary schools, parks and streets. The Auckland Airport International Terminal is named in her honour. Outside the terminal is a bronze statue of Batten waving with her right arm and holding flowers in her left, and inside the terminal the aviatrix's *Percival Gull* – in which she made her solo trip from England to Australia – is suspended from the ceiling. Another bronze sculpture of Batten is located in the main terminal of Rotorua Regional Airport, and memorial panels are installed in the building. I am sure my father resented the fact that she had been recognised but he had been forgotten. There is nothing in New Zealand even today, named after Oscar Garden. No parks or streets, not even in Otumoetai! There are no statues or panels or photographs of him at Auckland Airport. (In July 2019, a portrait of Oscar by Graham Hoete was installed at Tauranga Airport. An article about this is reproduced in the Afterword, p. 249.)

In 1977, New Zealand's TV2 aired a program on the history of Air New Zealand. There was no mention of my father. The interviewer said *Awarua* was brought out to New Zealand by Christopher Griffiths. Griffiths, who was interviewed, failed to correct the interviewer. Both Rose and May (my father's sisters) were furious that his name was not mentioned. In a letter to May, Oscar wrote that it wasn't the first time he had been left out of some of the early history: 'It leaves a sour taste sometimes.' He recalled:

I had hundreds of near misses over the years and am damned lucky to be alive. I lost count of the number of times I should have been killed (even on the Tasman) but I also had lots of bad luck. Still, I survived. I am in fact the only survivor of all the early long-distance pilots up to 1933.

Oscar was still looking for a 'first' or a 'record' to his name. But in 1977, he was not the *only survivor*. While most of his peers had died in crashes, including Bert Hinkler, Charles Ulm, Charles Kingsford Smith and Amy Johnson, there were others who had survived. he was not the only survivor. He had overlooked Cecil Arthur Butler, who broke the England-to- Australia record in November 1931 and had gone on to found Butler Air Transport, which later became Airlines of New South Wales. Butler died on 13 April 1980. And defining the time span as 'up to 1933' conveniently excludes Jean Batten, who was still alive at that time. She died in Majorca in 1982.

Even though my father did not go to any of TEAL's regular reunion gatherings, he and Mum both attended the 1978 occasion to celebrate the merger of New Zealand's domestic carrier National Airways Corporation with Air New Zealand. Morrie Davies, the Chief Executive of Air New Zealand, who had been my father's office boy at Mechanics Bay, gave a speech. He said he had been 'shivering in his shoes' when he went to my father's office for an interview. Evidently Oscar called out during the speech, 'Come off it, Morrie.' Mum recalled, 'Your father was a different man, like the man he used to be when I first met him, people giving him attention.' She was angry to discover the extent of his aviation accomplishments and asked him afterwards, 'How could you keep this from your children?' At this event, my parents were given a free trip around the world, first-class. They took this the following year.

This was the second time Oscar had been in a plane since leaving TEAL. They flew to Honolulu, where they stayed at the penthouse apartment of Illikai Hotel, belonging to Morrie Davis. Oscar complained it was 'too opulent'. From there, they flew to Los Angeles, where they stayed overnight before flying to London for a few days. Mum said Dad stayed in the hotel most of the time watching television, while she had a 'ball' visiting art galleries and museums, and shopping. They then took a train to Edinburgh and from there drove up to Tongue, where they stayed at the Ben Loyal Hotel.

Oscar at the celebration of National Airways Corporation merging with
Air New Zealand in 1978. He is with many of the TEAL pilots he had trained in
the 1940s and is in the front row to the left of the man with a white suit.

Oscar and Helen in Tongue in 1979. They are standing outside Dunvarrich
(Oscar's childhood home) with Gordon and Tott (Jessie) Burr, the owners at
that time.

Mum and Dad visited Oscar's childhood home, *Dunvarrich,* and the current owners, Gordon and Tott (Jessie) Burr, were thrilled to see him. That night Mum and Dad had dinner with the Burrs at *Dunvarrich* and talked long into the night. Knowing how divided my parents were about the family history, I am sure the scandal of Rebecca and Robert's acrimonious split was not mentioned. The next day they visited the original store established by Robert Garden Sr in the late 1800s, as well as the Tongue Primary School and the post-office, where the postmistress, aged 83, remembered my father. He wrote in a postcard to his sister Violet:

Staying here two days. Lots of memories. Very good reception from the Burrs. Son and wife of the Burr who took over from Dad. Very big business now. You can see big new garage and lots of cars in front of the house [Dunvarrich]. Will be in Orkney day after tomorrow. Prices are sky high everywhere.

They then sailed over to Orkney and were welcomed and entertained by Oscar's cousin, Duncan Bain, and members of his family. They visited the old store of Robert Garden Sr, the Merchant Prince of Orkney, as well as the St Magnus Cathedral. They only stayed one night before sailing back to John O'Groats and driving back to Aberdeen. By this time, Oscar had had enough and decided to go home early. Overall, he did not enjoy the trip. He hated the travelling, the noise, staying at strange places and the endless socialising. In spite of his 'love' and 'yearning' for Scotland, he couldn't wait to leave and return to Papakura.

It was around this time that I returned to Brisbane and fell in love with Kevin, a businessman who was a keen cyclist. Kevin was 15 years older than I was. The age difference was the same as that between my parents. But Kevin was not stingy and miserly. He was the opposite – generous, even careless at times. One of the first things he did for me was to build me a racing bicycle.

My first 'real home' was a charming Queenslander in the leafy suburb of Bardon. In 1981, Eamon was born, and 18 months later Natalya. I loved being a mother, and I discovered that I had a flair for renovating and redecorating the various houses we owned over the years. Even though I have a restless spirit, I have been luckier and more astute than my father in real estate decisions, and the improvements always added value. I have *made* money from the houses I have sold!

After I settled in Queensland, I saw my father about five times. I would fly over to Auckland and stay in a motel near my parents' place – Oscar would never have anyone stay – and would pop in to see him. These visits were short, maybe an hour at the most. It was all my father could cope with. It was all I could cope with. I would always feel uncomfortable around him. I could never be myself. The fear I had of him just never went away, even when I was an adult. He would invariably complain about the pain, 'My head goes right up here,' he used to say, shooting his hand up above his head. Each time I went over to New Zealand, I would soon feel sad and depressed and want to return home to Queensland. Each time I went to say goodbye, if I tried to give him a hug he would recoil and put his hand up to his forehead.

Even though my father complained that he had been forgotten, he didn't make it easy for people to write about him, to tell his story, because of his constant moving. Nevertheless, between 1960 and 1994 about 15 articles and book chapters on Oscar Garden were published (see Appendix 1). In his 1979 book *Airline* Ian Driscoll devotes a whole chapter – albeit a short one – to Oscar's flying career. Driscoll writes, 'Garden must be the most unnoticed of New Zealand's airline pioneers. It is the paradox of the professional pilot that the more competently and therefore uneventfully he flies, then completely does his individuality disappear into anonymity.'[160]

In 1982, in *NZ Wings*, John King wrote a lengthy article called, 'Whatever happened to OSCAR GARDEN?' He writes:

Oscar in 1990. He was always able to put on a cheerful face to outsiders.

Pilots who flew solo 50 or more years ago are not too common these days. Pilots who were flying commercially then are still less common. And those who flew from England to Australia, alone in an open cockpit biplane more than half a century in the past, and are still around to talk about it can be counted on the thumbs of one hand.

King mentions that 35 years ago, after a disagreement with TEAL over its future direction and policy, Oscar Garden severed his connections with aviation, but he now regrets it. These days, King says, he 'obviously enjoys talking about flying'.

There were also full-page features, including two in 1984 in Scotland's *Northern Times*: 'Salute to a Great Aviator from Tongue' and 'Tribute to road and air pioneers'. And in 1990, Murray Patterson wrote a long feature 'Sundowner of the Skies' for Christchurch's *Central Canterbury News*. Dad was chuffed with these. His spirit would be lifted when people dipped into his past, a time when he was happy, healthy and freer. For brief moments he could forget about his health. However, even though he had regrets about severing ties with the world of aviation, which had led in part to him being forgotten, he could not get over what happened to him at TEAL. Joy Hanna (nee Paterson), one of those first six stewardesses selected by Oscar in 1946, told me that he was still feeling hurt and bitter when she went out to visit him a few years before he died.

In the last 10 years of his life, my father's health problems worsened. He had difficulties sleeping and resorted to taking sleeping tablets. He had a variety of procedures on his left supra-orbital nerve. This nerve was first divided in 1976, and he had at least four subsequent operations, but they failed to help. His obsession with his health and fixation with surgery led one doctor to write, 'The man might be a potential "Munchhausen".' He saw almost every ear and nose surgeon in the North Island.

In 1988 he told a neurologist that the persistent pain above his left eyebrow was like a sharp instrument boring through his skull into his brain. He told another specialist the pain in his left eyebrow was a million times worse than it has ever been before, all because of the wrong sutures used by a surgeon who he would not name because 'he quite liked that chap'. The specialist noted that this is somewhat unusual because Oscar has not liked many of the other people who have treated him, and yet 'he is capable of holding a very cheerful account about how terrible it is and actually exhibits almost no evidence of being in pain, whatsoever.' Oscar was advised to go back to the surgeon he would not name and discuss it face to face as he was 'spending a considerable amount of time brewing over his imagined grievances'.

Of course, Dad would not have done this. He was incapable of resolving conflicts. It was fairly typical of people of his generation. Feelings were frozen and things left to fester. It was just one more layer of the huge plank of resentment Oscar carried, going back to his childhood and being sent to the Dollar Academy; the family being disinherited from the Robert Garden fortune; TEAL choosing more flying boats rather than the land-based DC4s he had lined up from America; and then missing out on the top job at TEAL after being The Boss all those years. And now he believed incompetent surgeons had damaged him.

These years were also miserable for Mum, as she was caught up in Oscar's ongoing health dramas and going along with him to various doctors. Reflecting on this time with him she said,

It wasn't a dull life, but fraught with difficulties. He was so self-centred. He was the meanest man I've ever known. He was miserly. But he had far more good points than I appreciated. He was very tenacious. It is sad looking back, as he was a capable, clever man but nothing ever came together. He had a lump on his shoulder that coloured and soured everything else. I wanted to leave him early on, would have been happy to, but later on I could never have left him as he was a pathetic figure on his own. He mellowed in the last few years and really appreciated me.

He said towards the end, 'I don't know what I would have done without you.' Maybe it was too much for him, being a father and breadwinner. He wasn't happy with me. He achieved a lot. Some people admired him; others were jealous. A few people in Tauranga said he grew tomatoes as he flew a plane. A born perfectionist. He was excellent at everything he did: at being a pilot, growing tomatoes ... but not a father or husband!

Mum recalled that once, soon after he retired, she decided to leave him. She was in their bedroom packing her suitcases when Dad walked in. Somehow, she fell over one of the suitcases and they both burst out laughing. Mum told me he then looked forlorn and said, 'I just can't help it. I can't help myself.'

In late 2005, I spoke on the phone to Mary Ewart, one of my mother's closest friends, who by that time was in a nursing home in Tauranga. I had not had any contact with her since I was a teenager. When I asked if she had been aware of my father's aviation feats, she suddenly fired up. 'It used to make me absolutely furious to hear the men, typical of men, you know, go on and on about your father's flying achievements when he used to treat your mother and you children so abominably.' She said she admired his tenacity, but didn't like the way 'he treated your mother or you children. I loved your mother and her mother [Ivy].' I was taken aback. I thought no one knew what had gone on behind our closed doors.

On one of my visits, however, Dad brightened up for a while and forgot about his head pain. I asked him how he went to the toilet on *Kia Ora*. But he didn't answer. He only grinned. He went on to tell me how he saw UFOs on his 1930 flight in *Kia Ora*. On another visit, we talked about religion, which he said he never had to study as his mother taught him everything. He said he believed in the coming 'rapture' and that Christ would return and take him away on a flying saucer. I told him I thought that was nonsense. He was very surprised when I told him I was an atheist and said he thought that I, out of all his children, would be a Christian and believe in Jesus. I did not tell him that religion, rather than being his saviour, had done him little good. He had never been able to throw off the cold, repressive force of Scottish Calvinism.

In 1990 my marriage ended. After we moved to Maleny it was clear that Kevin and I were moving in different directions. Rather than our lives becoming simpler and less stressful, Kevin threw himself into work, and we hardly saw him. I realised that in many respects I had married my father. Kevin is odd and eccentric and can be narcissistic and self-absorbed. If I became sick it was invariably 'not his reality'. He wanted me to be strong, capable and organised. He could not be there for me if I was vulnerable and needing help. Kevin is also a strong advocate of corporal punishment and at times could be quite harsh with the children. He was patriarchal in his attitudes. My place was in the home. I was the homemaker; he was the breadwinner. Like Oscar, he talks a lot about his health and his various aches and pains (some from past cycling injuries).

In spite of having counselling, I could hang on no longer. It was a heart-wrenching decision, and if I had my time again, I would do things differently. But I have never regretted my decision that the relationship had come to an end. Although I had a fantasy of us co-parenting, this was not to be. Kevin moved back to Brisbane, and I was a single mum with no job! The next few years would be a struggle for me financially, but it was also a time for tremendous growth as I threw myself into therapy. I stopped running from my past, sought help, and began to turn my ghosts into my ancestors. Dr Norman Doidge, author of *The Brain That Changes Itself*, explains, 'We are often haunted by important relationships from the past that influence us unconsciously in the present. As we work through them, they go from haunting us to becoming simply part of our history.' I was lucky. Some people stay in dead or toxic relationships for years, for decades, for their whole life. Like my mother. She often said to me, 'Just don't do what I did. Get trapped like me.'

In 1992, I found the courage to write Dad a letter, to be honest with him for the first time in my life. I told him how frightened I had been of him as a child, how much I suffered. He was shocked and told Mum to write and tell me he wanted no more contact. I saw him again a few years later. I had gone to South Auckland to do a five-day Elisabeth Kübler-Ross emotional healing course to externalise some of my suppressed rage and fear towards him, and afterwards visited my parents. There was no mention of my letter. The conversation was as stilted and strained as it always had been.

The Garden family tree is blighted, cursed not only by alcoholism, but also by mental illness and violence. This has caused intergenerational trauma that has had a ripple effect on my own life. I did not just inherit this pattern from the Gardens. It also came from my mother. She made allowances for bad behaviour; she excused my grandfather's (Robert Garden Jr's) alcoholism. She felt sorry for him, just as she felt sorry for my father.

Three weeks before my father passed away, I was standing at the stove cooking when suddenly I had the strongest feeling he was going to die very soon. I rang Mum and said, 'I think Dad's going to die soon.' She groaned, 'If only. I wish.' Then we laughed and wondered whether he would hang around for years. Two weeks later Mum rang to say Dad had been taken to Middlemore Hospital by ambulance and that the doctor said he only had a few days to live. I began making preparations to fly over, but later that day Mum told me not to come because he had picked up and there was talk of putting him in a nursing home. He also said he didn't want to see anyone. A few days later he was dead. He died alone, in the early morning of 2 June 1997. The cause of death was noted as 'Respiratory failure – days; lung cancer – years.' And yet in all the medical notes I obtained there is no mention of lung cancer. The hospital notes mention his acute anxiety. Mum said that a few days before he died, he told her, 'Well I will be up there in heaven because I haven't done anything wrong.'

I flew to Auckland that morning with my daughter Natalya. We were the only ones to be there with Mum for the first few days. Anna was in London. Robert was stranded in Palmerston North because his partner,

Marquita, had broken her leg orienteering in the Manawatau (south of the North Island). Luckily, they both had stopped in at Middlemore Hospital and spent some time with our father on the way there.

The next day Mum and I went to the morgue to say goodbye. My father was lying there on a high bed with a white sheet covering his body with only his head showing. I put my hand on his cold clammy forehead and read the Lord's Prayer. My mother didn't touch him, but said he looked like Jesus. She also lent over and whispered under her breath that he was a miserly bastard. I said, 'He is not here, Mum.' There was no funeral, as my father had bequeathed his body to Auckland Hospital for medical research. A few years later, his ashes were scattered on the waters of Mechanics Bay. Between 1940 and 1947 the big birds, *Awarua* and *Aotearoa*, with Oscar at the helm, had lumbered across this bay and descended gracefully to the water, sending a plume of spray into the air upon landing.

My father's death was barely mentioned in New Zealand newspapers. I thought that at least on his death he'd at last be remembered and acknowledged. I felt crushed. I needed to have a famous father. From when I was a child, the idea that he had once been this other person, a famous adventurous aviator, had somehow made his coldness and cruelty a little more bearable. But maybe that was my fantasy. What he had done wasn't that important. It was just him big-noting himself, as Mum used to say.

I had a dream a few weeks after his death. I went into my lounge and knew Oscar had been there. He had left this large wooden chest, much like the camphor chest he used to keep his flying things in. When I opened the chest there was a beautifully carved, old-fashioned telephone. I was thrilled. I knew [in the dream] that it meant I could ring him up whenever I wanted. Years later when I began to dig up his past, I'd often have conversations with him in my head. I'd tell him how angry or sad or amazed or astonished I felt. And I'd say, 'I'm telling *everyone* what I have found.'

I can only remember one thing my father praised me for, admired in me, and that was the ability to find things, to untangle knots. That skill has been put to good use in tracking down much of this story. His contributions to aviation spanned almost two decades. His epic flight in 1930 – especially the treacherous crossing from Wyndham to Alice Springs – ranks with the achievements of Charles Kingsford Smith, Bert Hinkler and Amy Johnson, who all died in crashes. Unlike his peers he survived to contribute much more. Yet what is his legacy? There is nothing anywhere. In spite of his flaws and foibles, Oscar Garden – my odd father – is one of history's great aviators. He deserves to be remembered.

There are times when I am out on my gorgeous mint-and-rocket-red Specialized Ruby bike, pedalling down one of the hills on the Sunshine Coast hinterland, even reaching speeds of 75 kilometres per hour, and I think of my father. I think of how he would have felt in his Gipsy Moth all those years ago, high above the earth, the rush of wind against him. A huge grin spreads over my face. It is the most glorious feeling. I am flying. I am free.

AFTERWORD

After the release of the first edition of *Sundowner of the Skies,* two unexpected things happened. One was thrilling, the other was deeply distressing, if not traumatic.

- A large mural of my father was unveiled at Tauranga Airport and now hangs in the Departure Lounge.

- My sister published her own book on our father.

Tauranga Airport: Oscar Garden no longer the forgotten aviator.

There is now a wonderful portrait of Dad installed at Tauranga Airport, New Zealand. Ingrid (Alys) Wicksteed the daughter of Mary Revfeim, a close friend of Mum's, gave a copy of my book to internationally renowned Māori artist Graham Hoete (known as Mr G) and said, 'You must do a portrait of Oscar.' And so he did. Alys has had a close friendship with the Hoete family, who also live in the Bay of Plenty, for many years.

I was at the airport for the unveiling and the Māori blessing – a very moving experience. Alys was there, along with the Hoete family, some Garden cousins and Alastair Barclay. Alastair is the son of Dad's cousin, Robin Barclay, who was our family doctor growing up.

The portrait now has an information stand next to it, the text for which I provided. It also features the cover of my book.

Sunlive, 12 August 2019
Tauranga's 'forgotten aviator'
honoured with mural by Kate Wells

https://sunlive.co.nz/news/217664-taurangas-forgotten-aviator-honoured-mural.html

Graham Hoete, or more commonly known as Mr G, unveiled his newest piece at the new Tauranga Airport terminal.

Mr G's work of art is a circular portrait of the late Oscar Garden, the first New Zealand resident to fly from the United Kingdom to Australia.

Tauranga Airport approached Mr G three months ago to create a feature piece for the new complex, and not long after, he learned about Oscar's story through Ingrid Wicksteed and thought it would be fitting to construct a mural of 'the forgotten aviator'.

"Ingrid was saying it would be cool if I could paint some kind of tribute mural of him somewhere in Tauranga because he lived here for 26 years," says Mr G.

"She told me his story and I was pretty much blown away, and I said actually, I've got the perfect spot for this."

After meeting with the council and airport representatives, Mr G went about his work and yesterday, he revealed his piece at a small gathering.

"My priority was presenting it to Mary, Oscar's daughter, just in a nice, respectful and intimate fashion.

"I wanted to make sure Oscar had a strong connection to Tauranga Moana, but also the fact that he was an aviation legend," says Mr G.

"It's quite funny, he brought this second-hand Gipsy Moth plane, flew it all the way from England to Australia, knowing the plane was called Kia Ora as well, he had a kiwi battler mentality.

"He went out and gave it a go and did it on a shoestring budget, and he was a humble man who didn't like to talk about himself."

Mr G says Oscar has unfortunately been a forgotten aviator, but he wants his art piece to educate people, so Oscar can be remembered.

The piece itself is a painted portrait, and in the frame Mr G incorporated Edinburg Castle and the Scottish tartan on the left-hand side to acknowledge his Scottish heritage, and on the right-hand side he has painted Mauao and a carving of a koru.

"It will bring back his connection to Tauranga Moana and Aotearoa."

Me with Graham Hoete at the unveiling of Dad's portrait on 11 August 2019.

My Sister's Book

I was delighted that Steve Braunias accepted my article for his Reading Room on *Newsroom*. He said: 'What a bizarre story! I love it ... The bigger portrait, with its psychological depth, is fascinating – this is a terrific yarn.' It was published on 5 April 2021. Steve told me it was a 'smash hit and widely read'.

https://www.newsroom.co.nz/sister-vs-sister

'Why my sister's book is a stab in the back'

Two sisters have written books about their father. One feels betrayed

I wrote a book about my father, the great Tauranga aviator Oscar Garden. Then my sister Annamaria did. My father's epic solo flight from London to Australia in 1930 is featured in my book *Sundowner of the Skies: The story of Oscar Garden, the forgotten aviator,* published by New Holland in 2019. But I first heard about my sister's book *Oscar Garden: A tale of one man's love of flying* in October last year, the day before it was published. A cousin sent me an email: "Have you seen this"?

It was a complete shock. I felt like I'd been stabbed in the back.

I discovered that no one in the family, apart from my brother Robert, knew she was writing it. She told me later she didn't want me to know in case I tried to stop it from being published: "I didn't know what the grounds for stopping it would be. I thought you could do anything."

Robert told me, "She got me to swear I wouldn't tell you. She did it pretty quickly, after your book was out, and I suspect she wanted to put a different perspective on it keeping away from family issues, as she didn't like that."

A part of me felt embarrassed. I had grown up feeling shame around my birth family, how strange we were. I couldn't wait to leave home, to get right away from my odd, dysfunctional family. "The mad Gardens", Mum called us.

My father was born in 1903 in Tongue, in the far north of Scotland, and emigrated to New Zealand in 1921. In 1937, he married Greta Norlén who he had met in Stockholm while doing night-flights; she was a receptionist at the hotel where he stayed. Their daughter Margareta (who later married novelist Maurice Gee) was born in 1940. They separated in 1944, and he met my mother Helen Lovell in 1945.

When I began to dig up my father's story in 2005, there was virtually nothing online – a Google search revealed a single entry on Oscar Garden, in the *Dictionary of New Zealand Biography*. My father was an unsung and forgotten hero of pioneer aviation until Sundowner of the Skies was launched.

Then I found my younger sister Annamaria had whipped up a book behind my back. She mentions in her author's note: "It took only eight months to write the basics … My brother, Robert, supported me totally in this."

*

Why, then, did my sister write this book? In the author's note, she writes: "I read my sister's biography … This was good but it was her version not my own. I needed to write my own. I wanted to tell a story that gave a complete picture of my father's life showing what an extraordinary man he was. Having had a good relationship with him I feel I am in a good position to write his story."

Fair enough. We are all entitled to write our own stories, our own versions. Her rendition of our father as a dashing, courageous aviator is actually not much different from mine – but miles apart in her rendition of Oscar Garden the man.

She recalls Dad telling "exciting stories" about his flying years when she was a child. My recollection is different. Dad worked long hours, seven days a week; when he came inside, we were not to disturb him. After our evening meal (no talking at the table) we were shooed outside. Although I was vaguely aware of Dad's life as an aviator, I don't recall him talking to us about his flying adventures. He seldom talked to us about anything, except to bark orders. He commanded our family as if he was still the captain of a flying boat.

A week after her book's release, Annamaria wrote on the NZ Book-lovers site, "I disagreed so strongly with my sister's rendition of my father that I put pen to paper and wrote furiously putting together my tale on Dad. When my brother read it, he said 'You and my sister had two different fathers'. He agreed with my version as being a closer picture of Dad."

I felt devastated reading their public attack on their own sister. I thought we'd always been on the same page about our father. Annamaria and Robert had both read the draft manuscript of *Sundowner of the Skies* that I sent to family members. I was relieved when no-one came back and said, that is not correct, that did not happen, Oscar was not like that. No-one said, don't write about family issues.

But now she and Robert are saying my book is, in effect, a lie.

*

My sister's book makes no mention of Dad's gambling addiction, his abuse, his mental struggles, including depression. No mention he was a miser – in Mum's words, "the meanest man I've ever known." No mention that Dad recoiled from human touch. He never hugged or kissed my mother, not even a peck on the cheek. He never held her hand, though sometimes clutched her wrist, even her throat. Mum said: "He had a cold streak, yet when a bird flew into the side of the glasshouse he would sit there with a saucer of water and some crumbs and stroke it. He wouldn't do this with humans."

Annamaria says he was "occasionally moving house". That's an understatement. Mum said, "There was always something wrong. Nothing was ever right for Oscar. On the move all the time." In their first 35 years together, they moved 23 times. Sometimes he sold up within nine months. Once he bought the place next door. Mum said that was an easy move. She just chucked stuff over the fence.

In *Sundowner of the Skies*, I interviewed many people, including relatives, friends of Mum, and pilots Dad trained. I included Mum's story, too. She was still alive when I began working on my book and wanted it to be a 'warts and all' account. She recalled: "He was excellent at everything he did, being a pilot and growing tomatoes, but not a father or husband." She'd say, "He was a bastard of a father. And a bastard of a husband."

Our half-sister Margareta and her husband Maurice Gee were a huge support during the research and writing of *Sundowner of the Skies*. We exchanged hundreds of emails. When the book was published, Maurice wrote, "I read with huge interest and admiration. What a story, what a character, (almost said what a monster?). He's an enigma, his poles are so far apart it's hard to believe he was just one man. Congratulations on a great story well told (How the hell did you survive?)"

Throughout her book, my sister emphasises Dad's positivity, "his optimistic nature", how much he "loved" this or that. But he was a negative and bitter person. His first marriage was acrimonious: Margareta recalls her mother Greta screaming and crying. His marriage to Mum was miserable: "We often fell out and went for days where we would not speak to each other. He had a lump on his shoulder that coloured and soured everything."

Annamaria's book mentions the "great houses" we lived in. When I was eight and she was six, we moved to a plain white stucco building with only two bedrooms. Annamaria and I had to stay in a small wooden hut about 100 yards away from the house; we'd go to the main house for meals and to have a bath. The hut had no internal walls or doors, only curtains. It had an outside dunny that stunk and was shrouded with spiderwebs; Dad would not let us use toilet paper, only newspaper. During storms sleeping in the hut was terrifying. I'd hide under the bed covers listening to the sound of the wind shaking branches of the large willow tree hanging over the roof.

My father would not have liked my book *Sundowner of the Skies*. My sister's book *Oscar Garden: A tale of one man's love of flying* is the book he would have wanted. He didn't just soar through the skies: he crash-landed the journey of his life on earth. And we are still picking up the pieces.

Appendix 1

Articles or book chapters on Oscar Garden published 1960–1994, after he left TEAL

1960, Leo White, 'This and That', *Whites Aviation*, p. 32.

1964, Dennis Burley, 'Otumoetai is now home to "Sundowner of the skies"', *Bay of Plenty Times*, 19 February.

1970, 'Oscar Garden – where are you?', *Eastern Evening News*, 6 November, p. 10.

1971, 'The epic flight of Mr Oscar Garden', *Eastern Evening News*.

1971, 'Flight to Australia', *Wings*, Norfolk and Norwich Aero Club, pp.26–31.

1979, Ian Driscoll, 'Garden', *Airline: the making of a national flag carrier*, Auckland: Shortland Publications, pp. 121–129. (Also pp. 143–145.)

1982, John King, 'Whatever happened to…Oscar Garden?', *New Zealand Wings*, pp. 42–45.

1984, 'Salute to a Great Aviator from Tongue', *The Northern Times*, 6 January, p. 4.

1984, 'Tribute to road and air pioneers', *The Northern Times*, 6 January.

1985, Ted Wixted, 'Oscar Garden', *North West Aerial Frontier 1919–1934*, Brisbane: Boolarong Publication, pp. 91–92.

1990, Robert Mannon, 'Adventurous budget traveller', *The Dominion Sunday Times*, 4 November, p. 7.

1990, Neil Rennie, 'Captain Oscar Garden', *Conquering Isolation*, Auckland: Heinemann Reed, p. 44.

1990, Jack Leigh, 'Hot-footing it to Sydney', *New Zealand Herald*, 21 April.

1990, Murray Patterson, 'Sundowner of the Skies', *Central Canterbury News*, 25 July, p. 6 & p. 14.

1994, Maurice McGreal, *A Noble Chance: one pilot's life*, Wellington: McGreal, p. 84 & p. 92.

Appendix 2

My Articles

2021, 'The incredible exploits of Oscar Garden', *Flypast*, 24 February.

2020, 'Sundowner of the Skies, *Flypast*, pp. 90–95.

2019, 'Oscar Garden: a Scottish-born Aviator', *The Scottish Banner*, Vol. 43, No. 5, pp. 30–31.

2013, 'The Sundowner of the Skies', *The Aviation Historian*, Iss. 5, pp. 12–25.

2008, 'Flying is Good for you', *Flight Path*, Vol. 19, No. 2, pp. 20–7.

2007, 'Sundowner of the Skies', *Living Orkney*, Iss. 19, June, pp. 14–25

2007, 'The Plane Facts', *Weekend Australian*, February 10, Travel, p. 5.

2007, 'Tracking the Truth', *Dotlit: the online journal of creative writing*, QUT, Vol. 6, Iss.1.

2007, 'He needed a drink, but they brought him boiled eggs!', *Northern Times*, January 19, p. 7.

2007, 'New motor service helped transform life in the North', *Northern Times*, January 12, p. 7.

2006, 'The First Landing', *Flight Journal* (Connecticut), December, pp.42–3.

2006, 'Flying is Good for you', *LogBook*, (Florida), Vol. 7, No. 4, pp. 28–33.

2006, 'Sunday Flying, Oscar Garden Charged', *New Zealand Memories*, Iss. 62, October/November, pp. 14–18.

2006, 'Plane Sailing', *The Southland Times*, Inform section, February 25, pp. C1- C2.

2006, 'Oscar for a Bay Aviator', *Bay of Plenty Times*, January 11, p. 13.

2005, 'Historical Hiccups in the South Island of New Zealand', *Flightpath*, Vol. 17, No. 2, pp. 28–31.

2005, 'Sundowner of the Skies', *Logbook* (Florida), Vol. 6, No. 4, pp. 22–9.

2005, 'Landing on Stewart Island', *New Zealand Geographic*, No. 76, pp. 20–3.

2005, 'Flight from the Blue', *The Christchurch Press*, October 15, Mainlander D7.

2005, 'When Sunday flying trips were banned', *Timaru Herald*, 6 September, p. 9.

2005, 'Off on a Wing and No Fear', *Timaru Herald*, 16 July, p. 21.

2005, 'To Australia on Two Spare Springs', *Otago Daily Times*, July 2–3, p. 4.

2005, 'Sundowner of the Skies', *The Journal of the Aviation Historical Society of Australia Inc.*, Vol. 36, No. 2, pp. 60–3.

2005, 'Oscar Garden: An Unsung Hero', *Pacific WINGS*, June, pp. 11–13.

2005, 'Sundowner of the Skies – Mary Garden takes flight with her father', *Weekend Financial Review*, 24–8 March, pp. 6–7 Review section.

Notes

1.   He was actually the fifth, but Francis Chichester is often overlooked because he had to wait several weeks in Libya for a replacement propeller to be sent over from England.

2.   Margareta Gee & Stephen Berry 2000, 'Garden, Oscar', *Dictionary of New Zealand Biography*, Vol. 5, www.TeAra.govt.nz/en/biographies/5g4/garden-oscar

3.   Collector of airmail stamps and covers; the covers need to have been 'carried on an aerial flight and bearing evidence of being flown', www.americanairmailsociety. org/resources/collecting-airmail/safe-landing

4.   These logbooks are the Engine Logbook and the Aircraft Logbook: 8/11/1927 to 11/06/1934. In June 1934, new log books were started, and it is not known what happened to those ones.

5.   *Sydney Morning Herald*, 18 October 1930, p. 15.

6.   *The Sun*, 5 November 1930, p. 13.

7.   *The New Zealand Herald*, 20 June 1945; *New Zealand Wings*, May 1947, p. 29.

8.   Ian Driscoll 1979, 'Garden', *Airline*, Auckland: Shortland Publications, p. 121.

9.   Howard Hazell 2010, *The Orcadian Book of the Twentieth Century*, Kirkwall: The Orcadian Ltd.

10.   Jim A. Johnston 1987, 'Robert Garden: Orkney merchant emperor' in *North Sutherland Studies*, Scottish Vernacular Buildings Working Group, Edinburgh, pp. 54–61, p. 54.

11.   Christopher J. Uncles 2003, *Memories of North and West Sutherland*, Ayrshire, UK: Stenlake Publishing, p. 73.

12.   Alexander McLeod, *Tanera Island*, unknown date. freepages.genealogy.rootsweb. ancestry.com/~coigach/tanera2.htm

13.   I have compared the relative real wealth which uses the RPI on this site: www. measuringworth.com/calculators/ukcompare

14.   Handwritten letter of a conversation with Embla Mooney by Ernest Marwick, 17 February 1963, Ernest Marwick collection, Orkney Archives.

15.   www.criterion.com/current/posts/3130-breaking-thewaves breaking-the-rules

16.   In the mid to late 19th, and early 20th century, these addresses were a way to thank people for significant contributions. They were art forms in themselves and often used highly sophisticated illustration techniques and calligraphy. www.nma.gov. au/ exhibitions/irish_in_australia/behind_the_scenes/illuminated_addresses

17.   The *Northern Times*, 18 February 1909.

18.   Robert took the address when he moved to New Zealand in 1915. After he died, it was left to May. Rose looked after it for many years before passing it on to my father who left it to my brother, Robert. Robert gave it to me in 2007, where it has hung on my lounge wall for some years. In 2019, the family decided to gift it to Strathnaver Museum, north Scotland: it was packaged up and shipped over.

19.   Petition Cs252/355, 9 September 1913, National Archives of Scotland.

20.   Petition Cs253/262, 28 October, 1913, National Archives of Scotland.

21. Meagan Lee Butler 2014, '"Husbands without wives, and wives without husbands": divorce and separation in Scotland, c. 1830–1890', theses.gla. ac.uk/5264/1/2014butlerphd.pdf
22. Catherine/Kate was a local girl, born in Tongue on 20 February 1873.
23. 270 Berryman Road, Manchester.
24. Rosalie Holland 1990, *Cave 1850–1990*, Cave: Cave Country Women's Institute, p. 43.
25. Ibid, p. 12.
26. Robin Charteris, *Otago Daily Times*, 6 April 1990.
27. 'Christchurch man's plan to fly from England to N.Z.', *The Sun* (England), 15 October 1930.
28. Marion Shepherd 1989, *Some of my Yesterdays*, Invercargill: Craig Printing Co., pp.100–101.
29. First Women's Cycling Club in Australasia formed, nzhistory.govt.nz/page/ first- womens-cycling-club-australasia-formed
30. 'Cycling in Christchurch: Then and Now', www.stuff.co.nz/thepress/news/70365737/ Cycling-in-Christchurch-Then-and-Now
31. 'The 1920s Overview', nzhistory.govt.nz/culture/the-1920s/overview
32. 'Speeding Alleged', *Ellesmere Guardian*, 28 January 1927, p. 4.
33. Hampton, Dan 2017, *The Flight: Charles Lindbergh's daring and immortal 1927 transatlantic crossing*, New York: HarperCollins, blurb.
34. Ian Mackersey 1998, *Smithy: the life of Sir Charles Kingsford Smith*, London: Little Brown and Company, p. 159.
35. 'Mr Oscar Garden's Solo Flight from England', *The Sydney Mail*, 12 November 1930, p. 17.
36. *The Sun* (Sydney), 5 Nov 1930, p. 13.
37. 'End of long flight in sight', *The Advertiser*, 6 November 1930, p. 19.
38. Selfridges closed its aviation department in 1936.
39. Aircraft dope is a plasticized lacquer, which tightens and stiffens the fabric, and makes them airtight and waterproof.
40. *The Sun* (England), 15 October 1930.
41. *The Sun* (England), 9 November 1930, p. 2.
42. Ibid.
43. The Hon. Mrs. Victor Bruce 1931, *The Bluebird's Flight*, London: Chapman & Hall Ltd, p. 80.
44. Ibid, p. 82.
45. *The Straits Times*.
46. The Hon. Mrs. Victor Bruce 1931, *The Bluebird's Flight*, London: Chapman & Hall Ltd, p. 91.
47. Ibid, p. 92.
48. In his log book, my father forgot to include 31 October so all the dates and places are wrong after the Rangoon entry.
49. The flight had taken 18 days and 11 hours. He'd left Lympne at 6:18am and arrived at Wyndham at 5.00pm, but 9.5 hours' time difference between England and Australian was allowed. See: 'Dramatic Air Race Ends', *The Border Watch*, 21 October, 1930, p. 1.

50. 'Oscar Garden reaches Wyndham: 18 days from England', *Sydney Morning Herald*, 5 November 1930.

51. 'Mother thankful', *Sydney Morning Herald*, 6 November 1930.

52. *Isle of Man Daily*, 5 November 1930.

53. 'Route and time: best amateur effort', *The Evening Post*, 25 November, 1930, p. 11.

54. 'Great achievement. Oscar Garden's leisurely flight from London to Canberra: First Australian Aerial Landing at Wyndham', *Sunday Times* (Perth), 9 November 1930, p. 3.

55. 'Greatest danger was starvation', *Newcastle Sun*, 2 July 1931, p. 7.

56. 'Blew in: Sky Sundowner', *The Sun* (Sydney), 5 November 1930, p. 13.

57. 'Out among the people' [by Rufus], *Advertiser and Register*, 21 April 1931.

58. 'Flyer Garden Today', *Daily Guardian*, 7 November 1930, p. 1.

59. 'Mr Garden's Flight: Arrival at Broken Hill', *Argus*, 7 November 1930.

60. 'Oscar Garden's flight', *Barrier Miner*, 7 November 1930, p. 1.

61. 'Girl in Green was waiting: flyer Garden met her at Mascot', *The Daily Guardian*, 8 November 1930.

62. nla.gov.au/nla.obj-161206403/view; nla.gov.au/nla. obj-161413436/view

63. paperspast.natlib.govt.nz/newspapers/As19380520.2.120.4?query=whye

64. *The Daily Guardian*, 7 November 1930, p. 5.

65. *The Daily Guardian*, 7 November 1930, p. 5.

66. 'Arrives in Sydney: Welcome at Mascot', *Sydney Morning Herald*, 8 November 1930, p. 13.

67. 'Oscar Garden at Sydney', *The Christchurch Press*, 8 November 1930.

68. *The Sun*, 7 November, p. 10.

69. Marion Shepherd 1989, *Some of my Yesterdays*, Invercargill: Craig Printing, p. 116.

70. *Isle of Man Examiner*, 7 November 1930.

71. Scott was an English aviator who settled in Australia in 1926. He committed suicide on 15 April 1946 using his military issue revolver.

72. *Wings*, Norfolk & Norwich Aero Club Ltd, 12 November 1971.

73. Warren Manger 2016, 'Mystery behind the death of aviator Amy Johnson may finally have been solved', *Mirror*, 29 December.www.mirror.co.uk/news/uk-news/mystery-behind-death-aviator-amy-9528648

74. 'Oscar Garden's Flight', *The Evening Post*, 14 November 1930, p. 9.

75. *The Daily Guardian*, 8 November 1930.

76. 'Another Tasman flight', *New Zealand Herald*, 6 November 1930, p. 10.

77. Terry Gwynne-Jones 1991, *Farther and Faster: Aviation's Adventuring Years, 1909–1939*, NSW: Allen & Unwin, p. 276.

78. 'Mr Oscar Garden's flight: mayoral welcome arranged', *Otago Daily Times*, 25 November 1930, p. 30.

79. 'Reception at Wellington today', *The Press*, 25 November 1930, p. 13.

80. 'Welcomed home', *The Evening Post*, 26 November 1930, p. 6.

81. 'Oscar Garden talks to Smithy', *Horowhenua Chronicle*, 26 November 1930, p. 8.

82. Douglas Walker 1986, *The Air Mails of New Zealand: Vol. 2 – the overseas flights 1928–1940*, The Air Mail Society of New Zealand, p. 42.

83. ralphwatson.scienceontheweb.net/profile.html

84. 'Oscar Garden arrives', *Christchurch Press*, 1 December 1930, p.17.
85. Ibid, p.17.
86. 'Blazing the trail: pioneers of the air', *Evening Star*, 4 December 1930, p. 17.
87. 'Lady in Distress: Airman's timely gallantry', *Poverty Bay Herald*, 8 December, 1930, p. 19.
88. 'Blazing the trail: pioneers of the air', *Evening Star*, 4 December 1930, p. 17.
89. Ibid.
90. Ian Mackersey 1992, *Jean Batten: The Garbo of the Skies*, London: Warner Books, p. 75.
91. 'Oscar Garden in New Zealand: His own account of his experiences', *The Isle of Man Times*, date unknown (early 1931).
92. 'Them Homies!', *Auckland Star*, 18 December 1930, p. 6.
93. 'Who are New Zealanders?', *Auckland Star*, 1 December 1930, p. 6.
94. 'Mr. Oscar Garden's Flight', *Auckland Star*, 20 December 1930, p. 8.
95. Rinker Buck 2001, *If We Had Wings: the enduring dream of flight*, New York: Crown Publishing.
96. 'Aviator honoured', *Ellesmere Guardian*, 30 December 1930, p. 5.
97. www.rootsweb.ancestry.com/~nzlscant/aero.htm
98. *Otago Witness*, 10 February 1931.
99. Mary Garden, 'Flight from the Blue', *Christchurch Press*, 15 October 2005, Mainlander D7.
100. Kaituhituhi Valledor-Lukey 2011, 'Three times ordinary', *Te Karaka*, pp. 17–18.
101. Robin Hyde 1937, 'Isle of the Glowing sky – Stewart Island and a Glass Box', *The New Zealand Railways Magazine*, Vol. 11, Iss. 11, 1 February, p. 27.
102. Mary Garden 2006, 'Plane sailing', *The Southland Times*, 25 January, pp. C1–C2.
103. On 17 May 1933, Mullan sold the plane to M. A. Scott of Hamilton. Scott in turn sold it to the Auckland Aero Club on 12 September 1933. The Auckland Aero Club had established a branch at Te Rapa using D.V. Bryant's farm on Sandwich Road. They used ZK-ACK to ferry instructors to Te Rapa each weekend, and eventually gifted the plane to the Waikato Aero club on 5 December 1937. On 11 October 1939, at the outbreak of World War Two, *Kia Ora* was impressed into RNZAF for a cost of £350 as NZ510. Used by 2 EFTs, New Plymouth. Converted to INST37 in mid-1941 with Whangarei ATC. Written off books at Hobsonville on 11 June 1946 and broken up.
104. *News Chronicle*, 8 July 1931.
105. 'Oscar Garden at Douglas: Intrepid airman visits his native island', *Isle of Man Times*, 8 July 1931.
106. www.afleetingpeace.org/index.php/14-business-and-pleasure/156-the-aerial-circuses
107. Spartan three-seaters became one of the mainstays of the pleasure flight trade in the 1930s.
108. 'Kingsford Smith: arrival in England', *Argus*, 9 October 1931, p. 7.
109. Ian Mackersey 1998, *Smithy: the life of Sir Charles Kingsford Smith*, London: Little Brown and Company, pp. 259–262.
110. Gerry de Vries 1991, *Wingfield – a pictorial history*, Cape Town: Gerry de Vries.

111. William Courtenay, 1937, *Airman Friday*, London: Hutchinson & Co., p. 149.

112. Ibid, pp. 149–150.

113. John Illsley 2003, *In Southern Skies – a Pictorial History of Early Aviation in Southern Africa 1816–1940*, Cape Town: Jonathan Ball Publishers, p. 202.

114. Letter Rebecca Garden wrote in 1934 to Mr. Savage, the Prime Minister of New Zealand.

115. The G-ABPZ was re-registered as ZS-ADP. It crashed in the sea off Cape Town on 12.12.1933.

116. Sold to John Stark, Allhallows, Kent; on-sold to E. A. Rance, Stag Lane 3.33 and finally reregistered in Ireland 6.34 as EI-AAT.

117. 'Engine failure: Garden comes down', *Evening Post*, 26 July 1931.

118. 'Oscar Garden looking for a position', *Stratford Evening Post*, 5 September 1932.

119. Ian Mackersey 1992, *Jean Batten: The Garbo of the Skies*, London: Warner Books, p. 76.

120. Ibid, p. 75.

121. wight.hampshireairfields.co.uk/sim.html

122. 'Flyer's Hope: solo to Dominion', *Auckland Star*, 8 March, 1934, p. 9.

123. 'Personal', *Horowhenua Chronicle*, 23 March 1935.

124. 'Mayor's flight to Blackpool', *Isle of Man Weekly Times*, 4 May 1935.

125. In April 1940, British Airways merged with Imperial Airways Ltd and became British Overseas Airways Corporation (BOAC).

126. John Gunn 1987, *Qantas 1939–1954*, Brisbane: University of Queensland Press, pp. 12–13.

127. Wilmot Hudson Fysh 1968, *Qantas at War*, Sydney: Angus & Robertson, p. 57.

128. *Sydney Morning Herald*, 25 June 1937.

129. The *Press*, 2 August 1937.

130. 'Trans-Tasman Airmail', The *Press*, 3 December 1938.

131. According to Warwick Pryce ('A Confusion of Identities – ZK-AMA', *NZ Wings*, July 1991, pp. 34–36), the three planes were initially registered for Imperial Airways: S884 as G-AFCY *Captain Cook*; S885 as G-AFKZ *Canterbury*; S886 as G-AFDA *Cumberland*. When released to TEAL, S884 became ZK-AMA *Ao-tea-roa*; S885 became ZK-AMB *Canterbury* and S886 became ZK-AMC *Awarua*. In May 1939, the name on S886 was changed to *Aotearoa* (unhyphenated) and S884 renamed *Awarua*. In August 1939, the registrations of the two planes were officially swapped. *Canterbury* was later renamed *Australia* and then changed to *Clare* when it was retained for war service with Imperial Airways.

132. Letter to Margareta, dictated to my mother by my father in 1993.

133. 'Tasman plane in Brisbane', *Courier Mail*, 28 March 1940, p. 2.

134. 'Second Flying Boat for Tasman service', *The Auckland Star*, 3 April 1940.

135. Wilmot Hudson Fysh 1968, *Qantas at War*, Sydney: Angus & Robertson, p. 108.

136. Vaughan Yarwood, 1988, 'Wings of Desire', *New Zealand Geographic*, Iss. 40, pp. 105–128.

137. www.australia.gov.au/about-australia/australian-story/flying-boats-of-australia www.australia.gov.au/about-australia/australian-story/flying-boats-of-australia

138. Radio interview 1990 with Noel Wesney, Radio Avon, New Zealand.

139. Jack Leigh 1990, 'Hot-footing it to Sydney', New *Zealand Herald*, 21 April.
140. Ian Driscoll 1979, *Airline: the making of a national flag carrier*, Auckland: Shortland Publications, p. 144.
141. Vaughan Yarwood 1988, 'Wings of Desire', *New Zealand Geographic*, Iss. 40, pp. 105–128.
142. Maurice McGreal 1994, *A Noble Chance: one pilot's life*, Wellington: McGreal.
143. Brian Cassidy 2009, *Flying Empires: Short 'C' class Empire flying boats*, Bath, UK: Queens Parade Press, citeseerx.ist.psu.edu/viewdoc/download?doi=10.1.1.463.3896&rep=rep1&type=pdf
144. Chris Parson, 'One very cool customer: Churchill, puffing on cigar and wearing dashing aviator glasses while being tailed by the Luftwaffe during "most daring flight of the whole war"', *Daily Mail*, 9 July 2012, www.dailymail.co.uk/news/article-2170684/Winston-Churchill-tailed-Luftwaffe-daring-flight-war.html
145. www.nzhistory.net.nz/page/liner-sunk-german-raiders
146. 'Reunion in Sydney: Tasman Pilot and his Swedish wife', *The Weekly News*, 12 February 1941.
147. *New Zealand Herald*, 19 June 1944.
148. *New Zealand Herald*, 15 August 1945.
149. Ian Mackersey 1990, *Jean Batten: The Garbo of the Skies*, London: Warner Books, 2nd ed., p. 348.
150. Letter to Sidney Holland, leader of New Zealand's National Party, 6 July 1948. Holland had requested his attendance in Wellington for a committee enquiry into another flying boat terminal in New Zealand.
151. His application was dated 23 April 1946.
152. Noel Holmes 1982, *To Fly a Desk*, Wellington: Reed, p. 87.
153. Maurice McGreal 1994, *A Noble Chance: one pilot's life*, Wellington: McGreal, p. 92.
154. *New Zealand Herald*, 6 May 1947, p. 7.
155. Ian Driscoll 1979, *Airline: the making of a national flag carrier*, Auckland: Shortland Publications, p. 144.
156. Correspondence with Mike Hart.
157. Ibid.
158. Maurice McGreal 1994, *A Noble Chance: one pilot's life*, Wellington: McGreal, p. 93.
159. Ian Mackersey 1990, *Jean Batten: The Garbo of the Skies*, London: Warner Books, 2nd ed., p. 351.
160. Ian Driscoll 1979, 'Garden', *Airline*, Auckland: Shortland Publications, p. 121.

About the Author

Mary Garden is a freelance writer, with a PhD in journalism (USC). She is also an avid cyclist and works in the family bicycle business.

Her first book *The Serpent Rising: a journey of spiritual seduction* (1988; 2003; 2020) is a memoir of her years in India in the 1970s where she fell under the spell of various self-appointed 'god-men'. It was one of the first books to shine the light on the danger of the guru-disciple relationship, especially for naïve Westerners.

Mary has been writing feature articles since 2002 and these have appeared in print newspapers and magazines, as well as online publications, worldwide.

She lives in the rainforest in Maleny on the Sunshine Coast hinterland with a dog called Ivy and a cat called Elsa.

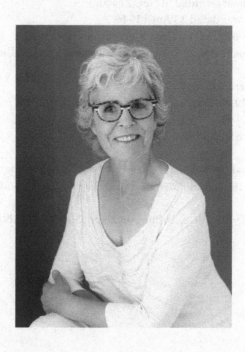

Acknowledgements

This book has been a long journey. It began in 2005, although I took a long break when Oscar's story seemed like a Herculean task. Many people have helped me along the way.

My deepest thanks to:
Those who helped my research: the aviation buffs, aero philatelists, historians, librarians, museum curators and readers of my articles who contacted me: 'My aunt went on a joyride with your father in 1931; here's a photograph of her in Kia Ora!'

The late Richard Hitchens of the Aviation Historical Society of Australia SEQ, who said in 2005 that my book should include 'the difficult bits' missing from my articles.

New Holland Publishers: Alan Whiticker, who loved Oscar's story and believed it was time for him to be remembered; Fiona Schultz and the team who created the first edition, a blue-and-gold wonder. Luke Harris of Working Type Studio, who helped with this new one, an eye-catching stunner.

Editors Judy Fredrikson, Samantha Miles and Elsie James, who did their magic shaping this book. For this edition, Glenine Hamlyn, not only an Elegant Owl, but an error-terrier, too.

Brian Day, who is wise and funny and always believed I could do it. Melinda Johnstone, my bright beta reader, who dived in boots and all. Debbie Greene, who hears all about the Mad Gardens while we pedal up mountains.

My half-sister Margareta and her husband Maurice Gee, who have been behind me from the beginning with boundless enthusiasm and have helped in countless ways. My cousin Rosemarie Toynbee who cheered me on and at the end said, 'It is magnificent. You put the huge jigsaw of the Garden family together.' That meant so much to me!

Writing friends, including Leigh Robshaw, Mary-Lou Stephens, Bianca Millroy and Gay Liddington. We writers need writers.

Mike Burge, especially for his support through the shock of my sister's book and reading drafts of my articles. You're a treasure, Mike.

Dan Oakman, cyclist and historian. His book *Oppy* came out about the same time as *Sundowner of the Skies*, so we've had lots to talk about. What a journey, Dan!

The enthusiastic readers and booksellers who have made sure Oscar is no longer the forgotten aviator. Jan Cornfoot of Rosetta Books, Maleny, who has been there for me with all the ups and downs and unexpected turns of *Sundowner of the Skies*.

Aviation museums in New Zealand and Australia, who have bought lots of copies, of course! 'Our aviation section leader, who is an ex-topdressing pilot, was absolutely enthused about your book at our Committee meeting last night.'

Special thanks to my dear cousin Gillian MacColl, who has helped in many ways, including the 2019 book launch at Classic Flyers, Tauranga, packing and posting books all over New Zealand, and supporting me through the latest Garden saga. Everyone needs a big-hearted cousin like Gillian.

Alys Wicksteed, whose mother was one of Mum's best friends. She knows the truth. Alys remembers Mum fleeing around to their house. Alys also told the renowned artist Graham Hoete (Mr G) that he *must* read my book and he *must* paint Oscar. Graham's amazing portrait of Oscar now hangs at Tauranga Airport. He looks over passengers sitting in the lounge waiting for their flights. How cool is that!

Tauranga City Council, especially former mayor Greg Brownness, Harry Mayer-Singh and Ray Dumble. Chris Walters, Operations Manager at Tauranga Airport. They all made things happen so that the unveiling of the portrait would be on the same day as my book launch in July 2019.

The warm and loving Mr G, and his parents, Graham and Kathy, who opened their arms and hearts: 'Kia ora, Nau mai piki mai ki Tauranga Moana Mary! Welcome to Tauranga Moana, Mary!'

Finally, my children, Eamon and Natalya, who always have my back. Always. You helped to heal me.